MW01221703

DEMAND GUARANTEES
IN
INTERNATIONAL TRADE

AUSTRALIA
The Law Book Company
Brisbane . Sydney . Melbourne . Perth

CANADA
Carswell
Ottawa . Toronto . Calgary . Montreal . Vancouver

Agents

Steimatzky's Agency Ltd., Tel Aviv;
N.M. Tripathi (Private) Ltd., Bombay;
Eastern Law House (Private) Ltd., Calcutta;
M.P.P. House, Bangalore;
Universal Book Traders, Delhi;
Aditya Books, Delhi;
MacMillan Shuppan KK, Tokyo;
Pakistan Law House, Karachi, Lahore.

DEMAND GUARANTEES

IN

INTERNATIONAL TRADE

by

ANTHONY PIERCE

M.B.A. M.I.Ex. (Grad.) M.C.I.M.

London
Sweet & Maxwell
1993

Published in 1993 by
Sweet and Maxwell Limited of
South Quay Plaza, 183 Marsh Wall,
London E14 9FT
Typeset by Tradespools Ltd., Frome
Printed and bound in Great Britain by Hartnolls Ltd., Bodmin

No natural forests were destroyed to
make this product: only farmed
timber was used and re-planted.

ISBN 0-421-43770-7

**A catalogue record for this book is
available from the British Library**

Printed and bound in Great Britain by
Hartnolls Limited, Bodmin, Cornwall
Index prepared by Alex Noel-Tod

© Anthony Pierce 1993

BIOGRAPHICAL DETAILS

Anthony Pierce M.B.A. M.I.Ex. (Grad.) M.C.I.M.

Managing Director of Export Risk Control Ltd., an export risk advisory and service company, specialising in export finance and the control of risks and hidden costs. Until 1987 Group Export Finance Manager and Treasury Operations Manager BICC plc, responsible for trade and project finance, control of contract bond exposure, analysis and control of contract risk, currency dealing and currency risk management. Formerly Export Credit Manager, The Plessey Company, with similar responsibilities. Holds a Masters Degree in Business Administration, having studied International Competitive Strategy at London Business School, International Trade and Finance at City University Business School and modern languages at London University.

Graduate of the Institute of Export and Member of the Chartered Institute of Marketing.

Former chairman CBI Performance Bonds Group, former member of the CBI Export Finance Committee and International Chamber of Commerce Ad Hoc Group on Contract Guarantees.

A former member of the BEAMA Export Credit Finance Committee, he is currently visiting MBA lecturer in Finance of Trade and Large Projects at City University Business School.

PREFACE

This is a long overdue book about performance bonds and guarantees.

Over the years much has been talked about the problems they represent for the exporter, his buyer and the banks and other financial institutions that provide the guarantees.

For those that are involved in international trade but are new to this important subject let me explain what the problem is. Many overseas buyers in public and major private sectors in strong negotiating positions insist that exporters provide bonds or guarantees to ensure that the terms of their tender or contract are adhered to.

These are intended to deter or penalise bad faith and non-performance and provide the buyer with a ready source of funds to help meet the cost of remedying the exporter's failure. For the uninformed exporter the lack of knowledge in this area can be very dangerous as he risks exposing his balance sheet to unwelcome contingent liability and his profit margin to unexpected erosion.

The object of this book is to explain the nature and role of the different types of bond and guarantee in relation to export tenders and contracts. It will highlight the problems, the risks and hidden costs, and give guidance on the monitoring and control of those risks and costs associated with bank guarantees payable on demand.

It is structured to be either read from cover to cover or dipped into as required.

The International Chamber of Commerce has been working on a set of uniform rules for such guarantees for over 20 years. Their earlier efforts received little support from the international business community because of the excessive bias in favour of the exporter, and legalistic overtones.

It is hoped that readers of this book will be awakened to the issues that the ICC have been addressing for so long and will see why it is so important to adopt wholeheartedly their new Uniform Rules for Demand Guarantees, ICC Publication No. 458, which approach the issues from a totally realistic and pragmatic point of view.

Anthony Pierce
26 May 1993

TABLE OF CONTENTS

		Page
Biographical Details		v
Preface		vii
Acknowledgements		xi
Chapter 1:	Introduction	1
Chapter 2:	Source and Nature of Guarantees	13
Chapter 3:	Text of Guarantees	39
Chapter 4:	Anticipating Unfair Demands	81
Chapter 5:	Project Guarantees	117
Chapter 6:	Cost of Issuing Demand Guarantees	135
Chapter 7:	Recourse-worthiness	149
Chapter 8:	Controlling the Risk of an Unfair Demand	157
Chapter 9:	Corporate Guarantees	213
Chapter 10:	International Code of Practice	219
Chapter 11:	Grading and Controlling Risks	259
Appendix A:	Bibliography	277
Appendix B:	Useful Addresses	281
Index		285

ACKNOWLEDGEMENTS

It would not have been possible to attempt this book without the help of those individuals and institutions actively involved in providing bond demand guarantees for export contracts.

A simple list seems inadequate to express my thanks to those who gave me support and encouragement as well as providing me with factual up-to-date material. Each deserves full recognition for their help:

Barclays Bank plc, London and Coventry
Association Belge des Banques – Departement Juridique et Fiscal,
    Brussels
Siemens AG, Munich
ORGALIME, Organisme de Liaison des Industries Metalliques
    Europeennes, Brussels
Commerzbank, Frankfurt
Hogg Robinson (Credit & Political) Ltd, London
VDMA – Verband Deutscher Maschinen- und Anlagenbau e.V, Abteilung
    Recht und Wettbewerbsordung, Frankfurt/Main
International Chamber of Commerce, Paris
ICC United Kingdom, London
Confederation of British Industry, London
The former Plessey Company
BICC plc
Balfour Beatty Ltd

In particular I would like to thank Jim Wood, now retired from BICC plc, whose support over many years helped me accumulate the knowledge, experience and background necessary to make such a book possible.

Acknowledgement is also due to the ICC for kind permission to reproduce the following publications:

ICC Uniform Rules for Contract Guarantees – 1978 Edition
ICC Publication 325 – ISBN 92.842.1140.9
Published in its official English version by the International Chamber of Commerce, Paris
Copyright c.1978 – International Chamber of Commerce (ICC)

Available from: ICC Publishing SA, 38 Cours Albert 1er, 75008 Paris, France
And from: ICC United Kingdom, 14/15 Belgrave Square, London SW1X 8PS, UK

ICC Uniform Rules for Demand Guarantees – 1992 Edition
ICC Publication 458 – ISBN 92.842.1094.1
Published in its official English version by the International Chamber of Commerce, Paris
Copyright c. 1992 – International Chamber of Commerce (ICC)
Available from: ICC Publishing SA, 38 Cours Albert 1er, 75008 Paris, France
And from: ICC United Kingdom, 14/15 Belgrave Square, London SW1X 8PS, UK

Finally, I would like to thank my wife Abeda for her help, advice and support during the more difficult moments in its writing.

Anthony Pierce

CHAPTER 1

INTRODUCTION

"We learn about geology the morning after the earthquake"
Emerson

It is common practice for many buyers, particularly overseas buyers in the public and major private sectors in strong negotiating positions, to insist that exporters provide bonds or guarantees as security to ensure that the terms of their tender or contract are adhered to.

This form of security has become an established part of international commerce, particularly in overseas civil engineering projects, and major sales, process engineering and defence contracts. They are the legal instruments used to guarantee to the buyer, *i.e.* the beneficiary, that the contractor or exporter will not prematurely withdraw from his tender (in the case of tender bonds) and is, purportedly, technically and financially capable of performing the underlying contract in accordance with its agreed provisions.

Guarantees can be called (*i.e.* payment demanded) if a tenderer fails to enter into an effective contract, or if there is actual or, in some cases, likely failure of the exporter to perform the contract properly. As such, they are intended to deter or penalise bad faith and poor performance for whatever reason. They provide the buyer with a ready source of funds which can be used to help meet the cost of remedying the exporter's failure.

Exporters have actively involved English and other European courts in this relatively new area of litigation, particularly with regard to the prevention of the unfair calling of bank demand guarantees.

Not all the court decisions have been completely consistent, although a general view has evolved which mostly favours the beneficiary, and generally fails to protect the contractually compliant exporter or contractor, who is required to provide such guarantees, against unfair demands for payment.

Purpose of This Book

The purpose of this book is to explain the nature and role of the different

1

types of bank demand guarantee in relation to export tenders and contracts. It will highlight the problems, risks and hidden costs, and give guidance on the monitoring and control of these risks and costs. It will also refer
to a number of the United Kingdom and other European court cases which
have contributed to the development of the current legal attitudes in
England and Europe. However, the author makes no claims to being a lawyer and makes reference to the various court cases only to help those lawyers who would like to delve deeper into the facts and circumstances of
each case. There are many lawyers who could make a valuable contribution to the legal literature on this subject by addressing it purely from the
legal viewpoint.

This book is aimed to help exporters, importers, commercial managers,
contract negotiators and bankers as well as lawyers gain a broader insight
into the problems and advantages of bank demand guarantees.

Whilst the book has been written in relation to exports and imports,
many of the issues relate also to domestic contracts where bank demand
guarantees are required.

The book is structured to enable the reader to understand in broad
terms, by reading Chapter 1, the general nature of demand guarantees, and
the related issues and problems. Subsequent Chapters then elaborate, offering where appropriate constructive help and advice on the issue and
control of bank demand guarantees, and the mitigation of the risk of unfair
calling.

The Growth of the Problems and Risks

Tender and contract guarantees have been a feature of international tenders and public works (and some private) contracts in developed countries
for many years.

The reasons are understandable. The interval between bidding for, and
completing, a contract can extend from just a few weeks to a number of
years. During this time, circumstances within the contractor's or supplier's
company, or technical, economic or political factors, could have delayed or
prevented the due fulfilment of the contract. The buyer, therefore, has a
need to find some means of protecting his financial interests.

Bank demand guarantees of a nature independent of the contract came
to wider international use and prominence following the economic recession in the developed countries of the early 1970s. This recession was attri-
buted at the time to the oil price hikes by the Middle Eastern and other
oil-producing countries, which became very rich at the expense of the developed world. The recession forced many Western exporters and contractors to look for contracts from these rapidly developing and, in most
cases, cash-rich markets.

As a result of the excessive liquidity of these oil-producing exporting countries (OPEC), the poorer non-oil-producing countries were able to take advantage of the extremely relaxed lending régime of the international banks with access to the OPEC cash deposits. With such loans, even the non-OPEC countries were able to place major contracts.

As the credits got bigger, so the size of individual contracts also grew, not only for civil works contracts, but also for supply and service contracts in the Middle East, Africa, the Far East, Latin America and the then Soviet Bloc countries.

There was an increase in the number and value of tender guarantees, and performance guarantees reflected the increased contract values. Massive advance payments were asked for, and paid, against advance payment guarantees. Exporters willingly agreed to provide these bank guarantees in exchange for obtaining cheap working capital in excess of their requirements to perform the contract.

The cost of this was the then little-understood and intangible *contingent liability* that built up on the exporter's balance sheet. This was seen in simple terms to be directly compensated for and secured by a tangible (although, as subsequently realised, diminishing) cash deposit. It was a short-term view of many who either failed to appreciate, or disregarded, the longer-term reality, and consequential risks to which they were exposing themselves.

Banks, for their part, found guarantees a valuable new source of fee income which could be earned simply by committing their own name and balance sheet to what was then considered a low-impact contingent liability. Their guarantees were purely of a financial nature secured against the adequacy of the exporter's assets or perceived credit-worthiness and, therefore, there was usually no need to vet in depth the exporter's technical and managerial ability to perform a contract.

They paid out cash on demand, up to the value of the commitment expressly stated in their guarantee, against claims made strictly in accordance with the guarantee. They took recourse on the exporter, often by a direct debit against his account.

Billions of pounds' worth of demand guarantees were issued by banks in this way. As a result, both the banks' and the exporters' balance sheets became loaded with contingent liability. At the time, this was not regulated by central banks, or viewed as a significant problem by accountants or auditors, as long as the guarantees were issued in the regular course of business.

However, the contingent liability was marked against the exporter's banking lines and, for the smaller company, subsequently became a serious constraint on its ability to borrow and (as the cash deposits from advance payments were spent) on their letter of credit, foreign currency dealing and overdraft facilities.

In many cases, this eventually restricted the size of contract the exporter could subsequently take on (see Chapter 7: "Recourse-worthiness").

Origins of Demand Guarantees

With the sudden excessive wealth of the oil producers, it was inevitable that some buyers would be cheated on their contracts by profiteers and charlatans. Many innocent buyers, with more money than international trading experience, suffered badly from the default of a few exporters who failed to perform their contracts and improperly banked contract payments and unearned advances.

Buyers found that it was too difficult, costly and slow to get retribution through the courts, and surety bonds and those contract guarantees payable against admitted default or arbitral award gave no speedy remedy in terms meaningful to the aggrieved buyer.

On another front, some honest exporters simply over-extended themselves with the size of contracts they took on and became insolvent through overtrading. This left buyers with unfinished contracts on their hands, and no means of recovering payments or imposing effective penalties on the exporter because of the international boundaries.

As a result, buyers, especially those with a duty to protect public funds, began to insist on the provision of more stringent unconditional bank guarantees payable simply on first demand, in support of tenders and contracts. These are guarantees issued independent of the contract and payable without contestation or objection by the exporter or his bank.

The Reaction of Exporters

Demand guarantees are rarely volunteered by the experienced exporter (except where absolutely necessary to release payments, or because of competitive pressure). On the other hand, many are provided by less experienced exporters believing them to be "harmless pieces of paper" standing between them and a new contract.

Some exporters believe that bank demand guarantees are simply a necessary appendage to a bid, or something only to be discussed in the final stages of contract negotiations. This is not the case. They give the buyer an effective instrument of control over the exporter, far exceeding the buyer's rights as expressed in the contract. They therefore need to be drafted and tabled for discussion early in the contract negotiations.

Terminology

The terminology surrounding bank demand guarantees can be confusing to purists with legal training. It has been developed by exporters, bankers and insurers rather than lawyers. As a result, it is often inaccurate from the legal point of view, but well understood by the layman. For example:

Bonds and guarantees

The actual words "bond" and "guarantee" have slipped into the vernacular. The documents to which they relate take various forms, having developed from the needs of international trade. However, the terms are often interchanged by commercial usage for no good legal reason.

Normally a bond requires no consideration since it is issued under seal, and a guarantee must be supported by consideration. However, in the present context, "bond" and "guarantee" should be regarded as simply meaning a "promise".

Whatever word is used to describe these instruments of payment, all bank guarantees include an undertaking to pay a certain sum of money when one party demands payment on the grounds that another has purportedly not fulfilled its contractual obligations.

Throughout this book a distinction will be made between surety bonds, contract guarantees and demand guarantees, but not necessarily between the words "bonds" and "guarantees". Each is given equal meaning for the sake of style unless the context otherwise dictates.

Buyers and sellers

In the context of guarantees issued in respect of contracts, sellers can be variously described as suppliers, exporters, contractors, principals, applicants, etc. Buyers are equally referred to as purchasers, customers, importers, clients, beneficiaries, etc., according to context.

Guarantor

The institution issuing the guarantee is variously described as the guarantor, surety, issuing bank, instructing bank, local bank or just simply bank, according to its legal constitution, role, location or context.

Types and Uses of Guarantees

There are several types of guarantee which exporters may be called upon to provide in favour of the buyer at particular stages of the sales transaction:

(a) *Tender bond (tender guarantee, bid bond)*
   In order to deter frivolous bidders, exporters are often required to submit a bid bond/tender guarantee with their tender for a contract, commonly for an amount between 0.5 and 5 per cent. of the tender price. Two per cent. is quite common for the supply of plant and machinery.
   The purpose of the tender guarantee is to protect the tender-inviting

authority from the failure of the tenderer to fulfil those obligations undertaken by him when submitting his tender.

They provide the buyer with a source of funds to help cover his additional unexpected costs should the successful tenderer not proceed with the contract when awarded to him; for example, by refusing to sign it or by failing to submit a performance guarantee where required.

A tender guarantee indicates to the buyer that the tenderer is serious and will neither withdraw his bid nor unilaterally depart from the conditions set out in the original tender. It gives some assurance that the exporter will sign a contract at the price and on the terms of his tender if it is awarded to him within the validity of the tender and tender bond.

There is an implication that, when the bid is supported by a reputable bank, the exporter is considered sufficiently financially sound to undertake the contract. Where a surety company issues the bid bond, it indicates that the surety company considers that the exporter is recourse-worthy, technically capable, and sufficiently competent to perform the contract if awarded.

The tender bond provides an assurance to the buyer that, on award of the contract, subsequent guarantee requirements to secure contractual performance and/or advance payments will also be forthcoming.

(b) *Performance guarantee (performance bond, completion bond)*

Performance guarantees are a means of ensuring completion of the contract or of extracting a financial penalty from the exporter if he fails to fulfil his obligations.

They provide the buyer with effective, and often unilaterally enforceable, security against the exporter's failure to perform the contract in accordance with its terms and conditions in due time.

It would be normal for a performance guarantee to replace by substitution any tender guarantee which may have been issued in connection with the same contract.

They usually contain an undertaking to pay a certain sum, typically between 5 and 10 per cent. of the contract value.

Performance guarantees are, in effect, penalty bonds, but have also been used by some buyers as a mechanism to secure payments from the guarantor due under a contract's liquidated damages clause, which is usually triggered to penalise late delivery; payments which under the contract should have first been sought from the exporter direct.

(c) *Repayment guarantee (advance payment/interim payment guarantee)*

Advance payments are often required to finance the initial pre-shipment stage of a contract, such as the cost of mobilisation/start-up on construction contracts, the purchase of special plant and capital equipment, materials, etc.

The repayment guarantee enables the buyer to recover all or part of his advance and progress payments in the event of the exporter not becoming entitled to payment under the contract.

Advance payments and progress payments generally amount to anywhere between 10 and 20 per cent. of the contract value. In the mechanical engineering and construction industries, it is customary to ask for and provide bonds against advance and mobilisation payments amounting to one-third of the contract price, which are often followed by interim progress payments.

Occasionally, bonding up to 100 per cent. of the contract has been required from exporters who have sought the equivalent cash advances. It would be normal for the amount of the advance payment guarantee to reduce *pro rata* to contract performance and payment.

(d) *Retention bond (payment bond)*

Retention bonds are used as security to release retained contractual payments that would otherwise be held by the buyer pending final acceptance or expiration of the contractual warranty period. They assure the buyer that these funds will be repayable by a reputable third party in the event of the exporter's failure to perform during this period. They are usually offered by exporters to improve their cashflow and release profit during the final phase of the contract.

A retention of payment is a mechanism to ensure that the exporter has a financial incentive to, for example, complete final tests or perform rectification work after installation or construction. It provides the buyer with a pool of funds to help defray the cost of employing an alternative contractor to complete such contractual obligations if necessary.

Typically, they can be for a value of 5 to 10 per cent. of the contract price.

(e) *Maintenance/warranty guarantee*

Where the contract does not provide for retentions, maintenance guarantees are normally requested, particularly in connection with construction contracts. Warranty bonds cover the warranty obligations of equipment suppliers.

Their purpose is to ensure that, once the contract has been completed, the contractor or exporter, having already been paid the full contractual price, will continue to fulfil his obligations during the maintenance/warranty period.

The amount should be set so as to provide sufficient funds for the buyer to bring in a third party to complete the maintenance/warranty obligations if necessary.

Typically, this is 5 per cent. of the contract price.

There are other forms of bond to be aware of, but which will not feature extensively in this book as they relate to beneficiaries who are not party to the main contract. These are:

(f) *Customs bond*

Customs bonds are provided in respect of a contractor's plant or samples and display material temporarily imported for a project or exhibition. They give the customs department in the buyer's country assurance that import duty will be paid if re-export does not take place by a set date.

The amount of the bond is related to the level of deferred duty based on the value of the item temporarily imported.

(g) *Freight bond*

Freight bonds are often associated, for example, with the international construction industry where special freight rates are quoted for the two-way transportation of the construction plant. They assure the shipping company that if the construction plant is sold off locally and not reshipped, then the unearned discount on the freight will be repaid.

Sources of Guarantees

Guarantees are issued on the instructions of an exporter by an independent and financially solvent third party, usually a bank, surety company or other sound financial institution. (The respective roles of banks and surety companies are covered more fully in Chapter 2: "Source and Nature of Guarantees".)

The Parties to a Guarantee

There are usually three parties involved in the provision of a guarantee:

(a) *The exporter (supplier or contractor)*

Also known in this context as the principal or applicant, who is to perform the work covered by the supply contract entered into with his overseas buyer.

(b) *The buyer (client or customer)*

Also known in this context as the beneficiary, to whom the guarantee is issued. The beneficiary is the only party that can claim under the guarantee (but see "Assignment of Guarantees", pp. 45 and 159).

(c) *The issuing bank or surety company*

Also called the guarantor. It is the party which issues the actual guarantee agreement (contract of indemnity) to the exporter's customer on provision of a written counter-indemnity from an instructing bank and/or the exporter.

Frequently, when the buyer or local regulations require, a local bank in the beneficiary's country is involved (often the correspondent bank of the exporter's bank) which issues the guarantee on the instructions of the exporter's bank, the *instructing bank*.

The local bank is the *issuing bank* which gives the promise to pay the guarantee sum on demand by the beneficiary. In such a case, the exporter's bank (in this context the instructing bank) counter-indemnifies the local bank (the issuing bank).

The inter-relationship of these parties is shown in Fig. 1, p.26, below.

Each party has a separate contract with one or more of the other parties. The English and European courts tend to regard each of these contracts as totally independent from each other and will not determine the obligations under one contract by reference to the terms of, or what happened under, any of the others.

Where the guarantee is independent of the contract, which is usually the case with bank demand guarantees, only the wording of each individual guarantee document can be relied on to provide the actual terms of the promise.

Conflicting Interests of Exporter and Buyer

When an exporter and his buyer enter into a contract, they agree that the exporter will perform the contract in accordance with its terms and conditions, and the buyer will pay him whatever is due. They both desire the contract to be completed as originally intended, or as amended by mutual agreement from time to time, at no extra cost or delay.

The conflict of interests between the exporter and his buyer is clear. The buyer needs a first-class independent guarantor to guarantee the bona fides of the exporter and to provide without undue delay an agreed sum of money in the event of default. He would ideally prefer a bank demand guarantee as the effective instrument to achieve his objectives. This gives assurance that cash is available to complete the contract, and helps to keep pressure on the exporter to perform his contract.

From the exporter's point of view, he wants to win the contract and give the buyer adequate assurances of financial strength and contractual competence. He needs to be able to satisfy the buyer that he has signed the contract in good faith and that he will complete it in accordance with its terms (not necessarily to the satisfaction of the buyer), or suffer the penalty of a claim on the guarantee. The exporter normally tries to achieve this without increasing his extra-contractual risks and costs.

He does not want to put in the hands of the buyer a demand guarantee instrument that can create excessive *coercive pressure* and possibly induce serious cashflow problems if a claim is made precipitously or even capriciously. He would prefer to offer a less onerous guarantee.

Initially, *surety companies* were able to reconcile this conflict of interests

with the issue of *surety bonds*. However, not all countries or buyers are prepared to accept such highly conditional bonds. As a result, bank guarantees or, in the case of the United States banks, stand-by letters of credit
evolved to fulfil the demands of many buyers.

The terms of a demand guarantee can often be very onerous, although
there are occasions when the experienced exporter can minimise risks by
agreeing equitable wording with his buyer.

Other exporters try to dilute their commitment and exposure to sudden
claims by offering the guarantee of their parent company, or of a major
partner(s) in a joint venture.

Yet others try to provide a so-called *letter of comfort* on the (wrong) assumption that they are non-binding, cheaper, and do not involve cost or
the commitment of the balance sheet of their parent company or independent third parties (see Chapter 9: "Corporate Guarantees").

In the final analysis, it is the party in the strongest negotiating position
that has the last say on the guarantee wording.

The Hidden Risks

The decision as to whether a guarantee commitment should be given and
on what terms is clearly the responsibility of the exporter. He therefore
needs to understand the commercial and legal implications of his decision.

There are many obvious risks, most particularly that of an unfair call,
which is addressed in detail in Chapter 8: "Controlling the Risk of an Unfair Demand". In addition, there are less obvious risks and costs such as:

Unreduced values

Advance payment and retention guarantees remaining unreduced or
unrecovered at the appropriate milestone in the performance of the contract have a penalty effect similar to that of a performance guarantee. This
is because they no longer secure for the beneficiary an unearned payment,
and the exporter will already have amortised the advance payment and retention in the performance of the contract. As such, they increase the risk of
loss for the exporter if not reduced or recovered at the appropriate time.

In addition, bank fees continue to be paid on the outstanding value of the
guarantee.

Aggregation of guarantees

Exporters are often requested to provide several guarantees under the
same contract. The aggregation of liabilities which results, together with
other unexpired or uncancelled guarantees associated with separate contracts, raises the exporter's risk profile and costs. In addition, a contingent

liability is created on the exporter's balance sheet that ties up bank lending lines, which become encumbered for further efficient use.

Expiry date

A bank demand guarantee has a particular disadvantage compared with a surety bond. When it has demonstrably reached a point when it should expire or reduce, often it does not. In many countries, express permission has to be sought from the beneficiary for cancellation or reduction. There is often the risk of considerable delay in obtaining this. In many cases the guarantee has to be physically returned for cancellation.

Extend or pay claims

Guarantees payable on demand, not requiring independent evidence of default by the exporter, are vulnerable to *extend or pay* demands from the beneficiary. If the exporter is not prepared to agree to extend the guarantee, the bank must pay. If he does agree to extend, then he incurs additional bank charges and possibly insurance premiums in cases where the guarantee has been covered against the risk of *unfair demand*.

Local laws and regulations

Many demand guarantees have to be issued by a bank in the country of the buyer. These will usually be subject to local laws and regulations. The local issuing bank will require precise instructions from the exporter's bank together with an *inter-bank counter-indemnity*. In turn, the exporter's bank requires a *counter-indemnity* from the exporter.

All these documents are legally independent of each other, and the laws and regulations governing each are not necessarily the same. This causes the exporter considerable difficulty when disputes arise and he tries to re-cover a payment made against an unfair claim by the beneficiary.

Texts of Guarantees

Chapters 3: "Text of Guarantees" and 4: "Anticipating Unfair Demands" give specimens of texts of guarantees. The extra-contractual risks imposed on the exporter by entering into a contract requiring demand guarantees, the problems and hidden costs are discussed more fully in Chapters 7: "Recourse-worthiness" and 8: "Controlling the Risk of an Unfair Demand".

The limited ability of exporters to resist onerous conditions, and the difficulty of different banks in interpreting guarantee wording uniformly (because of differing local practices, laws and regulations), led to the realisation that an internationally accepted code of practice was needed.

Code of Practice

Moves to establish uniform rules to regulate demand guarantees have been made by the United Nations Committee on International Trade Law (UNCITRAL), the International Chamber of Commerce (ICC) and the Committee of London & Scottish Clearing Banks (CLSCB). This resulted initially in the publication by the International Chamber of Commerce of Uniform Rules for Contract Guarantees (ICC Publication No. 325) in 1978 and subsequently Uniform Rules for Demand Guarantees (ICC Publication No. 458) in 1992.

This book will help explain:

(a) many of the issues which prompted the ICC to become involved with this aspect of international trade;
(b) how the ICC's first attempt to establish uniform rules to regulate guarantees failed to achieve broad international acceptance;
(c) how the success of their second attempt is thought to be more likely.

The ICC Rules are discussed in Chapter 10: "International Code of Practice".

Controlling Exposure

The insurance of demand guarantees against unfair call is covered in Chapter 8.

The issue, control and cancellation of guarantees is a matter of considerable importance, requiring systems that can monitor the degree of risk and level of exposure. These are covered more fully in Chapter 11: "Grading and Controlling Risks".

CHAPTER 2

SOURCE AND NATURE OF GUARANTEES

This Chapter explains the source and nature of the alternative forms of guarantee, when they can be used, the role of the issuer and the requirement for counter-indemnities.

Source of Guarantees

The guarantor that issues guarantees can be a surety company, bank or other similar financial institution. Whilst this book is intended to concentrate only on bank demand guarantees, it is nevertheless worthwhile understanding a little of what alternatives are available for comparison purposes.

Surety company bonds

The term "surety company" embraces both insurance and specialist surety companies. They may be specialists whose sole activity is suretyship, or they may be composite insurance offices. However, bonds issued by insurance companies are not insurance policies.

Surety companies usually issue bonds, without collateral security, after careful examination of the scope of the contract, its terms and conditions, and the financial, managerial and technical competence of the exporter. They would not issue a bond unless and until they were satisfied that the exporter was capable of performing the contract: through the bond the surety company is, after all, guaranteeing that the exporter has the appropriate ability and adequate resources to perform the related contract.

The amount of bonding a surety company will provide to an individual exporter or a single contract is limited, and can be less than the ceiling imposed by the exporter's bank. This is because they do not have a charge on the exporter's assets, nor can they monitor the exporter's financial health as closely as a bank with regular daily contact.

The surety company knows that every exporter has finite human, technical and financial resources and does not want him to overstretch himself contractually just because surety bonds do not absorb his banking lines.

The surety company therefore limits its support to what it considers a prudent level of contracting and bonding.

The main questions a surety underwriter would be concerned with when considering whether or not to issue a bond are:

(a) What is the financial standing of the exporter?
      (Although bonds issued in the surety market do not form part of the
      exporter's overdraft limit, the guarantor will naturally want to
      have more detailed, and up-to-date, information than would norm-
      ally appear in the exporter's published accounts.)
(b) Has the exporter sufficient liquidity to carry out the contract in ad-
      dition to his existing commitments?
(c) Is the cashflow of the contract acceptable?
(d) How competent is the exporter?
(e) Has he the technical ability and manpower to carry out the contract
      in question?
(f) Has he completed similar contracts successfully in the past?
(g) Has he sufficient and suitable plant for the performance of the work
      to be undertaken?
(h) After allowing for all contingencies, is the contract price adequate
      to produce a reasonable profit?
(i) Are the conditions of the contract and the obligations of the guaran-
      tee reasonable?
(j) What part of the work is to be sub-contracted and how has the ex-
      porter protected himself against the failure of major, or essential,
      sub-contractors?

In effect, the surety company underwrites the exporter's ability to manage and control his risks and working capital. Failure in this could lead to the exporter's default and non-performance. In such proven circumstances, the surety company settles the claim and takes recourse under a counter-indemnity (see below, p.28) provided by the exporter.

Buyers in most developed countries accept surety bonds for appropriate civil and process engineering projects as well as private and government supply, and supply and install, contracts.

However, some buyers, particularly in underdeveloped and developing countries, do not normally accept surety bonds because of their highly conditional wording, unless the exporter is in a strong negotiating position. In some cases, buyers are prevented from accepting surety bonds because of restrictive local regulations or development bank funding conditions.

Bank guarantees

Generally speaking, the main source of demand guarantees is banks. However, not all banks are acceptable to overseas buyers. The exporter's choice of bank can be restricted by the buyer's preference, local regulations, or by commercial, political or religious considerations.

Administratively, it is normally very easy, and often quicker, to obtain a demand guarantee from a bank than a surety company (unless the exporter is already well known to the surety company), because of the bank's general experience of its customer's affairs and its less detailed underwriting approach to guarantees. There is usually no specific assessment of the exporter's financial standing, resources, technical ability, management capabilities, skills and expertise.

Bank guarantees are mainly issued by one of the exporter's banks on the strength of the exporter's balance sheet, and the collateral security which the bank holds or requires.

Guarantees count as part of the exporter's credit ceiling, absorbing available capacity on his banking lines. As such, they are a restraint on the exporter's ability to take on too many contracts.

Other banks not holding any tangible collateral security would take a view of their exposure based on the strength of the exporter's balance sheet, reputation and general credit-worthiness. They would satisfy themselves that the exporter could withstand the financial impact of a call on the guarantee that would be reflected back through a counter-indemnity. In some cases, where they are unhappy with the security of a counter-indemnity alone, they may require a floating charge on the exporter's assets, or some other suitable and adequate security.

Nature of Guarantees

A distinction needs to be drawn between the nature of undertakings given by banks and those given by surety companies. In the case of the former, the bank undertakes to pay money if the buyer makes a demand in accordance with the wording of the guarantee. In the case of the latter, the surety company commits itself to see the contract completed in the event of the exporter's contractual failure. Only when this is not possible will they be liable to pay cash up to the maximum amount of their liability.

Benefits of Using Surety Bonds

Surety companies are usually unwilling to issue bonds payable on first demand because, unlike banks, their funds and investments are not structured to be instantly accessible to enable them to pay out large sums at short notice.

Surety's experience

As they insist on examining the contract, the experience of surety companies in this field gained from their range of clients can be of considerable benefit to the exporter. This requirement has in the past prevented the unwitting acceptance of unduly onerous contract conditions.

The surety company also takes a great interest in the performance of the contract and gains a valuable insight into the exporter's capabilities. Thus, over a number of contracts, a surety company will develop a close relationship with an exporter. Such a close relationship can lead to an increase in the level of bonding which the surety company is prepared to support at any given time, and speed up the bond issuing process.

In the event of the exporter defaulting on his contract, the surety company will either complete the contract by helping the exporter or by hiring in another company. When this is not possible, they will repay any costs the buyer may incur in completing the contract up to the amount of the bond.

Beneficiary to prove default

The surety bond usually contains a condition that if the exporter duly performs and observes all the terms of the contract or, failing this, remedies the default, then the bond is void and a valid claim under it cannot be made. Failing this, the beneficiary is indemnified for the loss he can actually show he has suffered.

There is, therefore, no incentive for the beneficiary to make false claims; but there is every incentive to work with the surety company to ensure that the contract is completed with the minimum of delay and disruption.

Where the exporter is unwilling to admit a breach of contract, the onus is placed upon the buyer to prove default by the exporter. There is provision in the bond for settlement of disputes between the buyer and the exporter, usually through the courts or arbitration.

In the event of a dispute, therefore, making an effective claim against a surety bond can be slow and costly because of the arbitral process. As a result, surety bond claims usually favour the exporter's cash position since there can normally be no unexpected, precipitous outflow of working capital under the counter-indemnity to the surety company.

It follows that it is in the interests of the exporter to try to persuade the buyer to agree to a contract providing for surety bonds. Experience shows, however, that many buyers are not willing to contemplate the risk of delays, which can run to many months, while arbitration procedures take place to establish the necessary independent proof of default. Therefore, they insist on demand guarantees issued by banks.

New ICC Rules for Surety Bonds

In conjunction with leading surety companies, the International Chamber of Commerce is to publish uniform rules for surety bonds. These codify the existing practice of surety companies for the issue of bonds and payment of claims, where the obligation of the surety depends on the duties and liabilities of the exporter under the contract. They are called Uniform Rules for Contract Bonds, and will be published in September 1993.

Bank Guarantees

Many buyers prefer bank demand guarantees. A first-class bank demand guarantee provides the beneficiary with:

(a)   an indication of the exporter's good faith;
(b)   an independent financial guarantee; and
(c)   access to cash on demand from a reputable third party.

Issuing bank guarantees

For the exporter who is recourse-worthy, the mechanics of issuing a guarantee are straightforward. He simply instructs his chosen bank in writing to issue a bank guarantee in favour of the buyer.

Before issuing a guarantee, a bank needs to know what type of guarantee needs to be issued, the amount, the expiry date or expiry event, and the documents against which they should make payment. The bank then either issues the guarantee direct to the exporter's customer or through a correspondent bank in the customer's country.

In many cases, but not all, the tender document or contract stipulates the content, or even the required wording, of the guarantee. If no text is stipulated or agreed, then the exporter will either ask the bank to use its own standard text for the buyer's country (see Chapters 3 and 4), or agree an appropriate text with his lawyer and/or bank.

Once issued, a bank guarantee is irrevocable and cannot be cancelled or recovered without the beneficiary's consent. As with letters of credit, amendments can normally only be made with the mutual agreement of all parties, *i.e.* the beneficiary, the exporter and the guarantor. However, there can be exceptions to this, in respect of the validity and amount where the buyer can make unilateral demands (see Chapter 8: "Controlling the Risk of an Unfair Demand").

There are two basic types of guarantee issued by banks in respect of export contracts; guarantees payable:

(a)   on accepted or proven default; or
(b)   on first demand.

The former are drafted only to permit payment to be made should the exporter admit default, or a pre-agreed independent third party certify default, or the buyer obtain an arbitral or equivalent judgment through a court of law against the exporter.

The latter permits payment on first demand, often without the need to provide proof of default by the exporter.

As the exporter's cashflow, and perhaps solvency, depends on the distinction, it is necessary to understand the difference between these two forms of guarantee. The nature of the exporter's liability under each of them is clearly very different.

Default guarantees

Guarantees payable on accepted or proven default can be *dependent on*, or *independent of*, the contract. They usually state that they are payable only if the exporter is in breach of his contractual obligations.

As such, payment of a claim is dependent on:

(a)   the bank's interpretation of the contract and the exporter's performance under it in respect of a *dependent* guarantee; and/or

(b)   the exporter's acceptance of the claim or an independent report or arbitration award in favour of the beneficiary in respect of an *independent* guarantee.

Dependent guarantees

Dependent guarantees require interpretation of the contract to establish where the exporter has defaulted, and are not normally liked by banks. Traditionally, banks are checkers of documents, for example, shipping documents presented against letters of credit. So guarantee wording saying "payable in the event the exporter fails to perform the contract" would not normally be accepted by an experienced bank.

This would require them to have read and understood the contract, and then to make quality judgments about whether a purported default is sufficient to justify a claim under the guarantee.

Banks do not consider themselves particularly skilled at evaluating whether or not an exporter has performed his contract (unlike a surety company, which has a tradition of employing assessors and loss adjusters whose aim is to keep liability to a minimum).

In some countries, particularly in Europe, such dependent guarantees are also referred to as *secondary* or *accessory obligations*, because they have to be read in conjunction with the contract.

Dependent guarantees in law

In France, Belgium and Germany, the system of issuing dependent guarantees is more codified than in the United Kingdom. Dependent guarantees are known as *statutory* or *civil code* guarantees.

Such guarantees are agreements under which one party agrees to be answerable for the debt or default of another, the primary debtor (exporter). In France, such *cautionnements* come under the French Civil Code, Art. 2011. The German equivalent is the *Bürgschaft*, and is covered in the German Civil Code, s.18, Arts. 765–778.

Throughout continental Europe, the law is fairly uniform as regards the rights of the guarantor:

(a) the guarantor's liability cannot exceed that of the principal debtor (although the guarantor would be prudent to put a ceiling on the level of his commitment);

(b) the terms of the guarantee agreement cannot impose more onerous terms on the guarantor than those applicable to the principal debtor (*e.g.* English common law, French Civil Code, Art. 2013);

(c) if the underlying obligation of the exporter is illegal in any respect, the guarantor is discharged from his obligation (French Civil Code, Art. 2012; *Coutts & Co.* v. *Browne-Lecky* [1947] K.B. 104).

Unless the guarantor has specifically waived these rights in the guarantee agreement, the beneficiary of the guarantee must first exhaust his remedies at law against the principal debtor (exporter) before turning to the guarantor for payment of any unpaid balance due.

These waivers are common in practice, and usually include a statement that the guaranteeing bank recognises that it is an unlimited joint co-obligor with the exporter, so that the beneficiary can proceed, at his own choice, against either the exporter (principal debtor) or the bank (guarantor) for the whole or only part of the whole amount, due as a result of the exporter's default (see, for example, French Civil Code, Art. 2021).

In France, the guarantor may avail himself of any defence against payment to which the exporter is entitled (French Civil Code, Art. 2036), and is discharged if the beneficiary of the guarantee, by act or omission, fails to preserve fully all rights against the exporter which pass to the guarantor by subrogation (French Civil Code, Art. 2037). Since the promulgation of the Law No. 84–148 of March 1, 1984, this right cannot be waived contractually. (Source: *International Financial Law Review*, December 1986, p. 11.)

Under English common law, if the buyer grants the exporter an indulgence without the consent of the guarantor, the latter is freed from his obligation to the buyer. Such indulgence may be given, for example, by an extension of the time for the exporter to perform his contract, or by the release of a co-guarantor, or of another security used to ensure the exporter's performance.

Some guarantees contain a clause whereby the guarantor gives the buyer advance consent in the guarantee text to grant an indulgence. Such advance consents are perfectly legal.

In August 1978, the International Chamber of Commerce published a set of rules, Uniform Rules for Contract Guarantees (ICC Publication No. 325, "the 325 Rules"), which dealt with dependent contract guarantees issued by banks and surety companies payable on only proven default. These Rules were intended to establish "the principle of the need to justify a claim under a guarantee, to invest guarantee practice with a moral content". These Rules are discussed in Chapter 10: "International Code of Practice".

Independent guarantees

Guarantees payable on accepted or proven default can also be *independent* of the contract. Proof of default usually has to be in the form of:

(a)   the exporter's written admission of default;
(b)   an independent report of default (for example, an engineer's report under a civil engineering contract); or
(c)   a certificate of arbitration awarded or other legal proceeding in favour of the beneficiary.

Where the guarantee requires the beneficiary to submit his claim together with one of the above documents, no judgment is required of the bank except to check that the documents comply with the guarantee.

Such guarantees are acceptable to both the issuing bank and to the exporter, because there is little likelihood of a sudden unexpected outflow of cash from the exporter's account.

They are also equitable in respect of the buyer, as he can receive immediate payment from the bank on proof of default.

However, although equitable, such guarantees calling for independently produced documents are not always acceptable to buyers. For many buyers, arbitration is too slow and expensive, and ties up scarce resources. Bank guarantees payable on *first demand* are, therefore, preferred.

First demand guarantees

This is a category of guarantee that is often heavily biased in favour of the buyer.

Bank demand guarantees are *autonomous* of the underlying commercial contract. They are *primary* or *independent* guarantees and must be complete in themselves. As such, they do not require reference by the bank to the exporter, to a third party, to the related commercial contract, or to any other documents for proof of the exporter's contractual default, save those specified in the guarantee (if any) for interpretation of the obligations of the bank to pay a claim.

Banks require exporters to ensure that the guarantee wording is clear and unambiguous as it is not the function of the bank to arbitrate or decide whether the grounds for a claim are justified, only whether it is in accordance with the guarantee. The obligations of the issuing bank are purely financial.

The advantage to the beneficiary of a bank guarantee payable on first demand is that the claim procedure is extremely simple. Beneficiaries are able to secure cash payment quickly in the event of an *alleged dispute* so that they are placed in the strongest negotiating position.

The principal characteristics are:

(1) The bank's commitment is to pay up to the amount of its guarantee only if the beneficiary makes a compliant demand.

A compliant demand is a claim for payment supported by such documents or statements as may be specified in the guarantee (if any). Thus, if the issuing bank receives a demand which *appears on the face of it* to comply with the terms of the guarantee, the bank must pay. The nature of the bank's obligation does not involve it in deciding whether the documents are correct. The bank pays immediately and the exporter has no right to object.

(2) Payment of the guarantee is independent of the contract and all its protective clauses. A bank is not involved in deciding whether or not the respective contractual obligations have or have not been performed.

Banks have no means of judging whether or not the beneficiary has a justified grievance against the exporter under the contract and therefore proper grounds for a demand on the guarantee.

(3) The issuing bank will take recourse on the exporter.

As a matter of prudence, some banks may first take recourse on the exporter to cover their position and then pay the demand. Having paid a demand, there is the serious risk that the beneficiary may never repay a wrongfully demanded payment. This could, for example, be because of his insolvency or other commercial, political, economic or regulatory factors.

Nature of Demands

All bank guarantees are payable on *first demand* as long as the demand is compliant with the guarantee wording. However, the nature of the demand can vary. This affects the degree of risk to which the exporter is exposed.

There are three types of demand guarantee:

(a) Independent documentary demand guarantee;
(b) Demand guarantee requiring the beneficiary's statement of default;
(c) Simple demand guarantee.

How the beneficiary makes a demand on the guarantee depends on the
type of guarantee issued.

Independent documentary demand guarantees

These are payable "on demand" when supported by a document or
documents referred to in the guarantee. They usually require a statement
giving the reason for the claim and/or documentary evidence of default,
for example, a bill of lading showing that shipment took place on a date after the contractual due delivery date, an inspection certificate stating that
the quality of the goods was less than the contract specified, or such other
documents as are stated in the guarantee.

Demand guarantee requiring payment against beneficiary's statement

Guarantees can be payable "on demand" against the buyer's own statement of the reason for the claim. No independent evidence of default is required. As such, exporters should regard these guarantees as being almost
as dangerous as *simple demand* guarantees. The only difference is that the
unscrupulous beneficiary has to make a *deliberately false statement* of the exporter's default to fulfil the guarantee's requirements.

The issuing bank will usually accept any statement or document complying with the guarantee at face value unless there is *obvious fraud*.

Simple demand guarantees

Some guarantees provide for payment on "simple demand" without ex-
planation, justification or contestation. Simple demand guarantees are like
discounts, and as such nobody willingly concedes them. However, they
may have to be given in order to win a contract.

Like discounts, a payment under a guarantee is a direct drain on profitability. A discount is a finite sum with little risk of hidden costs. There is no
uncertainty about how much is conceded to win the business or when. On
the other hand, there is considerable uncertainty about the ultimate cost of
giving a simple demand bank guarantee and the nature of the risk. This
very much depends on the attitude of the beneficiary, the location of the
issuing bank, and the laws and regulations to which the guarantee is
subject.

The simple demand guarantee totally protects the buyer against actual,
threatened, or *imagined* default of the exporter.

For the exporter, it is like a blank cheque and constitutes cash in the
hands of the buyer, paid without any condition or evidence that the
buyer's demand is fair and justified.

Some prudent exporters would rather decline a contract than accept one
that was too heavily or unfairly secured by simple demand guarantees.

If a bank receives a demand against a simple demand guarantee, it must pay the beneficiary without reservation or any legal obligation to refer back and consult its customer, the exporter.

The exporter has no right to object to such a claim before it is paid, nor right of protest under the guarantee after payment.

Buyers may require such inequitable "simple demand" guarantees because they are an unavoidable requirement of local financial authority regulations. However, more frequently, it is because insufficient confidence and trust have been established between the two parties to the supply contract or, occasionally, between their respective financial authorities.

For many exporters and banks alike, guarantees issued payable on "simple demand" have become a real concern. They recognise what a powerful *coercive* weapon unscrupulous beneficiaries have in their hands, with which they can make unreasonable demands, *particularly after the contract is completed*. The risk of an unfair call hovers constantly over the exporter's head like Damocles' sword, and in times of recession banks have to be concerned about the continuing solvency of their customer.

Many banks do not concede simple demand guarantees willingly or as a matter of course. However, some European banks do prefer to issue them on this basis. They consider that an attempt to impose prior conditions to payment is likely to be resisted by the beneficiary. In the opinion of some European banks, conditional or documentary guarantees defeat the commercial objectives of a bank guarantee.

However, other banks, including those in the United Kingdom, together with exporters, have been more resistant to the request for simple demand guarantees. They recognise how dangerous they are to the exporter's cash-flow and solvency, and therefore the bank's ability to take recourse.

Independent guarantees in law

Banks regard their demand guarantees (*Garantie* in Germany and *garantie à première demande* in France and Belgium) as independent (primary or abstract) of the underlying commercial contract and although this autonomy has been challenged in the English and European courts, legal opinion has consistently supported the banks in this view (see Chapter 4: "Anticipating Unfair Demands").

Such independent demand guarantees first began to appear in the mid-1960s, concurrently with the expansion overseas of European contractors and suppliers. In France such guarantees, unlike their *cautionnements*, are not based on any statutory authority, unless the French Civil Code, Art. 1134 (which validates all contracts not violating public policy and which is often referred to in case law on guarantees payable on first demand), can be said to constitute a legal basis. In Germany, likewise, the *Garantie* is not dealt with at all in national law.

The issuing bank, and ultimately the exporter who counter-indemnifies the bank for any payment it is required to make, takes the risk of the beneficiary demanding payment, even though it may not be justified through default of the underlying commercial contract.

Under the terms of a demand guarantee, the issuing bank must unconditionally pay to the beneficiary the claimed amount up to the value of the guarantee when a demand is made in accordance with the guarantee.

Non-compliance by the buyer with the conditions of the autonomous underlying commercial contract, and even its illegality, or the buyer's insolvency (preventing subsequent repayment of an improper claim), cannot be used by the bank as defences to avoid the obligation to pay.

Central Bank Constraints—Risk Asset Ratios

In addition to the credit-worthiness of their customers, a further constraint on the provision by banks of demand guarantees is the ceiling on the total value of guarantees a bank will want to issue because of central bank constraints.

In the United Kingdom, for example, there are over 500 banks, of which just under half are branches of foreign banks. Most foreign banks are supervised by their own financial authorities, to whom the Bank of England looks for assurances on the overall soundness of the bank. So far as United Kingdom-incorporated banks are concerned, they are required to have permanent capital as a stable resource to cushion any losses. The bank's capital requirements have been based for many years on a system known as the *risk asset ratio*, a system which was enshrined in the E.C. Solvency Ratio Directive (Directive 89/647: [1989] O.J. L386/14), implemented in the United Kingdom from December 1990. The purpose of this is to weight a bank's assets. These are broken down into broad categories according to their degree of riskiness. Balance sheet items have been typically weighted as follows:

Cash = 0 per cent.;
Treasury bills = 10 per cent.;
United Kingdom Government stocks = 20 per cent.;
Guarantees on commercial loans, etc. = 100 per cent.;
Commercial loans = 100 per cent., etc.
(Source: "Bank of England Fact Sheet", May 1993.)

Bank guarantees and stand-by letters of credit, being off-balance sheet risks, have a risk weighting of 50 per cent.

The *capital assets* of a bank (also known as the capital base) are calculated as a percentage of the portfolio of risk-weighted assets. This percentage is the *capital ratio*. Each bank is set an individual capital ratio by the Bank of England, taking into account risk factors arising from the nature and business of the bank. Typically this is about 10 per cent. of the weighted capital assets. A higher ratio is set for a bank with inexperienced management or a high concentration of risk, or dependent on certain types of company, economic sector or country.

The Bank of England expects banks to report to it large exposures to individual customers and countries.

The significance of risk asset ratios, or their equivalent in other countries, is that whilst the issue of bank demand guarantees is a useful source of fee income to banks, the *contingent liability* which they create can tie up more profitable lending capacity.

Banks put a limit on the extent that their balance sheets are used to secure the issue of guarantees. They also endeavour to charge fees for guarantees which, in a competitive situation, best maximise the return on balance sheet utilisation.

Competitive Charges for Guarantees

Banks usually like issuing demand guarantees, in many cases to adjust their lending portfolios from high-risk loans to developing countries to a more stable fee-based business.

Different banks, particularly foreign banks, will have different capital ratios, and therefore pricing differences will arise. As a result, it is possible to obtain competitive fees from banks of different nationalities. This competition can be exploited by the larger, more informed, exporter. Smaller exporters tend not to be of interest to most foreign banks based in the United Kingdom.

In certain circumstances, there may be advantages in shopping around selectively, especially where exporters are in a position to request banks to provide a package which includes both bank guarantees, letters of credit and/or export finance supported by the national credit insurer.

This will maximise the benefits to the bank of using its balance sheet for contract guarantees and will encourage competitive pricing.

Competitive charges are also achievable from banks that have special expertise, or close links with banks in particular overseas countries.

However, it is true to say that with some banks, as with any other commercial organisations, exporters only get what they pay for. Many banks quote low fees, but give no help and advice on the risks and wordings of guarantees. On the other hand, some banks may let the exporter use the banks' unwillingness to issue simple demand guarantees as a means of persuading the buyer to accept less onerous bond wording.

Banks earning an economic fee are more likely to co-operate more actively with an exporter in the recovery and cancellation of a guarantee. This can be essential where the exporter is operating at the limits of his banking lines. Many exporters have to turn down business because of their lack of banking capacity caused by an excessive loading of their balance sheet with bank guarantees.

Direct Guarantees Issued in the Exporter's Country

Many demand guarantees are issued by the exporter's bank direct to the buyer. These are sometimes referred to as *direct* guarantees. The relationship of the parties is as shown below:

Figure 1

Direct guarantee: instructing and issuing process

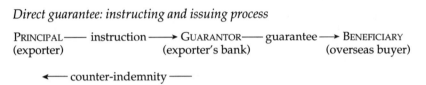

Wherever possible, the exporter should try to get the buyer to agree to accept a direct guarantee issued by the bank in the exporter's country. This can give the exporter greater control over the risks and costs.

Indirect Guarantees Issued in the Buyer's Country

However, overseas buyers often require guarantees issued to them by national banks in their own country. In some cases this is a local regulation over which the buyer has no control. These are sometimes referred to as *indirect* guarantees. In this case, the parties involved are the exporter (principal), the exporter's bank (instructing party), the correspondent bank (issuing bank and guarantor) and the buyer (beneficiary).

The risks and costs increase because they are subject to local laws, regulations and loyalties and influenced by local political vicissitudes. It is usual that the local issuing bank is fully indemnified by the exporter's bank, which in turn is indemnified by the exporter. It will also charge fees.

The relationship of the parties to an *indirect* guarantee is as shown below:

Figure 2

Indirect guarantee: instructing and issuing process

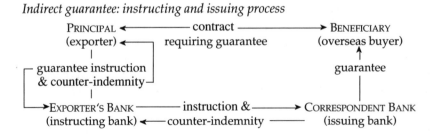

The exporter will usually have to ask his own bank to instruct a suitable *correspondent bank* in the buyer's country to issue the guarantee.

The correspondent bank would only accept issuing instructions against the security of the exporter's bank's *counter-guarantee*. This is because the correspondent bank normally has no relationship with the exporter and no alternative payment security to rely on in the event of a claim by the beneficiary on the guarantee.

From the exporter's point of view, locally-issued guarantees should be avoided if possible, because it is more difficult to control unjustified claims payable overseas where more than one bank is involved. Any action to stop payment must, in these circumstances, be directed towards the issuing bank in the buyer's country.

Where locally-issued bank guarantees cannot be avoided, the exporter should try to get the guarantee issued by a *local branch* or *affiliate* of his own bank. This does not get round the problem of local laws, regulations and jurisdiction, but will give him the opportunity to negotiate a single composite fee for the involvement of two affiliated banks. This way the exporter's bank maintains some control over the commitment, and is better placed to recover the guarantee or avoid any bank charges after its expiry.

A major disadvantage to the exporter of *indirect* guarantees is that, once the local issuing bank has paid a claim, payment by the exporter's bank (instructing bank) cannot be considered unjustified, even if the demand on the guarantee by the buyer was in itself unjustified.

Issuance and Indemnification

The guarantor bank becomes involved from the moment it receives written instructions from the exporter to establish a guarantee in favour of the buyer.

The instructions would, among other things, have to specify the guarantee wording that had been agreed. The buyer may have prescribed a certain wording from which neither the exporter nor the bank can deviate, or the exporter may have been in a position to agree wording with the buyer, or the bank may be allowed to use one of its recommended published specimens.

In order to make sure that it will be reimbursed in case it has to make payment under the guarantee, the bank will thoroughly check the exporter's credit-worthiness, as well as the security, collateral, etc., offered.

The bank will also require a counter-indemnity in writing (see p.28). This will authorise it to honour the beneficiary's demand immediately, without having to ask for reasons for the claim or check its justification. It also relieves the bank of the obligation of having to refer to the contract between the buyer and the exporter, notwithstanding any possible objections the exporter might have.

The exporter's indemnity will include an undertaking to pay the bank's commissions and to reimburse it for all its expenses, damages, losses, etc., resulting from the bank complying with the exporter's instructions.

Counter-indemnities

The issue of a bank guarantee involves the commitment by the bank to an *irrevocable obligation*. The bank's national and international reputation is dependent upon its prompt compliance with such obligations. The situation is similar for surety companies when they issue surety bonds. Therefore, guarantees and bonds are not given lightly, and certainly not without a back-to-back commitment from the exporter.

In return for the bank's or surety company's agreement to issue a guarantee or bond in writing on behalf of the exporter, the exporter will usually be required to provide an *indemnity* committing him to reimburse the guarantor's payment and costs in the event of a claim.

Under English law, a guarantor has a right to indemnity against the person guaranteed, but guarantors, irrespective of nationality, nevertheless normally request a written counter-indemnity. The contract of indemnity is a two-party arrangement. The exporter undertakes to hold the bank or surety company harmless if it suffers loss as a result of a claim. In other words, the indemnity is a *primary* obligation on the part of the exporter. (This compares with the *secondary* obligation of the three-party relationship associated with the common law guarantee. Here the buyer has a claim against the exporter, and the guarantor undertakes to pay the buyer if the exporter fails to remedy his default.)

The contract of indemnity is valid even if the underlying contract guaranteed is flawed by invalidity (*Coutts & Co.* v. *Browne-Lecky* [1947] K.B. 104).

The extent of the indemnity is encapsulated in the wording of the counter-indemnity. It is an area of significant risk for the exporter. The wording is often all-embracing, counter-indemnifying guarantors for everything they do, or even fail to do, in relation to the issue, maintenance and cancellation of the guarantee.

The majority of banks and surety companies use their own standard forms of counter-indemnity. These vary considerably in terms, conditions, and complexity. The exporter should ensure that his liability under the indemnity is not open-ended as to value, reason for claim or validity. Most standard form counter-indemnities contain a *conclusive evidence clause*, which makes it virtually impossible for the exporter to dispute the validity of any claim. Exporters need to study the terms of the required counter-indemnity most carefully (and if necessary take legal advice) before instructing the bank to issue a bank demand guarantee.

One method of restricting exposure is for the exporter to give individual counter-indemnities for each guarantee issued, particularly high-value guarantees, even though a single omnibus indemnity covering all guarantees issued by a single bank is administratively more convenient.

Exporters also need to ensure that the individual counter-indemnity refers to the specific guarantee in question, for example, by attaching a copy of the guarantee as issued and initialling it as "relevant thereto" when he signs the counter-indemnity.

Counter-indemnities which automatically reimburse the banks, for example, through direct debits, should be resisted. There is a strong argument for only using banks with whom there is no directly debitable bank account.

Exporters should try to ensure that the counter-indemnity restricts the bank to claims for reimbursement of amounts it has actually paid against a demand, and then only if the claim has been made by the buyer or the bank's overseas correspondent in strict compliance with the conditions of the guarantee.

The following specimen counter-indemnity from Barclays Bank permits payment of a claim without any requirement for Barclays to verify that the claim was made by an authorised person or that the claim documents are genuine. As mentioned above, it contains a *conclusive evidence* clause.

Counter-indemnity to bank

(Source: Barclays Bank Group.)

To: Barclays Bank PLC

1. The consideration for this indemnity shall be your giving and/or procuring the giving by your correspondents of a bond, indemnity, guarantee or other obligation in the terms of the copy endorsed hereon or attached hereto (which I/we have verified and signed) ("the Obligation").
2. I/we [jointly and severally] for myself/ourselves and my/our legal personal representatives hereby
   2.1 agree to keep you indemnified from and against all actions, proceedings, liabilities, claims, demands, damages, costs and expenses in relation to or arising out of or appearing to you to arise out of the Obligation and/or your indemnity in respect thereof and to pay to you on demand all payments by you in consequence thereof or arising thereout whether directly or indirectly; and
   2.2 irrevocably authorise you to debit to any of my/our account(s) with you all such payments, losses, costs, charges, damages and expenses, and further agree that you shall be at liberty without any notice or further or other consent from me/us to apply or transfer any money now or at any time hereafter standing to my/our credit upon account deposit or any other account in payment or in part payment of any such sums of money as may be or hereafter may from time to time become due or owing to you from or by me/us hereunder or to a suspense account and that you may refuse payment of any cheque bill note or order drawn or accepted by me/us or upon which I/we may be otherwise liable and which if paid would reduce the amount of money standing to my/our credit as aforesaid to less than the amount for the time being so due or owing to you from or by me/us as aforesaid; and
   2.3 irrevocably authorise and direct you to make any payments and comply with any demands which may be claimed or made or appear to

you to be claimed or made under the Obligation and/or your indemnity in respect thereof without reference to or further authority confirmation or verification from me/us and agree that any payment which you shall make in accordance or appearing to you to be in accordance with the Obligation and/or your indemnity in respect thereof shall be binding upon me/us and shall be accepted by me/us as conclusive evidence that you were liable to make such payment or comply with such demand and further that you may at any time determine or procure the determination of the Obligation and/or your indemnity in respect thereof; and

2.4 agree (without prejudice to any other provision of this indemnity) that any demand made upon you and/or your correspondents for payment of sums specified in the Obligation shall for all purposes relating to this indemnity be deemed to be a valid and effective demand and you and your correspondents shall be entitled to treat it as such notwithstanding any actual lack of authority on the part of the person making the demand if the demand appears on its face to be in order and

2.4.1 the demand is made by or through a bank or any other person carrying on a banking business, or

2.4.2 the demand appears to you or your correspondents to be made by or on behalf of the beneficiary; and

2.5 agree (without prejudice to any other provision of this indemnity) that in the event that the Obligation stipulates that a demand made upon you and/or your correspondents shall be accompanied by any document or documents then, provided that it or they appear on their face to be in accordance with the terms of the Obligation, such document or documents shall for all purposes relating to this indemnity be deemed to be genuine and in accordance with the terms of the Obligation; and

2.6 agree that my/our liability hereunder shall also apply to any extension or renewal of the Obligation (whether in the same terms or otherwise and whether arising with my/our agreement or by operation of law or otherwise) and/or your indemnity in respect thereof to the intent that all agreements, undertakings and authorities herein shall continue to be binding on me/us in relation to the Obligation and/or your indemnity in respect thereof as so extended or renewed; and

2.7 agree (without prejudice to any other provision of this indemnity) that (at your discretion and/or the discretion of your correspondents and entirely at my/our risk) you and/or your correspondents may use the telex system or other telegraph service of any country or any other recognised telegraph or transmission system for the purpose of giving the Obligation or sending any message relating or appearing to relate to the Obligation and/or your indemnity in respect thereof and in this connection I/we specifically release and indemnify you and your correspondents (and each of you and them) from and against the consequences of your and/or their failure and/or the failure of any other person to receive any such message in the form in which it was despatched and from and against the consequences of any delay that might occur during the course of the transmission of any such message.

3. This indemnity shall be governed by English Law and shall be additional to any other indemnity which you now or hereafter may hold.

Signed this   day of   19   by me/us, (or by
and   on behalf of   pursuant to a resolution of the Board of Dir-

ectors dated   19   a copy of which is hereto annexed/in your
possession).

Witness's Signature
and Address

(Note: The wording of the counter-indemnity may vary depending, for example, upon whether the counter-indemnity relates to a single bank guarantee or a number of guarantees which may be issued in the future.)

Inter-bank Counter-indemnities

There is often more than one counter-indemnity in the bonding chain, as
the buyer may require a guarantee to be issued by his local bank. If so, this
will require an instruction and counter-indemnity from the exporter's
bank (instructing bank).

The instructing bank will, in turn, require a counter-indemnity from the
exporter. Every link in the chain is a separate unconditional legal
undertaking.

The exporter is not party to the inter-bank agreement and counter-
indemnity, the wording of which he never sees and which may be subject
to a different law and jurisdiction to that governing the exporter's instructions and indemnity to his own bank. He has little or no influence over the
chain of independent liabilities that links him with the buyer, yet is required to carry all the costs arising from the whole process of issuing a
guarantee and maintaining its effectiveness, and ultimately the risk of a
demand.

The exporter's risks increase the more parties there are in the chain. He
has no control over costs, except perhaps those of his own bank, nor over
subsequent unfair claims.

The inter-bank counter-indemnity is a totally independent obligation.
This view has been upheld in a French case heard in the Cour de Cassation,
Chambre Commerciale, on March 18, 1986 (*Banque Egyptienne M.I.S.R.* v.
Banque de l'Indochine et de Suez et Banque de l'Union des Mines (1986) 17
Recueil Dalloz-Sirey 163).

This means that the claim on the counter-indemnity by a bank which
issued a guarantee on behalf of the exporter is not automatically unjustified even when the claim on the guarantee by the beneficiary is unfair
(*Esal (Commodities) Ltd. and Reltor Ltd.* v. *Oriental Credit Ltd. and Wells Fargo
Bank N.A.* (unreported, Court of Appeal, July 31, 1985)).

However, a claim by the issuing bank under the counter-indemnity from
the instructing bank would *probably* be unjustified if the beneficiary had
not made a claim. This depends on the wording of the counter-indemnity
between the banks. The issuing bank need not necessarily pay the beneficiary's claim before claiming under the inter-bank counter-indemnity.

In many cases, the counter-indemnity risks are more onerous than the
underlying bond itself because they are *open-ended*. If the buyer calls the

guarantee, the local bank pays and debits the exporter's bank, which debits the exporter.

A claim against an inter-bank counter-indemnity may be considered *fraudulent* if the bank which issued the guarantee, together with the beneficiary, co-operated in a fraudulent way, especially when the bank knows, or ought to know, the fraudulent nature of the claim against the guarantee.

This point on the co-operation between the beneficiary and the issuing bank was clarified by the French Cour de Cassation, Chambre Commerciale, on December 11, 1985 in the case *Banque Téjarat* v. *Soc. Auxiliaire d'Entreprise et Crédit Lyonnais* (1986) 19 *Recueil Dalloz-Sirey* 213.

The Swiss Cour de Justice de Génève on September 8, 1982 and on September 29, 1983, also ruled on this point (*U.B.S.* v. *I.P.I. Trade International et Banque Melli Iran* [1984] *Dalloz* 93).

Figure 3

Legal links between contract guarantees and counter-indemnities

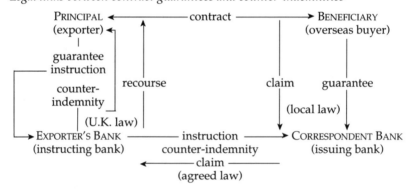

This shows the separate and unrelated legal relationships at each stage of the guarantee-issuing process. The exporter carries full liability for the risks and costs, but has no control over the process once he has given his instructions and counter-indemnity to his bank to issue a demand guarantee.

Three separate laws and jurisdictions could be involved in the bonding process. The exporter has no say in the wording of the counter-indemnity given to the correspondent bank. There is no legal link between the contract, the guarantee and associated counter-indemnity. Each has independent legal status. Therefore, any legal safeguards in the contract do not normally get reflected in the guarantee, and the counter-indemnity(s) can create risks beyond those contained in the guarantee.

Stand-by Letters of Credit

In the United States, contract guarantees in the form of surety bonds are the domain of surety companies such as Chubb, Frank B. Hall and Federal Insurance, etc.

Banks compete for this lucrative bonding business using a different financial instrument, because they are prohibited by federal banking regulations from issuing contract guarantees, so they resort to *stand-by letters of credit* to guarantee the performance of contracts. They are mainly used by United States banks which are incorporated as national associations. They enable the buyer to obtain payment in the event of the exporter being in default, by presenting to the advising or confirming bank the documents specified in the letter of credit.

Stand-by letters of credit are subject to the International Chamber of Commerce's Uniform Customs and Practices for Documentary Credits 1983 Revision (ICC Publication No. 400 (No. 500 from January 1, 1994), "UCP"). As such, they are independent of the underlying contract and provide for the buyer the same degree of protection as bank guarantees.

From the exporter's point of view, the UCP contains protective clauses which, for example:

(a)   stipulate the minimum requirements for the presentation of any claim and supporting documents; and

(b)   make it clear to both parties how banks will view the authenticity of claim documents presented.

They offer the exporter an opportunity to avoid the risk of an unfair call. They set out clearly the responsibilities of the issuing bank as regards payment of claims. In particular, there can be no confusion about validity and expiry dates. They ensure that the credit expires on its due date, unless an extension requested by the beneficiary is also mutually agreed by the exporter and his bank.

The advantage of this instrument is that the claiming documents have to be agreed before the letter of credit can be opened. Payment by the issuing bank can only be made on receipt by it of a *compliant demand* by the beneficiary. This can be either in the form of a simple request for payment, a request supported by a statement containing the reasons for the call, or a request with a statement plus supporting documentary evidence. This choice gives the exporter an opportunity to negotiate out of any payment documents which would in effect give the buyer cash on simple demand without a reason being stated.

Not all buyers are prepared to accept stand-by letters of credit. Equally, many exporters are not prepared to use them because they are a significant drain on banking lines, being treated by most banks, and other governing central financial institutions, as a *liability*, and not as a *contingent liability* with a lower reserve asset weighting, which is usually the case with bonds.

In certain circumstances, it may be possible for exporters outside the United States to persuade buyers to accept stand-by letters of credit, especially if the buyer is known to deal with United States exporters.

Chapter 3 explains the minimum requirements to be included in a guarantee and gives a number of specimen texts called for by overseas buyers.

A brief commentary against each draws attention to omissions and risks they contain, mainly from the point of view of the exporter.

Chapter 4 provides specimen texts of guarantees as suggested by recognised English and European institutions.

Annex: Inter-bank Counter-guarantees

Michael Vasseur, Professor of Commercial Law at the Paris University for Law, Economics and Science has been able to provide some valuable research on the attitude of French courts to the *autonomy* of the inter-bank guarantee. This is required when the exporter's bank has to issue a guarantee through a bank in the buyer's country. The issuing bank requires a means of securing payment from the instructing bank in the event of the beneficiary making a claim against the bond.

Vasseur's research reveals that the bank demand guarantee (*primary guarantee*) is not the only autonomous undertaking; the *counter-guarantee* between the instructing bank and the issuing bank is also an autonomous undertaking.

It is autonomous in respect of the primary guarantee as well as of the basic contract. The French Commercial Chamber called it so in its judgments of November 27, 1984, December 12, 1984 and February 5, 1985 ([1985] D.269, note Vasseur).

The Commercial Chamber chose the adjective "*autonomous*" in preference to "*independent*" previously used by authors who wished to distinguish precisely the nature of the inter-bank guarantee from the bond, which is a collateral, *i.e.* dependent on the main debtor's commitment.

The Commercial Chamber considered that the word "*autonomous*" had the advantage of expressing, with considerable emphasis, that:

(a) the undertaking of the banker granting a guarantee or counter-indemnity was his own commitment, even if he accepted it at the principal's request ((1986) D. 213, note Vasseur (Com.));

(b) the primary guarantee and counter-guarantee are in no way influenced by the basic contract; and additionally

(c) the primary guarantee is in no way influenced by the counter-guarantee.

Consequentially, the French Cour de Cassation arrived at the following conclusions:

(a) The bank cannot avail itself of defences the exporter could use against the beneficiary on account of the failure to carry out, or the faulty implementation of, the contract (Com., October 17, 1984);

(b) The arbitration clause included in the basic contract can have no bearing on the application of the letter of the guarantee (Com., December 20, 1982);

(c) Amendments to the basic contract, or the alleged invalidity of this contract, are without any influence on the bank's commitment (Com., December 20, 1982). However, some share the view that invalidity resulting from a breach of mandatory laws (*e.g.* a contract for the purchase of illicit drugs) may be a valid exception.

More specifically, the Commercial Chamber, in its judgment of November 2, 1985 ([1986] D. 213, note Vasseur) in the case *Dypra* v. *Banque Vernes*, logically drew from the autonomy of the counter-guarantee that the scope of the counter-guarantee is not necessarily the same as that of the primary guarantee. The inter-bank counter-guarantee may be broader than the guarantee; it is not confined to the latter.

Similarly, it is true that the counter-guarantee is autonomous *vis-à-vis* the primary guarantee; that while the guarantee could be a collateral security, *i.e.* a genuine bond according to the French Civil Code, the counter-guarantee would still be an autonomous on-demand guarantee ([1987] D. 17, note Vasseur (Com.)).

From the fact that the guarantee and inter-bank counter-guarantee are autonomous, the courts have drawn the following consequences:

(a) The banker who is the counter-guarantor and whose counter-guarantee is claimed by the banker who is the primary guarantor cannot request the latter to justify that the beneficiary claimed the guarantee in writing or that it was paid by the said banker, if no such provision was included in the counter-guarantee ([1985] D. 269, note Vasseur (Com.); Somm. 174, obs. Vasseur (Com.); Somm. 176, obs. Vasseur (Paris));

(b) The fact that the beneficiary's claim against the primary guarantor was fraudulent does not vitiate by fraud the claim against the counter-guarantee by the banker who was the primary guarantor, as long as there was *no fraudulent collusion* between the said banker and the beneficary; and

(c) It does not matter whether the claim against the primary guarantee was made outside the time limit; the only thing that matters is whether the counter-guarantee was claimed within the agreed period of time ([1987] D. 17, note Vasseur (Com.)).

The autonomy of the guarantee and the inter-bank counter-guarantee, and the fact that the banker's commitment is his own, are also reflected in the fact that the banker is not bound to request the principal's permission before paying, nor even to advise him.

If he usually advises him, that is up to the banker and is quite all right; but according to a judgment by the Grenoble Court of Appeal of November 12, 1987 ([1988] Somm. 247, obs. Vasseur), he is not compelled to do so unless it was agreed between the principal and the bank.

The bank must pay. If it resists, it can be sentenced to pay to the beneficiary, not merely interest in arrears but damages under the Civil Code, Art. 1153.

Such a resistance will be found to be dilatory and in bad faith since, as a professional, the banker cannot misunderstand the nature and characteristics of the obligations he accepted, and pretend that it was no more than a collateral bond (Com., December 20, 1982; [1988] D. Somm. 240, obs.

Vasseur (Com.)).

The Paris Commercial Court on February 15, 1984 rendered a judgment—reversed subsequently by the Court of Appeal ([1986] D.I.R. 157, obs. Vasseur)—inflicting damages on a bank that had not paid a counter-guarantee after being advised of an arrestation, later withdrawn, precisely because it *was* subsequently withdrawn.

This also results from a judgment of the French Commercial Chamber of October 7, 1987 ([1988] D. 265, note Vasseur) in the related field of documentary credits, stating that an *attachment* by the exporter cannot prevent the bank from fulfilling the direct commitment it has undertaken *vis-à-vis* the beneficiary.

It is true that in other circumstances the Paris Court of Appeal ruled in a judgment of December 3, 1984 ([1985] D.I.R. 240, obs. Vasseur) that by paying a guarantee in spite of a sequestration of goods ordered by a judge and not withdrawn, the bank had failed to respect the courts and their decisions.

CHAPTER 3

TEXT OF GUARANTEES

Chapters 1 and 2 explained the different types of guarantee and their sources, how they are issued and the requirement for counter-indemnities.

The purpose of this Chapter is to distinguish between high-risk and low-risk texts, and to show how the differing interests and negotiating strengths of the buyer and the seller are reflected in the text of the guarantee.

What is considered desirable by overseas buyers is often viewed as unreasonable by the exporter, and may even be unacceptable to the guarantor.

This Chapter provides specimens of a wide range of texts that have been drafted to meet the needs of specific contracts and buyers. It highlights the risks that have arisen either through poor drafting, locally imposed texts, or weak negotiating by the exporter.

(Chapter 4 provides specimens of recommended guarantees published by English and European institutions.)

Drafting Guarantees

Exporter's objectives

The objective of the exporter is to provide the lowest value guarantee, with the least onerous wording, to win a contract, and to ensure that it cannot be used to exert unfair financial or coercive extra-contractual pressure on him.

Exporters in a very strong negotiating position are able either to win contracts without conceding onerous guarantees, or with guarantees that are not unilaterally enforceable. This usually gives them the opportunity to establish the cause of any claim without first suffering a sudden outflow of cash.

Buyer's objectives

In principle, the buyer seeks a guarantee which effectively protects those contractual interests of particular concern to him, such as proper performance, warranty, or refund of an unearned advance payment. It is for him to ensure that there is such control over the exporter that he completes the contract. He therefore needs the guarantee to be readily enforceable.

However, some buyers achieve excessive control over the exporter through unreasonable one-sided guarantee wording and undue influence over their local bank.

Guarantees in International Trade

The variable nature of international trade is such that two guarantees are rarely the same, although there are key features common to all. Often it is easier to modify a near suitable text than to draft an original.

All guarantees should contain the following minimum information:

(a)   name of the beneficiary;
(b)   name of the guarantor;
(c)   name of the exporter/applicant;
(d)   purpose of guarantee;
(e)   date guarantee commences (effective date);
(f)   date guarantee expires and becomes unenforceable;
(g)   maximum amount guaranteed;
(h)   any reduction provisions;
(i)   manner of claiming payment;
(j)   documents to support a claim; and
(k)   law and jurisdiction.

It is the omission of some of these key items, or their inclusion in terms biased against the exporter, that usually creates the risk of an *unfair* demand for payment under the guarantee, and often renders virtually impossible the recovery of claims paid.

Guarantee wording needs to be clear and unambiguous, and the obligations of the guarantor not open to interpretation. The text should reflect commercial prudence and be so drafted that:

(a)   its terms are consistent with those of the commercial contract;
(b)   the amount payable under a claim is finite;
(c)   the guarantor knows when to pay;
(d)   its date for coming into effect, validity period, expiry date and reduction clauses are clear and workable;
(e)   the reason and procedure for making a claim are specific;
(f)   it contains no express conditions which make the risk open-ended and compel the exporter to *"top up"* the value after a call, or automatically extend its validity period;
(g)   there is a procedure for settling disputes; and

(h)   it complies with the prevailing laws and regulations, especially in the buyer's country.

The shorter and more succinct the wording, the greater the clarity. However, excess brevity should be avoided if this can result in key terms and protections being omitted.

It is generally considered reasonable that a buyer should be able to have the contract completed and, if this fails, to recover from the exporter or a third party some or all of his losses up to the value of the guarantee.

It is, however, unreasonable that the buyer should be able to claim the value of the guarantee when the exporter:

(a)   has not materially failed to perform the contract;
(b)   has defaulted but has rectified the default;
(c)   has failed to rectify the default but has paid the contractually due penalties to the buyer; or
(d)   has defaulted for reasons totally outside his control, such as buyer's default, political events, natural disasters, etc.

In lesser developed and developing countries, the form of wording of a guarantee or aspects of the guarantee, such as place of issue, validity, method and timing of claim, etc., is often imposed on the parties by local laws or banking regulations.

Formal requests for tenders usually incorporate the text of the guarantees that the exporter will be required to have issued in the event the contract is awarded to him. Only in certain circumstances are such guarantees negotiable. This depends on the extent to which the exporter can qualify his tender to leave the door open for further discussions and negotiation.

The text of guarantees can be considered under many headings, but low- and high-risk are the most suitable for our purposes.

Low-risk Texts

Guarantees that cannot be unilaterally called by the beneficiary are not usually at risk of an unfair demand.

Guarantees written by surety companies or banks permitting payment only on admitted or proven default offer the exporter the lowest-risk text. In an exporter's ideal world, all guarantees would be issued in the wording of surety companies. These work on the premise that it is the intention of all parties to the guarantee to see the contract completed. The obligation of a surety company is to see that this is achieved if the contractor defaults on his contractual responsibilities.

Surety bonds are accessory bonds of *secondary* obligation, and dependent for their interpretation on the tender or contract. A claim can only be made after the exporter has failed to comply with the conditions of the underlying tender or contract, and only then after the buyer's remedies under the tender or contract have been exhausted and resulted in failure. The surety company has every incentive to help the exporter fulfil his contractual obligations and reduce the liability, to avoid paying out the full value of the surety bond.

Specimen surety bonds

The following are typical specimens of tender and performance bonds issued by surety companies.

A key feature is that the guarantee remains *null and void* until the exporter has defaulted and has neither put right the default nor paid the claim.

Tender bonds

This example is silent on the governing law and jurisdiction. Failure to provide a contract performance bond is a reason to call the tender bond.

To:...
Ceylon...Board

Contract No...   Project Description...

BY THIS BOND WE...whose registered office is at...(hereinafter called the Tenderer) AND...whose registered office is at...(hereinafter called the Surety) are held and firmly bound unto the Ceylon...Board, Colombo, Sri Lanka (hereinafter called the Employer) in the sum of...(...) for the payment of which sum the Tenderer and the Surety bind themselves their successors and assigns jointly and severally by these Presents.

Sealed with our respective seals and dated this...day of...19...

WHEREAS

(1) The Employer has invited the Tenderer and other persons to complete Tenders in similar terms for the provision, execution and maintenance of the specific works and to submit the same for consideration by the Employer.

(2) The Tenderer herewith submits to the Employer a Tender in accordance with such invitation and has agreed by the above-written Bond to provide security for the due performance by him of the undertakings and obligations in the Tender on his part contained.

NOW THE CONDITION of the above-written Bond is such that:

(a) if the Tender is accepted by the Employer within one hundred and twenty (120) days from the...day of...19...and the Tenderer shall have provided a Surety in accordance with his undertaking in paragraph...of the Tender, or

(b) if the Tender be not accepted within the said period of 120 days, or

(c) if before the expiration of the said period of 120 days a Tender from an-

other person for the execution of the Works shall have been accepted by
the Employer

THEN this obligation shall be null and void but otherwise the Tenderer and Surety will pay the Employer the full amount of this guarantee as liquidated damages and no alteration in the terms of the Tender nor any forbearance nor any
forgiveness in respect of any matter concerning the Tender on the part of the Employer shall in any way release the Surety from any liability under the above
written Bond.

SIGNED SEALED AND DELIVERED by the said...
in the presence of...
THE COMMON SEAL OF...was hereunto affixed
in the presence of...

Performance bonds

The following is a dependent guarantee which reduces *pro rata* to shipment. It is silent on the governing law and jurisdiction.

To:...
Indonesia

KNOW ALL MEN BY THESE PRESENTS:

That we...(full name and address), hereinafter called the CONTRACTOR, and...
(full legal title), hereinafter called the SURETY, are held and firmly bound
unto...(full name and address) as Obligee, hereinafter called the BUYER in the
amount of...(figures and words) for the payment whereof the CONTRACTOR
and the SURETY bind themselves, their heirs, executors, administrators, successors and assignees, jointly and separately, firmly by these Presents.

WHEREAS the CONTRACTOR has by written agreement dated...19...entered
into a contract with the BUYER for the supply and installation of...in Indonesia
in accordance with the terms of the said Contract which is hereby referred to and
made part hereof as if fully set forth herein.

NOW, THEREFORE, THE CONDITION OF THIS OBLIGATION IS SUCH, that
if the above bounden CONTRACTOR shall well and truly keep, do and perform
each and every, all and singular, of the matters and things in the said CON-
TRACT set forth and specified to be by the said CONTRACTOR kept, done and
performed, at the times and in the manner in said contract specified, or shall pay
over, make good and reimburse to the BUYER, all loss and damage which the
BUYER must sustain by reason of failure or default on the part of the CON-
TRACTOR so to do, then this obligation shall be null and void, otherwise shall remain in full force and effect.

PROVIDED THAT the said amount of...(figures and words) shall be reduced automatically by five percent of the CONTRACT VALUE pro rata to each shipment
on acceptance thereof in accordance with the terms of the Contract.

Sealed with our seals and dated this...day of A.D...19...

IN THE PRESENCE OF:
...(Contractor)   (Seal)
...(Surety)   (Seal)

Most performance bonds do not reduce as the contract progresses. In the following example, which is governed by local law and jurisdiction, payment is against a claim with the engineer's supporting statement of default.

To:...
Tanzania

WHEREAS by a Contract dated the...day of...19...(the Contract) and made between...(the Contractor) and the NATIONAL CORPORATION, Dar es Salaam, Tanzania (the Employer), the Contractor has agreed to execute, complete and maintain the...Project and Related Works (the Works) as therein mentioned in conformity with the provisions thereof and

WHEREAS it is a requirement of the Contract that the Contractor shall provide Sureties and whereas...and...(jointly called the Sureties) have agreed to execute this Performance Bond and deliver the same to the Employer,

KNOW ALL MEN BY THIS BOND we the Contractor and the Sureties are held firmly bound unto the Employer in the sum of...in the lawful money of...for the payment of which sum the Contractor and the Sureties bind themselves and their Assignees jointly and severally by these Presents.

THIS BOND shall be irrecoverable and payable to the Employer on demand without any need for notarial or judicial proceedings, subject only to the payment condition stipulated below.

PAYMENT herein shall be made by the Sureties to the Employer upon receipt by the Sureties of a written demand from the Employer stating, firstly, that the Contractor is in default of his obligations under the Contract and, secondly, a description of the nature of such default and a certificate in writing from the Engineer appointed in relation to the Contract confirming the statements of the Employer in his demand with respect to the default of the Contractor. The liability of the Sureties hereunder shall cease upon receipt by the Sureties of a copy of the Certificate of Completion issued by the said Engineer and thereafter this Bond shall not be valid for any purposes whatsoever and shall be returned to the Sureties.

NOW THE CONDITION of the above-written Bond is such that if the Contractor shall duly perform and observe all the terms, provisions, conditions and stipulations of the Contract on the Contractor's part to be performed and observed according to the true purport, intend and meaning thereof, or if on default by the Contractor the Sureties shall satisfy and discharge the damages sustained by the Employer thereby up to the amount of the above-written Bond, then this obligation shall be null and void but otherwise shall be and remain in full force and effect but no alteration in terms of the said Contract or in the extent or nature of the Works to be built or constructed, erected, delivered and maintained thereunder and no allowance of time by the Employer or the said Engineer under the said Contract nor any forbearance or forgiveness in or in respect of any matter or thing concerning the said contract on the part of the Employer or the said Engineer shall in any way release the Sureties from any liability under the above-written Bond.

THIS BOND shall be governed by and construed in accordance with the laws of the United Republic of Tanzania.

IN WITNESS WHEREOF we have hereunto set out our hand this...day of...19...

Signed ...

In practice, the commercial philosophy of surety companies is closer to that of insurance companies than to that of banks. Their objective is to minimise the cost of getting a contract completed. This reduces the recourse they need to take on the exporter.

It is in the exporter's interest to provide guarantees with surety bond wording because there is little risk of a sudden outflow of cash in the event of a claim by the beneficiary, whether *fair* or *unfair*. For this reason some buyers are unwilling to accept such bonds.

Bank requirements

A bank guarantee is usually a guarantee *independent* of the contract. Unlike surety companies, a bank pays only against the documents specified in the guarantee as being necessary to support a claim.

Banks usually require to see and approve the guarantee wording before they agree to issue it. Some provide their own preferred text. Others have been known to seek amendments to texts that have already been agreed and incorporated into the contract. This usually only occurs when the bank considers the agreed text to be unclear or ambiguous as regards the responsibilities of the bank.

Care should be taken to draft guarantees in precise terms, and to check early with the issuing bank that the proposed text is acceptable, operable and effective in the way the exporter intended it to be.

It may be necessary to seek independent legal advice from an experienced source in the buyer's country, particularly, in some cases, where the guarantee has to be issued by a local bank and subject to local law.

Banks normally require that any guarantee they are asked to issue should comply with the following criteria:

(1) The guarantee should be for a finite sum of money either in sterling or in a specified foreign currency. The guarantee must not place upon the bank an obligation to complete a contract or to rectify defects, the bank's obligation being confined to the payment of the defined sum of money;

(2) The wording of the guarantee should be precise and unambiguous and, in particular, the circumstances in which the bank has to pay a claim under the guarantee must be clear. Banks will not enter into a commitment which involves acting as arbitrator between their customer and the buyer in connection with a claim;

(3) The guarantee should provide for termination on a specified date or on an indisputable event, *e.g.* the issue and production to the bank of a specified architect's or engineer's certificate;

(4) The beneficiary should not be able to assign the guarantee (although this does not prevent the proceeds of a claim being assigned).

The exporter needs to table his preferred guarantee wording *in the early stages of negotiation* and get it agreed by the beneficiary and the issuing bank. There is often no reason why a specimen guarantee should not be included in the quotation with the exporter's other conditions. Once it is tabled, the parties can negotiate the contract and guarantee wording in tandem. This approach helps to keep risks in focus during contract negotiation. The guarantee should not introduce more risks than those accepted by the exporter in the contract.

The exporter's ability to negotiate reasonable wording in the guarantee depends on:

(a)   the attitude of the buyer and exporter;
(b)   the experience and negotiating skills of the exporter and his banking and legal advisers;
(c)   the strength of the respective negotiating positions; and
(d)   precedents that have already been set.

Not all exporters give the necessary attention to the negotiation of the text of bank demand guarantees. It is often an issue they prefer to *avoid* during discussions with the buyer. As a result, they leave it until they know they have a good chance of signing a contract.

Unfortunately, this is when the buyer is in the strongest position to dictate the nature of the guarantee as the exporter, by this time, has used up most of his negotiating points. In a competitive situation, they often concede guarantees capable of unfair demand, despite the dangerous precedents they set. *Some exporters prefer to concede high-risk guarantees rather than risk losing a contract.*

An experienced exporter would want to negotiate guarantee wording which restricts the reasons for a call to only those events of default which materially impact on the buyer. He would seek to avoid loose, all-embracing, omnibus wording which permits the buyer to call the guarantee for minor defaults of minimal material significance, or for no reason at all, as in the case of *simple demand bonds*.

Every concession the exporter is asked to make that could affect his ability to complete the contract profitably needs to be considered in the light of the buyer's ability to call the guarantee.

When faced with a request for a guarantee, the exporter has several options:

(1)   agree to give no guarantee at all;
(2)   offer his own, or parent company's guarantee (however, this could create problems in controlling potential risk of open-ended liability: see Chapter 9: "Corporate Guarantees");
(3)   give a surety bond where default has to be admitted or proved;
(4)   give a bank guarantee payable against written demand supported

by the beneficiary's statement plus documents—preferably independent documents proving default;

(5) give a bank guarantee payable against written demand plus the beneficiary's statement only, *i.e.* the beneficiary must support his demand by stating that the exporter has failed to perform his contractual obligations, preferably also indicating how he has failed;

(6) offer a stand-by letter of credit payable against a claim supported by documents/statements detailed therein provided by the buyer;

(7) offer a simple demand guarantee, *i.e.* requiring no statement and no documents (a) issued by exporter's bank; or (b) issued by local bank.

Some banks are prepared to issue guarantees with low-risk wording similar to that of surety companies, provided that the circumstances resulting in a valid claim are readily verifiable by the bank without reference to the underlying contract, or provided that the documents against which claims have to be paid are clearly stated.

Advance payment guarantee

Guarantees against advance payment would fall into this category; for example, the following advance payment guarantee, which requires documentary proof of default by the exporter and reduces against independent proof of performance.

To:...
Tanzania

THIS DEED OF GUARANTEE made on the...day of...19...by...of...(hereinafter called the Bank) of the first part and...a Body Corporate, incorporated in and under the laws of the United Republic of Tanzania and having its registered office at..., Dar es Salaam, Tanzania (hereinafter called the Employer) of the second part.

WHEREBY the Bank by these Presents unconditionally guarantees payment to the Employer of a sum of...(amount in figures and words) in the lawful currency of...for the payment of which the Bank and...(hereinafter called the Contractor) and their Assigns and Successors are jointly and severally liable.

This guarantee shall be irrevocable and the sum guaranteed hereunder shall be payable to the Employer on written demand without any need for notarial warning or judicial proceeding and without recourse being first had to the Contractor subject only to the payment conditions stipulated below.

PAYMENT herein shall be made by the Bank to the Employer upon receipt by the Bank of a written demand from the Employer stating that the Contractor is in default of his obligations under the Contract and a certificate in writing from the Engineer appointed in relation to the Contract confirming the statement of the Employer in its demand with respect to the default by the Contractor.

WHEREAS the Employer and the Contractor have signed an agreement on the...day of...19...for the execution, completion, and maintenance of the... (hereinafter referred to as the Contract) in conformity with the provisions of the Contract,

AND WHEREAS it is provided in the Contract that the Contractor shall be entitled to payment by the Employer of an Advance Payment on the Contract of... (figures and words) in the lawful currency of...on condition, INTER ALIA, of production of a Bank Guarantee conforming with the provisions of the said Contract,

NOW THE CONDITION of the above mentioned guarantee is such that if the said Advance Payment shall have been fully recovered by the Employer by way of deductions from sums due to the Contractor or otherwise but without taking into consideration any claim by the Contractor for any set-off or if on the coming to the end of the Contract the Bank shall have paid to the Employer on demand any balance of the said Advance Payment which shall not have been recovered as above then this Guarantee shall become null and void but otherwise shall be and remain in full force and effect, and no allowance of time or any indulgence shown by the Employer to the Contractor shall in any way release the Bank from any liability under the above written Guarantee.

PROVIDED ALWAYS THAT the amount guaranteed at any time shall not exceed the amount of the said Advance Payment less the amount repaid by the Contractor by deduction from the interim payments made to the Contractor on the Engineer's Certificates, in accordance with the terms of the Contract.

Production by the Contractor to the Bank of the relevant Engineer's Certificates shall be conclusive evidence of the reduction of the amount guaranteed.

PROVIDED ALWAYS THAT the Bank shall be under no liability hereunder unless and until the aforementioned Advance Payment has been credited to the account of the Contractor; namely on the books of...

The liability of the Bank hereunder shall cease on receipt by the Bank of a Copy of the Certificate issued by the Engineer appointed in relation to the Contract stating that the Advance Payment has been repaid in full and thereafter this Guarantee shall not be valid for any purpose whatsoever and shall be returned to the Bank.

This Guarantee shall be governed and construed in accordance with the laws of the United Republic of Tanzania.

IN WITNESS WHEREOF we have hereunto set our hand this...day of...19...

Signed...(Contractor's bank)

High-risk Texts

From the exporter's point of view, guarantees with a high risk are those that are drafted to be payable when a demand is made in strict accordance with its text, irrespective of the exporter's rights under the related contract. Guarantees should not be payable automatically (although there have been some cases where this point has been conceded (see specimen performance guarantee, p. 53)).

Demand guarantees are separate legal documents containing a *primary* obligation, independent of the underlying contract. The risk is that a demand can be made unfairly unless some measures are drafted into the guarantee to prevent this.

Banks are disinclined to issue guarantees which could involve them in disputes between the buyer and the exporter. To be acceptable to a bank, a guarantee must not place upon the bank the burden of examining whether or not conditions laid down in the contract have been met. The bank is not in a position to do this, and will refuse to act as an arbitrator between the buyer and exporter.

However, even guarantees payable on first demand can still have some degree of protection for the exporter such as:

  (i)   a fixed or determinable expiry date;
 (ii)   governing law and jurisdiction;
(iii)   value reduction clauses;
 (iv)   claim documents, etc.;
  (v)   maximum liability.

The guarantee wording should not only prevent unfair and capricious claims but should also be sufficiently precise to discourage the exporter from preventing the bank from honouring a prima facie valid claim by the beneficiary.

When drafting guarantees to be tabled with the buyer, it is often very difficult to know what level of protection the buyer will permit the exporter to enjoy.

Bank demand guarantees issued in accordance with (a) below offer the lowest risk of an unfair call. Category (c) guarantees are the most dangerous, as they enable the beneficiary to claim payment at any time, even when the exporter is not in default.

Advice from banks or friendly exporters who have dealt with the same buyer can be extremely useful in deciding which of the following is the most appropriate form of guarantee wording:

 (a)   payment on demand supported by documents within the control of the exporter or an arbitrator. Demand must be in writing accompanied by a statement giving details of the nature of the exporter's default, and supported by documentary evidence. The documents may or may not be independent (*i.e.* issued by a third party), depending on what the buyer and exporter have agreed to be included in the guarantee;

 (b)   payment on demand together with the beneficiary's *unsupported* statement of the default. Demand must be in writing accompanied by a statement from the beneficiary saying in what respect the exporter had defaulted on the contract. This is still a demand guarantee with the control of the situation entirely in the beneficiary's hands. For genuine grievances, there should be no reason why a beneficiary should refuse to provide this information;

(c) payment unconditionally on first demand. This is the highest risk. Payment is on *simple* first demand. This means no statement explaining the nature of the default, no requirement to prove default, just a demand in writing to the bank to pay. From a negotiating position, such a guarantee is clearly very advantageous for the beneficiary—however, not at all good for the exporter.

The bank, as guarantor, looks at the guarantee wording to ensure that it contains clear information about who is entitled to make a claim, how and when. If a demand is compliant, then they will pay the beneficiary.

The experienced exporter would choose (a) above. He would seek to negotiate a text requiring the beneficiary to submit a demand together with:

(a) the written admission of default by the exporter and a statement saying that the amount claimed should be paid;

(b) an independent engineer's certificate stating the nature of the exporter's default and the amount to be paid under the bond; or

(c) an arbitral award in favour of the beneficiary ruling that the exporter is in default and stating the amount due to be paid under the guarantee.

Where bank guarantees incorporate such conditions, there is no implied obligation on the bank to complete the contract, but simply to pay the beneficiary.

Where the parties to the contract are reasonable and financially sound, and the chosen law and jurisdiction have sufficiently developed to form a balanced and unbiased view of a dispute between an exporter and his buyer, there should be no reason why guarantees permitting payment of a claim against admitted or proven default should not be used.

However, legal and arbitral procedures can be a slow and expensive process. Buyers have a business to manage and contracts to finish. They do not wish to see cash due to them delayed because of protracted legal proceedings. Equally, they do not wish to tie up senior management's time and effort, or to pay for hiring costly lawyers, to pursue their case through court.

Settlement of disputes

Inexperienced buyers were particularly vulnerable during the early 1970s at the time of the excessive Middle Eastern oil price increases when exporters suddenly found a very rich buyer's market. Buyers were badly let down by the performance of some exporters who, subsequently, were confronted by buyers prepared to pay high prices, but who wanted very tight demand guarantee wording in return. As a result, many disputes arose over whether subsequent demands on guarantees were *fair* or *unfair*.

As can be seen from the specimen demand guarantees detailed below, in most instances the wording is not ideal, but certainly not atypical. Often guarantees are silent or unclear in areas of validity and expiry, reduction mechanisms, etc. In many cases, the governing law and jurisdiction are omitted from the text.

Unlike contracts, which usually have a disputes settlement procedure, many of the guarantees issued do not go into this detail, so in the event of a dispute the courts have first to decide on the applicable law and jurisdiction.

It is necessary to be specific on this subject and, where appropriate, to ensure, where permitted, that the law and jurisdiction governing the bank guarantee are the same as that of the contract, so that disputes under both legal documents can be heard in the same court or arbitral proceedings. The risk of extra and hidden costs for not achieving this is all too apparent.

It was the inconsistent standard in drafting, the lack of clarity in interpreting the guarantee wording and the unnecessary risks that this created for all parties concerned with the issue (particularly those banks finding themselves in the middle of legal disputes) that encouraged the reassembly of an International Chamber of Commerce Working Party on Guarantees to attempt the drafting of a set of key guidelines on demand guarantees acceptable to all, the ICC Uniform Rules for Demand Guarantees (ICC Publication No. 458, "the 458 Rules").

The 458 Rules include an arbitration procedure which can be relied on if they are incorporated into the demand guarantee by reference (see Chapter 10).

Badly-drafted demand guarantees not only run the risk of an unfair demand but also, as can be seen from some of the following specimen texts, the risk of:

(i)   open-ended validity;
(ii)   extra charges;
(iii)   hidden costs; and
(iv)   non-recovery of unfairly claimed payments.

The purpose of detailing these texts is to demonstrate just how varied and biased the text can be. They can be used as warnings against bad drafting, or more positively as models from which to draft more suitable guarantees appropriate for the country concerned. (Chapter 4 provides specimens of guarantees suggested by respected national and international institutions.)

Tender guarantees payable on simple demand

Tender guarantees are dangerous because there is no underlying protective contract for the exporter to resort to in the event of a dispute. The exporter has the least control over *simple demand tender bonds*. They can be
issued in several forms, for example, a tender bond which can be automatically extended until the performance bond is issued.

To:...Public Authority
Abu Dhabi   Tenderer:...
United Arab Emirates   Tendered Amount:...

We hereby guarantee to pay to the Government of Abu Dhabi a sum of UAE
DH...(amount in words) representing...% of the amount tendered, as a guarantee for the due and proper performance of the Tenderer's liabilities.

This guarantee shall be paid to the Government on first demand, without conditions of proof.

This guarantee shall be valid up to...(90 days from the latest date fixed for submitting tenders) and if the tenderer, on whose behalf this guarantee is issued, is
awarded the Contract, its validity shall be automatically extended until such
time as the Performance Bond, required under the Contract terms, is lodged with
the Government.

Signed...(Bank)

A second example would be a tender bond which remains valid until the
issue of the performance bond. In this case, cancellation depends on the
physical return of the tender bond. Being issued in the buyer's country, it
will be subject to local law, although the bond is silent on this point.

To:...
Cairo

BID LETTER OF GUARANTEE NO...

With reference to the offer of Messrs:...in connection with the adjudication of the
Tender No...for the supply of...WE hereby undertake to hold at your disposal,
as Provisional Deposit, free of interest and payable in cash on your first demand,
and notwithstanding any contestation by the tenderers, the sum of...

This Undertaking remains in force until a decision is taken on the tender and (in
the event of the whole or part of the tender being accepted) until such time as the
above mentioned tenderers have provided such Final Guarantee Deposit as may
be required by you, but will in any case, automatically expire on the...day
of...19...

Consequently, any claim in respect thereof should be made to us by the...at the
latest. Should we receive no claim from you by that date, our liability will cease
"ipso facto" and the present Letter of Guarantee will definitely become null and
void.

Please return to us this Letter of Guarantee on expiry date for cancellation.

Signed...(Bank in Egypt)

The following tender bond is payable on simple demand without any need to explain why a claim is being made. In the unlikely event of a dispute over the bond conditions, local law and jurisdiction will apply.

To...(Beneficiary)
Saudi Arabia

LETTER OF GUARANTEE FOR PRELIMINARY DEPOSIT NO ...

Dear Sirs,

Since Messrs...(the Tenderer) have tendered for the supply of...We...(local registered bank)...Branch, unconditionally guarantee to pay to you upon receiving your first written notice requesting payment of an amount not exceeding S.R...(Saudi Riyals...) being two (2) percent of the value of their offer as submitted in accordance with the conditions of the tender.

The validity of this guarantee starts from...and extends up to the end of the...day of...month of the year 19...You should submit request for payment of the value of this guarantee within the period of its validity.

Any dispute over the interpretation of the conditions of this letter of guarantee shall be subject to the regulations of the Kingdom of Saudi Arabia.

Yours faithfully
...(Bank)

Some buyers require a cash deposit but will accept a tender bond in lieu of a security deposit from offshore suppliers and contractors.

To:...
Singapore

TENDER SECURITY DEPOSIT

THIS GUARANTEE is made the...day of...19...by...having its registered office at...(hereinafter called the Guarantor).

WHEREAS

(1) ...of...(or whose registered office is situated at)...(the Tenderer) is desirous to tender to...(public authority buyer) and having its address at...Singapore (the Beneficiary) for the...as specified in the Tender Document of the Tender in consideration of the payment of a sum (referred to in the tender and hereinafter as the Tender Amount).

(2) The Tenderer is required by Clause...of the Tender to deposit, at the time of submission of the Tender, a sum equivalent to 1% of the Tender Amount (hereinafter called the Tender Security Deposit).

(3) At the request of the Guarantor, the Beneficiary agreed to accept this Guarantee in lieu of the Tender Security Deposit in cash upon the terms and conditions hereinafter stated.

NOW IT IS HEREBY AGREED as follows:

1. In consideration of the Beneficiary agreeing to the request of the Guarantor to accept this Guarantee in lieu of the Tender Security Deposit in cash, the Guarantor hereby guarantees the Beneficiary that the Guarantor shall forthwith pay to the Beneficiary on demand the sum of Singapore Dollars (S\$...) amounting to 1% of the Tender Amount being the Tender Security Deposit (the Guaranteed Sum).
2. Until receipt of the Guaranteed Sum, the Beneficiary may apply and utilise it in all respects as if it were the Tender Security Deposit deposited under Clause...of the Conditions of Tendering.
3. The Guarantor shall not be discharged or released from this Guarantee by any arrangement made between the Tenderer and the Beneficiary with or without the consent of the Guarantor or by any alteration in the obligations undertaken by the Tenderer or by any forbearance whether as to amount, time, performance or in any other way.
4. This Guarantee shall take effect immediately and shall continue until...or any extended period thereof.

Dated this...day of...19...
Signed by...for and on behalf of...
In the presence of...

Performance guarantees payable on simple demand

Performance bonds are to ensure that the exporter completes his part of the contract. The most onerous are *simple demand performance bonds*. In his first example, the guarantee validity is automatically extendable.

To: Government Department
Abu Dhabi

GUARANTEE—PERFORMANCE BOND

We hereby guarantee to pay to the Government of Abu Dhabi a sum of UAE DH...(figures and words) representing...% of the Contract sum, as a guarantee for the due and proper performance of the Contract.

This guaranteed sum shall be paid to the Government on first demand without proof or conditions.

This guarantee shall be valid until ... (date scheduled for Completion of Contract) and shall, before expiry, be automatically renewed until the Final Acceptance Certificate has been issued or until advised by the Finance Department that the Contract has been fulfilled.

Signed ...

The following performance bond is subject to local law and remains valid until the contract is completed. Proving completion of a contract to the local issuing bank may not always be easy, especially where contracts have a permitted weight or quantity tolerance and a letter of credit is never totally utilised. The guarantee may never be returned for cancellation until the letter of credit has been fully exhausted, which could prove impossible to achieve.

To:...
Benghazi

LETTER OF GUARANTEE FOR THE DUE EXECUTION AND PROPER PERFORMANCE OF CONTRACT

Dear Sirs,

With reference to the Contract concluded on...between... Benghazi, Socialist People's Libyan Arab Jamahiria (the Company), and Messrs ... (the Supplier) for the delivery of...(the Goods) for the Contract Price of...(currency, figures and words).

We hereby irrevocably and unconditionally guarantee the Supplier up to the sum of 5% of the Contract Price, *i.e*...(currency, figures and words) for the due execution and proper performance of the Contract.

We undertake to pay to you on your first demand in writing to us any amount you may claim up to and not exceeding this sum, notwithstanding any contestation by the Supplier or any other third party.

This letter of guarantee shall be valid until the fulfilment of the Supplier's obligations and guarantees under the Contract, *i.e.* until completion of the supply of...

Should we receive no claim from you up to the date of expiry of this letter of guarantee our liability shall become null and void.

Please return this letter of guarantee as soon as its validity expires.

Signed:... (Local Libyan bank)

Some performance bonds can be automatically payable or extendable on expiry. For example, the following is issued by a local Syrian bank and therefore subject to local law. The neutrality of any local legal process will always be a question on the exporter's mind.

To:...
Syria

LETTER OF GUARANTEE NO ...

This is to inform you that we hereby guarantee...(name of exporter) jointly, severally and indivisibly for an amount of...(figures and words) only in respect of... (the Goods).

This Guarantee is valid until...and cannot be cancelled during its validity without your written consent.

We undertake to pay to your order in cash the above mentioned amount upon your first written demand.

In case we do not receive such a claim we will be obliged to pay the countervalue of this Letter of Guarantee on its expiry date to your order in cash without need for any procedure on your part or necessity for advice, unless we proceed to extend or to renew this guarantee.

We declare that we choose...as our domicile in all that concerns the application of the provisions of guarantee.

Yours faithfully
Commercial Bank of Syria...Branch

Advance payment guarantees payable on simple demand

An exporter can achieve a short-term improvement to his cash-flow by obtaining an advance payment, but expose his balance sheet to long-term risk in the process. For example, the following is a guarantee payable on simple demand. It does not reduce *pro rata* to performance and is valid until it is formally cancelled after it has expired. It has to be returned for cancellation unless the beneficiary approves the cancellation in writing. It is silent on governing law and jurisdiction.

> To: Abu Dhabi Company
> Emirate of Abu Dhabi
>
> Whereas Abu Dhabi Company has entered into a Contract No...for...(description), and
>
> Whereas Abu Dhabi Company shall effect an advance payment against presentation from...(the Seller) of a Letter of Guarantee issued by a bank in favour of Abu Dhabi Company as guarantee in support of the fulfilment of the obligations undertaken by the Seller in respect of the above mentioned Contract.
>
> We...Bank with main office in...guarantee to Abu Dhabi Company on behalf of the Seller for the amount of US$...(...amount in words).
>
> This Guarantee is in your favour for the punctual and good performance by the Seller of works in compliance with the obligations stated in the aforementioned Contract.
>
> We...Bank do hereby bind ourselves formally, firmly, irrevocably and unconditionally to pay the amount not exceeding the sum of US$...(...amount in words) against your first written demand and this notwithstanding any objection of whatever nature by the Seller or any other authorities and without necessity of any legal or judicial proceeding.
>
> This Guarantee will stand valid for the whole amount until...(date).
>
> This Guarantee has to be returned to us as soon as all obligations provided in the Contract are fulfilled by the Seller or until it is actually returned to us or until you approve the cancellation.
>
> Signed:...(Bank)

The following guarantee is payable on simple demand. It reduces *pro rata* to the buyer paying the exporter and is subject to local law and jurisdiction.

> To: Directorate General of...
> Muscat
> Sultanate of Oman
>
> ADVANCE PAYMENT BOND NO...
>
> Whereas...(the Contractor) has been awarded a contract dated...for the construction, completion and maintenance of...(the Contract) for the value of Rials Omani...(figures and words) and in consideration of your making an advance

payment of R.O...(figures and words) to the Contractor being...% (...percent) of the Contract value, by this Bond WE...whose address is...guarantee to pay you a sum not exceeding R.O...on your first written demand without reference to or contestation on behalf of the Contractor.

It is understood that our liability towards you will be progressively reduced by the amount repaid to you by the Contractor as contained in the Certificates and Payments against the said advance payment.

This Bond will be effective from...and shall be valid until... or until the amount of the advance payment is fully recovered, whichever is the later.

This Bond should be returned to us upon expiry or upon fulfilment of our undertaking, whichever is the earlier.

...(Authorised signatories of a locally registered bank)

With guarantees payable on a simple demand, there is nothing to stop a buyer cashing a bond relating to one contract because he is dissatisfied with the performance of the exporter on another, totally separate, contract. In the following example, an attempt has been made to solve this problem, but the solution is not watertight as the buyer can remain silent on the reasons for the claim. The bond can reduce *pro rata* to performance. The local bank is strict as to the responsibilities of the buyer, but equally the exporter has to settle any disputes in accordance with local law and jurisdiction.

To: Secretariat of...
Benghazi
Libya
Our Ref.:...

Dear Sirs

At the request of Messrs...(the Contractor) we undertake to pay to you, on first written demand, irrespective of any contestation of the tenderer, the sum of... (figures and words) in connection with the advance payment against Contract No...provided any repaid instalments are automatically reduced from the gross amount of the guarantee.

This Guarantee covers the advance payment made specifically in connection with the above mentioned Contract No...and does not cover any other contract. This Guarantee is valid up to...and any claim must be received by us in writing during official banking hours on or before this date. No claim received thereafter will be entertained whether entirely or partly. It is imperative, therefore, that all claims under this Guarantee should be submitted to us in writing within its validity date.

Please return to us this Guarantee and any other relative extension (if any) on its settlement or expiration or cancellation.

Yours faithfully
Signed...(Local Libyan bank)

When banks issue advance payment guarantees, they need to know when they have to pay a claim without reference to any other legal document. In the following guarantee, not only is there no expiry date in the guarantee itself, but the bank has to have details of the contract to understand what obligations are stated in the contract documents. These may conflict with the guarantee which also says that the guarantee is payable on first demand. Such ambiguity causes considerable problems for the guarantor. From the exporter's point of view, the guarantee is undesirable as it does not reduce as the contract progresses. This has the effect of converting an advance payment guarantee into a performance bond.

To: The Minister of. . .
Kuwait

Your Excellency:

Messrs. . .have declared that their offer to the Tender. . .has been accepted. We hereby guarantee to put at the disposal of the Ministry of. . .for the Government of Kuwait the amount of K.D. . .(figures and words) against the advance payment guarantees referred to in the Contract Documents.

This Bond shall be free from any interest and will be paid in cash upon the Ministry's first request in any form required without any rights to delay, oppose, or stop payment on our part, the Contractor's or any of his Representatives whatsoever.

This Guarantee shall be deemed valid until the time specified and will be under the obligation of the conditions and regulations of the Contract Documents for the supply and erection of. . .

Very truly yours
Signed. . .(Local bank in Kuwait)

It is dangerous to tie a claim under a guarantee to a specific event; in this case, the presentation of shipping documents under a letter of credit. It is quite normal for letters of credit to be extended for many reasons outside the exporter's control. It is also common for buyers to refuse to extend letters of credit. If this were to happen in respect of the following guarantee, the exporter's advance payment guarantee could be properly, but unfairly, called. The guarantee does not reduce *pro rata* to shipment and payment and therefore the exporter's risk of exposure increases as the contract progresses.

To:. . .
Iran

Dear Sirs

RE: ADVANCE PAYMENT GUARANTEE NO. . .

In consideration of the fact that according to the terms and conditions of Letter of Credit No. . .for. . .(figures and words) opened by your good selves with us in favour of. . .(the Supplier) an advance payment of. . .(figures and words) representing. . .% (. . .percent) of the contract value may be made against a Bank Guarantee.

We. . .Bank hereby engage ourselves irrevocably and unconditionally to refund to you the effected down payment up to the aggregate amount of. . . upon your first demand and without delay and without the necessity of any judicial or administrative action to be lodged in case the Supplier fails to present to us on or before. . .the shipping documents called for under and in conformity with the terms of Letter of Credit No. . .

Our obligation under this Guarantee is valid for a period of one month beyond the expiry date of the Letter of Credit, namely the close of business on. . .and will be extended to cover any extensions to the above said Letter of Credit.

Your claims, if any, under this Guarantee must be presented to us in writing within seven days after the expiry date of the Guarantee after which date our liability shall cease and upon the opener's confirmation to this effect.

Yours faithfully
Signed. . .Local Iranian bank

Tender guarantee payable on demand against beneficiary's statement

Less onerous than simple demand guarantees are those bonds requiring documentation to support a claim. The worst case is where the beneficiary can make a written *unsupported* statement on the nature of the alleged default. An example of such a guarantee is as follows.

To:. . .
Bangladesh. . .
(Date). . .

WHEREAS. . .(hereinafter called "the Bidder") has submitted its bid dated. . .for the supply of. . .under invitation to bid reference No. . .(hereinafter called "the Bid").

KNOW ALL MEN by these Presents that WE. . .of. . .having our registered office at. . .(hereinafter called the Bank) are bound up to. . .(hereinafter called the Purchaser) in the sum of. . .(amount in currency figures and words) for which payment well and truly made to the said Purchaser the Bank binds itself, its successors and assigns by these Presents, sealed with the Common Seal of the said Bank this. . .day of. . .19. . .

THE CONDITIONS OF THIS OBLIGATION ARE

1. If the Bidder withdraws its bid during the period of bid validity specified by the Bidder on the bid form, or
2. If the Bidder, having been notified of the acceptance of its bid by the Purchaser during the period of bid validity:
   (a) fails or refuses to execute the contract form, if required, or
   (b) fails or refuses to furnish the Performance Bond in accordance with the Instruction to Bidders,

WE undertake to pay to the Purchaser up to the above stated amount upon the receipt of its first written demand, without the Purchaser having to substantiate its demand and without reference to the Bidder provided that in its demand the Purchaser will note that the amount claimed by it is due to it owing to the occurrence of one or both of the two conditions, specifying the occurred condition or conditions.

This guarantee will remain in force up to and including thirty (30) days after the period of bid validity...(150 days from bid opening date)...and any demand in respect thereof should reach the Bank not later than the above date.

...Signature of bank

In some cases, the guarantee permits the buyer to extend the guarantee *unilaterally*. If the bank or exporter is unwilling to extend the guarantee, then it becomes *automatically* payable without any need for the buyer to make any further claim.

To:...
Iran...
(Date)...

Whereas according to invitation to bid No...dated...concerning the purchase of...(goods) Messrs....(the Supplier) have decided to participate in the said tender and a guarantee for...(amount) should be submitted by the tenderer.

This bank hereby guarantees the Supplier vis-à-vis...(the Purchaser). Should the Purchaser inform this bank in writing that the Supplier has been recognised as successful bidder, but has failed to sign the relevant contract or submit the required performance bond under the contract within the specified period we undertake to pay immediately upon the first notification...(guarantee amount...in Rials)...to the Purchaser without it being necessary for the latter to prove the refusal or produce any reason, issue a declaration or act through administrative or judicial channels.

This guarantee is valid up to the close of business on...(expiry date) and will be extended for any period asked for by the Purchaser.

Should the bank not be in a position or not agree to extend this guarantee and/or if the Supplier fails to provide the means for its extension and make the bank agree to such extension then the bank undertakes to pay the amount referred to above to the order of the Purchaser without it being necessary for the latter to make a new claim.

Signed...BANK MELLI, Iran

The following tender bond is payable on demand if the buyer claims that the exporter has withdrawn his offer before the bid expires. It is issued by a local bank and therefore subject to local law and jurisdiction. It is most unlikely that any unfair payment under the bond could be recovered from a bank in the buyer's country.

To: Central Tender Committee
Kuwait

Sir:

We have the honour to inform you that we guarantee Messrs...for the amount of...K.D. in order to allow them to submit an Offer for supplying and erecting...

This guarantee shall remain valid for a period of ninety (90) days after the date specified for opening of offers by the Central Tenders Committee.

In the event of Messrs...withdrawing their Offer prior to the expiration of this Guarantee we shall pay immediately upon your request in spite of any opposition from the other party mentioned an amount of...K.D. aforesaid above in cash.

Very truly yours
Signed...(Local bank)

In the following example, the guarantor is obliged to pay against written notice from the buyer that the exporter has defaulted on the terms of the tender bond. The exporter does not receive any notice from the bank, nor is he allowed to defend himself, counterclaim, etc. The exporter is also responsible for paying net of present and future taxes, levies, withholdings, etc. The bond is subject to local law which for many years was based on the texts of the Koran and not geared to Western commercial legal concepts.

To:...
Saudi Arabia

FORM OF TENDER SECURITY

We the...Bank (the Guarantor) hereby irrevocably and unconditionally guarantee to...(the Company), subject only to the monetary limitation hereinafter specified, that... a...(legal status) (the Tenderer), having submitted the accompanying tender dated...A.H. ...A.D. for...(the Work), shall not withdraw such tender for any reason during the period specified therein and, if the Company accepts the tender, shall enter into a contract with the Company for the Work in accordance with the terms and conditions of such tender and shall furnish such security or securities as may be specified in the tender for the faithful performance of such contract and shall provide such certificates of insurance as may be specified in the tender.

In the event of the Company, in their absolute discretion, giving written notice to us of any failure of the Tenderer to perform or fulfil any of the acts or obligations set forth in the preceding paragraph, we hereby unconditionally and irrevocably undertake, without any right of defence, set-off or counterclaim whether on our behalf or on behalf of the Tenderer and without the requirement of any notice or demand to the Tenderer, to pay to the Company the sum of S.R...(Saudi Riyals...).

Such written notice of the Company shall be conclusively binding on us for all purposes under this Tender Security.

We further agree that any payment made hereunder shall be made free and clear of, and without deduction for or on account of, any present or future taxes, levies, imposts, duties, charges, fees, deductions or withholdings of any nature whatsoever and by whomsoever imposed. Payments to be made hereunder will be effected by transfer to an account in your name at such bank in Saudi Arabia as you shall stipulate or in such other manner as shall be acceptable to you.

This Tender Security shall be valid until the end of the...day of...19...A.D., and any request for payment hereunder must be received by us before such date.

This Tender Security shall be governed by and interpreted under the laws of the Kingdom of Saudi Arabia.

Signed and sealed this...day of... 14...A.H. corresponding to the...day of... 19...A.D.

...(Signature)

In some cases, the buyer requires assurances from the exporter's bank that the exporter is not overextending himself financially on the contract. This no doubt reflects the experiences of some buyers who had contractors default on contracts that were too large for them to handle. An example is the following text from Saudi Arabia.

To: Ministry of...
The Kingdom of Saudi Arabia
...(Date)

LETTER OF GUARANTEE FOR PRELIMINARY DEPOSIT

His Excellency,

Since Messrs...(the Contractor) have tendered for the supply of...(the Contract) we...(Name of Bank)...hereby irrevocably and unconditionally guarantee the payment to you of Saudi Riyals...being 1% of the total value of their offer and accordingly covenant and agree as follows:

(a) On the Contractor's failure to fulfil any of the conditions of the Contract as determined by you in your absolute judgment the Guarantor shall forthwith on demand made by you in writing and notwithstanding any objection by the Contractor pay you such amount or amounts as you shall require not exceeding in aggregate the above mentioned amount of Saudi Riyals...(amount) by transfer to an account in your name at such bank in Saudi Arabia as you shall stipulate or in such other manner as shall be acceptable to you.

(b) Any payment made hereunder shall be made free and clear of, and without deduction for or on account of, any present or future taxes, levies, imposts, duties, charges, fees, deductions or withholdings of any nature whatsoever and by whomsoever imposed.

(c) The covenants herein contained constitute unconditional and irrevocable direct obligations of the Guarantor. No alteration in the terms of the Contract or in the extent or nature of the work to be performed thereunder and no allowance of time by you or other forbearance or concession or any other act or omission by you which, but for this provision, might exonerate or discharge the Guarantor shall in any way release the Guarantor from any liability hereunder.

(d) This guarantee shall remain valid and in full force and effect up to the end of the...day of...of the year...by which time any claim hereunder must be received by the agent of the Guarantor in Saudi Arabia namely...(Local Bank).

(e) The Guarantor represents and warrants that the amount of this guarantee plus all other facilities granted by them to their client...(Client) in connection with their work executed in Saudi Arabia does not exceed twenty (20) percent of the total of the paid up capital and reserves of the Guarantor.

(f) This guarantee is governed by and construed in accordance with the laws and regulations of the Kingdom of Saudi Arabia.

...(Authorised signature...Bank, Head Office)

In some countries, such as Syria, India, Pakistan, Thailand, Turkey, Saudi Arabia and Abu Dhabi, local banking regulations can over-ride bond wording, particularly in respect of validity. In the following example from Syria, it would be essential to recover and then cancel the bond physically; otherwise, Central Bank of Syria regulations would permit claims to be made even after the bond expired.

To: Syrian Arab Republic
Public Establishment
Damascus

Dear Sirs,

GUARANTEE NO...

We are informed by...(the Tenderer) that they are submitting an offer to you for the supply of...under Tender No...and in this connection they have requested us to issue our Guarantee.

In consideration of your permitting the Tenderer to participate in the said Tender, we...(Bank name and address) hereby irrevocably undertake to pay to you the sum of...despite any objection by the Tenderer upon receipt by us of your first demand in writing accompanied by your declaration stating that the amount claimed is due by reason of the Tenderer not fulfilling his obligations in accordance with the terms and conditions of the Tender, the signatures on such demand to be authenticated by your bankers.

ALWAYS PROVIDED THAT:

1. Our liability is limited to an amount not exceeding...(in words)
2. Our Guarantee will come into force on...19...and will expire on...19...and any claims must be received by us at this office in writing on or before that date when it will become of no effect whatsoever whether returned to us or not.

Yours faithfully
Signed...Bank
Countersigned...

The maximum amount of an exporter's liability is not always restricted to the amount of the bond. In the following example from Turkey, issued by a local bank and therefore subject to local law and jurisdiction, interest is to be calculated and paid from date of claim to date of payment.

To:...
Turkey
No...

PROVISIONAL LETTER OF GUARANTEE (BID BOND)

Whereas this Bank stands as joint and several surety for the debtor and as joint and several co-debtor for the sum of...being a provisional guarantee fund which, in compliance with the relevant law and on the estimated cost, the bidder is obliged to deposit for fulfilment of the requirements of the specification pertaining

to the tender to be held on...covering...opened by...and in which the bidder...will participate.

WE undersigned hereby state and undertake, on behalf of the Bank and as responsible representatives with full power to affix our signature, that the guarantee amount will be paid immediately and without delay in cash, in full to you or
to your order upon your first written demand, stating that the bidder has not
abided by tender conditions and/or not deposited performance guarantee funds
calculated on the basis of the bid amount within the period in the specification
starting from the date at which the bidder is notified that he has been awarded
the contract, together with legal interest for the days to be elapsed between the
date of such written request and the date of actual payment, without need to
issue a protest or to obtain a court order for the bidder's consent.

This letter of guarantee has been issued upon the counterguarantee of...
(instructing bank) No...dated...which we received from...situated at...(exporter's country)

Signed...(Local Turkish bank...branch)

Some guarantees permit claims to be made within a certain period after the
expiry date. This enables the beneficiary to enjoy the full validity of the
bond as he does not have to start claims procedures before the bond expires. In the following example from Venezuela, the issuing bank also has
to obtain exchange control and any other government approvals necessary
to remit claim payments.

To:...
Venezuela
Date:...

Dear Sirs,

                          TENDER BOND NO...

In consideration of your inviting our customer...(the Bidder) to tender for contract ref:... we hereby irrevocably guarantee to pay you a sum not exceeding...on demand in writing if the bidder withdraws or amends his tender in
whole or in part without your consent before the expiry of its validity (including
any extension thereof) or, on being awarded a contract by you, does not provide
the required performance bond.

This guarantee shall remain in force up to and including...19...(expiry date), and
any claim hereunder must be lodged with us in writing within one month of that
date.

No change in the constitution of the Bidder and no giving of time, neglect or forbearance on your part in enforcing the obligations of the said tender shall prejudice or affect our liability under this guarantee.

We bind ourselves to obtain any governmental or other permission which may
be necessary to remit the above sum to you in accordance with this guarantee.

Signed by...
For and on behalf of...Bank

Performance guarantees payable on demand against beneficiary's statement

Buyers require performance guarantees to ensure contracts are properly performed. In many cases, this includes the contractor's obligations during the warranty period. In the following example from Bangladesh, the performance guarantee is governed by and interpreted under local law and jurisdiction and includes an obligation to indemnify the buyer against consequential liability arising from the contractor's failure to perform, but only up to the amount of the bond.

> To:...
> Bangladesh
>
> We...(the bank) hereby irrevocably and unconditionally guarantee to...(the Employer), subject only to the monetary limitation hereinafter specified, that...Ltd. (the Contractor) shall well and truly perform and fulfil all the undertakings, covenants, terms and conditions of the Contract dated...(the Contract) between the Employer and the Contractor for the...and of any extensions thereof that may be granted by the Employer and during the term of any warranty period set forth in the Contract, and that the Contractor shall well and truly perform and fulfil all the undertakings, covenants, terms and conditions of any and all changes, modifications, additions, or amendments of the Contract that may hereafter be made, and that the Contractor shall also fully indemnify, defend, and hold harmless the Employer from all cost, liability, and damage that it may suffer by reason of the failure of the Contractor to do so.
>
> In the event the Employer, in its absolute discretion, gives written notice to us at any time of any failure of the Contractor to perform or fulfil any of the acts or obligations set forth in the preceding paragraph, we hereby unconditionally and irrevocably undertake, without any right of set-off or counterclaim, whether on our behalf or of the Contractor, and without the requirement of any notice or demand to the Contractor, to pay to the Employer the sum of...being an amount equal to...percent (...%) of the Contract price as set forth in the Contract; such written notice of the Employer shall be conclusively binding on us for all purposes under this Performance Security.
>
> We further agree that any changes, modifications, additions, or amendments that may be made to the terms and conditions of the Contract, or to the work to be performed thereunder, or in the payments to be made on account thereof, or any extensions of the time of performance or other forbearance on the part of either the Employer or the Contractor to the other, shall not in any way release us from continuing liability hereunder, and we hereby expressly waive all notice to us of any such change, modification, addition, amendment, extension or forbearance.
>
> This Performance Security shall be valid until the end of any and all of the warranty periods specified in the Contract, and any requests for payment hereunder must be received by us on or before such date.
>
> This Performance Security shall be governed by and interpreted under the laws of the country of Bangladesh.
>
> Signed and sealed this...day of...19...

The following performance guarantee from Chile is exceptionally penal.

Not only can it be called against the simple statement from the beneficiary that the exporter has failed to perform the contract, but the validity is also unilaterally extendable on the mere request of the beneficiary.

To:...
Chile

IRREVOCABLE GUARANTEE NO...

In accordance with Contract Reference...of EMPRESA NACIONAL DE... (EMPRESA) awarded to...(the Contractor), we...(the Guarantor) hereunder establish on orders from the Contractor and in favour of EMPRESA our unconditional and irrevocable guarantee in the amount of...(figures and words), which we undertake to pay without need of prior court order or arbitration, at the first request of EMPRESA, either by letter, cablegram or telex, indicating that the Contractor has failed to perform the terms of the Contract Reference.

Payment will be made without considering any objection whatsoever.

This Guarantee will be valid until...(date of expiry of guarantee) and will be extendable on mere request of EMPRESA to us.

...(Name of issuing bank)
...(Signature of authorised officers of the issuing bank)[1]

Not all claims under performance guarantees need relate to actual losses. In the case of a contract funded by the Kuwait Fund for Arab Economic Development for a Gambian buyer, the bank had to indemnify the buyer against *actual, estimated* or *expected* defects and shortcomings. The guarantee validity was also automatically extended as the contract completion date was extended, but in successive six-month steps.

To:...
Gambia

1. Whereas the Ministry of... the Republic of Gambia (the Employer) has awarded a contract for...(the Contract) to...(the Contractor).
2. And whereas the Contractor is bound by the said Contract to submit to the Employer a Performance Guarantee for a total amount of...(...).
3. Now we underwriters, the legal representative of the...Bank (the Guarantor), and fully authorised to sign and to incur obligations in the name of the Guarantor, will guarantee the Employer the full amount of...(...) as stated above.
4. After the Contractor has signed the aforementioned Contract with the Employer, the Guarantor is engaged to pay the Employer any amount up to and inclusive of the aforementioned full amount upon written order from the Employer to indemnify the Employer for any liabilities or damage resulting from the defects or shortcomings of the Contractor, whether these defects or shortcomings are actual or estimated or expected.
    The Guarantor will deliver the money required by the Employer immediately without delay and without the necessity of a previous notice or of

---

[1] Issued outside Chile. In some cases Chilean Empresas may require two performance bonds, each for 10 per cent. of the value of the contract. The first will be due to expire 30 days after provisional acceptance date and the second 30 days after final acceptance date.

judicial or administrative procedures and without it being necessary to prove to the Guarantor the defects or shortcomings of the Contractor.

5. This Guarantee is valid for the contract period plus an additional twelve (12) months maintenance period after acceptance of the work by the Employer.

6. At any time during the period in which this Guarantee remains valid, if the Employer agrees to grant extension of time to the Contractor or if the Contractor fails to complete the Works within the time for completion as stated in the Contract, or fails to discharge himself of the liabilities or damages as stated under 4 above, it is understood that the Guarantor will extend this Guarantee under the same conditions for the time needed by the Contractor to complete the Works and to discharge himself of any liabilities or damages under the Contract.

7. Until the Employer has issued an instruction to the Guarantor to the effect that this Guarantee can be released, the Guarantor undertakes, notwithstanding the validity periods as stated under 5 above, to extend the validity under the same conditions for successive periods of six (6) calendar months at a time and to forward the appropriate extension documents to the Employer.

As a declaration of good faith for this Guarantee, we the legal representatives of the Guarantor hereby sign and seal this Guarantee on the date of...19...

Signed...
Witness...

Performance guarantees with an open-ended validity date and a finite time from receiving a claim to make payment are to be avoided if possible. The following guarantee from Greece states that the performance bond can only be terminated on its physical return to the issuing bank with a written request to cancel. The issuing bank has also to certify that it is not exceeding its Treasury-imposed financial limits.

To: Hellenic...Limited
Athens

We hereby certify that by means of this Performance Bond we...(the Guarantor) unconditionally guarantee to you on behalf of...(the Contractor) of...(the Works) for the payment made by you of an amount of...(figures and words) to which our liability is limited and which amount you can determine as due in your absolute judgment from the enforcement of the whole or part of the guarantee due to non-observance of any of the terms of the Contract by the Contractor.

Such decision reached by your Board of Directors will be binding upon ourselves and will not be challenged by us and we waive all rights of division as well as under any decision or order of a court pursuant to Clause numbers 853, 862, 863, 867 and 868 of the Civil Code.

We are obliged to pay to you (without our objecting), within three (3) days of a notice having been received by ourselves, such sum demanded up to the above mentioned limit.

This Performance Bond is indefinite in duration and it can only be terminated by the return of this Performance Bond on receipt of written notice from yourselves.

We certify that the total sum of all our performance bonds, including the sum under this Performance Bond, does not exceed the limit of our Bank as determined by the Treasury.

Yours faithfully
...(Guarantor bank)

In some cases, even upsetting the buyer can result in a valid claim. In the following wording from Indonesia, the bank has to pay if the buyer claims simply because he *expects* the contractor to default. Claims can be made up to two months after the contract guarantee period has expired. The contractor has to prove to the bank that the bond has expired and can be cancelled.

To: Government Buyer
Jakarta

(1) Whereas...of...(the Buyer) has awarded a Contract for the supply and erection of...to...(the Contractor).

(2) And whereas the Contractor is bound by the said Contract to submit to the Buyer a Performance Bond for the total amounts of...(figures and words) ...(Indonesian Rupiah amount in figures and words) equivalent to ten percent of the Contract amount.

(3) Now we Underwriters responsible and representative of...situated at... (the Bank), and fully authorised to sign and to incur obligations in the name of the Bank, hereby declare that this Bank will guarantee the Buyer the full amounts as stated above.

(4) The Bank is engaged up to the aforementioned full amount to indemnify the Buyer for any liability or damage resulting from the defaults or shortcomings of the Contractor in performing and observing all the terms, stipulations, provisions and conditions of the said Contract, whether these defaults or shortcomings are actual or estimated or reasonably expected, upon written order from the Buyer.

   The Bank will deliver the money required to the Buyer immediately without delay and without the necessity of a previous notice or a previous judicial or administrative procedure and without the necessity to prove to the Bank the defaults or shortcomings of the Contractor.

(5) The Performance Bond is valid up until two (2) months after expiry of the guarantee period specified in the Contract.

In witness whereof the Contractor and the legal representatives of the Bank hereby sign and seal this Contract on the date of...19...

Witness...   Contractor...
Witness...   Bank...

The following is an example of a simple demand performance guarantee. The bank will pay immediately on demand for any reason stated by the beneficiary. The validity can be extended on the *unilateral* request of the beneficiary. If the bank is unhappy with the quality of the security it is getting from the exporter, it can refuse to extend and pay the claim instead, taking recourse on the exporter, thus weakening further the exporter's financial position.

To:...
Teheran

With reference to a contract (the Contract) relating to...(the Goods) concluded between...(the Supplier) and...(the Purchaser) and by the request of the Purchaser for the good performance of the undertaking accepted in accordance with the Contract in respect of the Goods, we...(the Bank) hereby guarantee and undertake, if it is noticed by the Purchaser that the Supplier has offended from their liabilities under the Contract, to pay immediately after receipt of the first written demand to or to the order of the Purchaser up to a total of...(figures and words) in Rials any amount in respect of this guarantee under any subject or reason ascertained by the Purchaser without any need for issuance of declaration form or execution of any action through administrative legal or other authority or proving the neglect untruth or correctness.

This Guarantee is valid until the official closing time on...(expiry date) and is extendable for any period requested by the Purchaser.

Should the Bank not be able or willing to extend the validity hereof or should the guarantee party not provide the necessities of the extension and obtain the concurrence of the Bank of the extension then the Bank undertakes to pay without any need for a second demand the said sum in favour or to the order of the Purchaser.

Signed...(Bank)

Sometimes it is not always possible for the exporter to establish constructive performance. In the following example from Pakistan, the beneficiary is the sole judge of the successful completion. The bond can be extended indefinitely until the beneficiary is satisfied.

To: Director General...Department
Pakistan

FAITHFUL PERFORMANCE OF CONTRACT NO...

WHEREAS Messrs...(hereinafter called the Contractor) have requested us to furnish a Bank Guarantee in your favour in the sum of...(figures and words) as performance bond against Contract No...dated...on the Contractor placed through the Director General...Department for...

WE HEREBY AGREE

(1) to make an unconditional payment of...to you on demand without any further question or reference to the Contractor, on the Contractor's failure to perform the Contract of which you will be the sole judge.
(2) to keep this guarantee valid and in full force from this date up to the time of the due and faithful completion of the Contract under reference or till...whichever is the later. The successful execution of the Contract will be intimated by the Director General.
(3) to extend the period of the enforceability of their Guarantee if such extension be necessary or desired by you of us.

All claims thereunder must be submitted to the Bank of...on or before the said expiry date after which this guarantee will become null and void and should be returned to us. Irrespective of its return, we consider ourselves fully discharged from any obligation thereunder after the said expiry date.

For the Bank of. . .
Signed. . .(Manager)

In the following guarantee, the guarantor will pay on demand against any claim stating that the buyer has not fulfilled any of the conditions of the contract. The bank does not have to check this statement or refer back to the contractor. However, the beneficiary must lodge his claim within the validity of the guarantee with the guarantor's agent in the beneficiary's country. Here is another example of where the beneficiary is concerned that the guarantor is not too dependent on the contractor's business in one country by getting the guarantor to warrant that their exposure to the contractor does not exceed 20 per cent. of the assets of the guarantor.

To: Ministry of. . .
The Kingdom of Saudi Arabia

LETTER OF GUARANTEE FOR FINAL DEPOSIT

Since you have awarded our clients Messrs. . .(the Contractor) a contract (the Contract) for. . .(description and identity of project) we. . .Bank (the Guarantor) hereby irrevocably and unconditionally guarantee the payment to you of Saudi Riyals. . .(figures and words) being five percent (5%) of the value of the Contract and accordingly covenant and agree as follows:

(a) On the Contractor's failure to fulfil any of the conditions of the Contract as determined by you in your absolute judgment the Guarantor shall forthwith on demand made by you in writing and notwithstanding any objection by the Contractor pay you such amount or amounts as you shall require not exceeding in aggregate the above mentioned amount of Saudi Riyals. . .(amount) by transfer to an account in your name at such bank in Saudi Arabia as you shall stipulate or in such other manner as shall be acceptable to you.

(b) Any payment made hereunder shall be made free and clear of, and without deduction for or on account of, any present or future taxes, levies, imposts, duties, charges, fees, deductions or withholdings of any nature whatsoever and by whomsoever imposed.

(c) The covenants herein contained constitute unconditional and irrevocable direct obligations of the Guarantor. No alteration in the terms of the Contract or in the extent or nature of the work to be performed thereunder and no allowance of time by you or other forbearance or concession or any other act or omission by you which but for this provision might exonerate or discharge the Guarantor shall in any way release the Guarantor from any liability hereunder.

(d) This guarantee shall remain valid and in full force and effect up to the end of the. . .day of. . .of the year. . .by which time any claim hereunder must be received by the agent of the Guarantor in Saudi Arabia namely. . .(Local Bank).

(e) The Guarantor represents and warrants that the amount of this guarantee plus all other facilities granted by them to their client. . .in connection with their work executed in Saudi Arabia does not exceed twenty (20) percent of the total of the paid-up capital and reserves of the Guarantor.

(f) This guarantee is governed by and construed in accordance with the laws and regulations of the Kingdom of Saudi Arabia.

...(Authorised Signature)
...Bank, Head Office

Sometimes the terms and conditions of the contract are, or are incorporated in, those of the tender. In the following example, the performance bond can be claimed for failing to fulfil the terms and conditions of the tender. Payment will be made against the beneficiary's own uncorroborated statement of the exporter's default. There is often little opportunity for the exporter to negotiate the terms of a tender open to international competitive bidding.

To:...
Venezuela

Dear Sirs,

BOND NO...

We are informed by...(the Supplier) that they have received Order No...for the supply of...(the Contract) and in accordance with the terms of the Contract they are required to furnish a Performance Bond in the amount of...

Now, therefore, in consideration of the foregoing Order, We...Bank hereby undertake to pay to you upon receipt by us of your first demand in writing, accompanied by the documents mentioned in paragraph 3 below, an amount not exceeding...in the event of the Supplier failing to fulfil its obligations in accordance with the terms and conditions of the said Order

PROVIDED THAT:

(1) Our liability shall be limited to an amount not exceeding...
(2) Our Bond will come into force on...and will expire on...and any claims hereunder must be lodged with us in writing on or before the latter date.
(3) Any claim hereunder must be accompanied by your declaration stating that the amount claimed is due by reason of the Supplier having failed to fulfil his obligations in accordance with the terms and conditions of Tender No...

...Signed

Advance payment guarantees payable on demand against beneficiary's statement

Many advance payment guarantees are drafted and negotiated to meet the requirements of specific contracts. Reduction clauses are incorporated to reflect the profile of the contract performance. In the case of the following example, reduction is to an agreed new amount on a fixed or earlier determinable date. A claim can only be made against the guarantee if the exporter does not repay the outstanding advance payment. Payment has to be made unconditionally on first demand within 14 days of a claim. The guarantee expressly states that it cannot be assigned. This does not necessarily mean that the proceeds of a claim cannot be assigned.

To: Administracion Nacional
Paraguay

WHEREAS Administracion Nacional...(the Buyer) has awarded a contract dated...19...for...(the Contract) to...of...(the Contractor) for...(the Works), and WHEREAS the Contractor is bound by the Contract to submit to the Buyer an advance payment guarantee amounting to...(figures and words) as provided in Article...of the Contract.

NOW WE...(the Bank) hereby declare that the Bank shall guarantee the Buyer the full amount of...(figures and words) provided that the said amount shall reduce to...(figures and words) on the date one year after the date of issue of this guarantee or earlier, when all the plant (as defined in the Contract) has been delivered in accordance with the Contract.

The Bank hereby indemnifies the Buyer up to the value of this guarantee against any loss or damage which the Buyer shall actually sustain by reason of the Contractor failing to deliver goods and/or to render services as required by the Contract and in the event of such failure refusing to repay all or the relevant part of the advance payment referred to above.

This bank guarantee shall be unconditional and payable on first written demand by the Buyer specifying the goods which the Contractor has failed to deliver and/or the services which the Contractor has failed to render, and the amount of the advance payment which the Contractor has refused to repay.

The above-mentioned written demand may be presented to the offices of the Bank's local subsidiary company......Branch who will telex advise the Bank of the contents of the demand. On receipt of the branch's tested telex, the Bank will remit funds to the said branch in order to honour this guarantee in accordance with its terms within 14 days after the presentation of the written demand.

This guarantee is valid until the issue of Final Acceptance Certificate under Article...of the Contract for the whole of the Works, after which date no claim hereunder will be entertained and this guarantee shall automatically be cancelled and the Buyer shall return the same to the Contractor.

This guarantee is personal to the Buyer and is not assignable.

Signed...(Bank in contractor's country)

Some guarantees are drafted to include reference to the contract. This may be an attempt to make claims against an autonomous, independent guarantee less clear and more ambiguous, as it forces that guarantor to ask whether the exporter has fulfilled his obligations under the contract. This is the case with the following guarantee. In addition it is unclear whether interest is charged on the full down payment, or only the part that has to be repaid.

To:...
Poland

We have been informed that a Contract No...dated...(the Contract) was concluded between...(the Buyer) and...(the Supplier) for the supply of goods and/or services.

The terms of payment in respect of the Contract are stated in Clause...of the Conditions of Purchase of the Contract and according to these a down payment of five percent (5%) i.e...(figures and words) shall be paid by the Buyer to the Supplier.

Accordingly, we the undersigned give this irrevocable guarantee to the Buyer to refund the down payment to the Buyer on the first demand of the Buyer transmitted to us in writing in the event the Supplier fails to fulfil his obligations in respect of delivery as stated in the Contract.

We also undertake that in the event of a refund of the down payment by us we shall pay interest to the Buyer at the rate of eight (8%) percent per annum calculated from date of receipt of the down payment by...Bank Ltd. for the account of the Supplier to the date of refund to the Buyer hereunder.

This guarantee is valid until completion of all deliveries of goods and services under the Contract or until...19...whichever is the earlier after which date this guarantee shall become null and void whether returned to us or not and reduces pro rata to value of deliveries made and services rendered.

This guarantee shall be construed and interpreted according to the Laws of England and be subject to the jurisdiction of the English Courts.

Our liability hereunder shall in no case exceed...plus interest at 8% per annum as stated above.

Signed...Bank Ltd, London

Many countries are short of convertible currency and ration it through an import licensing system. In Turkey, as can be seen from the following text, any advance payment has to be refunded if the exporter has not shipped the goods at least one month before the import licence expires. Interest is charged as well as, in some cases, non-performance penalties. The guarantee is issued by a local bank subject to local law and jurisdiction (Decree/Serial No. III No. 13). There is no provision in this guarantee for reductions *pro rata* to performance.

To:...
Turkey

Under the contract of...(date) No...concluded between your company and...(the Seller) residing at...(city) in...(country) your company has to make an advance payment of...(figures and words) to the Seller representing...percent of the value of...(the Goods) that is to be delivered by the Seller.

After this amount has been transferred by the Central Bank and paid to the Seller, in the event that the goods relating to the effected advance are not shipped from...(country) to Turkey at least one month before the termination of the span of importation we hereby undertake that we will ensure the refund of the same amount to our country in the same foreign currency together with its legal interest (and, should it be included in the contract, with the monetary indemnity of the failure) without obtaining a writ and/or a protest against the Seller and/or the Seller's consent.

This guarantee has been issued on the basis of the guarantee of...(date) No...of...Bank situated at...

Signed...(Local Turkish bank)

Advance payment guarantees which are particularly penal are those for a high value, non-reducing and payable on first demand. In the case of the following guarantee, the exporter will start with a positive cashflow but finish with a 20 per cent. bond payable on first demand still in the hands of the buyer.

To: Ministry of Finance and National Economy
The Kingdom of Saudi Arabia

Since you have awarded our clients Messrs...(the Contractor) a contract (the Contract) for...(the Project) and since you have agreed to reimburse to the Contractor an advance payment (the Advance Payment) up to twenty (20%) percent of the value of the Contract, we...Bank (the Guarantor) hereby irrevocably and unconditionally guarantee the payment to you of S.R...(figures and words) representing the amount of the advance payment and accordingly covenant and agree as follows:

(a) On the Contractor's failure to fulfil any of the conditions of the Contract as determined by you in your absolute judgment the Guarantor shall forthwith on demand made by you in writing and notwithstanding any objection by the Contractor pay you such amount or amounts as you shall require not exceeding in aggregate the above mentioned amount of Saudi Riyals...by transfer to an account in your name at such bank in Saudi Arabia as you shall stipulate or in such other manner as shall be acceptable to you.

(b) Any payment made hereunder shall be made free and clear of, and without deduction for or on account of, any present or future taxes, levies, imposts, duties, charges, fees, deductions or withholdings of any nature whatsoever and by whomsoever imposed.

(c) The covenants herein contained constitute unconditional and irrevocable direct obligations of the Guarantor. No alteration in the terms of the Contract or in the extent or nature of the work to be performed thereunder and no allowance of time by you or other forbearance or concession or any other act or omission by you which but for this provision might exonerate or discharge the Guarantor shall in any way release the Guarantor from any liability hereunder.

(d) This guarantee shall remain valid and in full force and effect up to the end of the...day of...of the year...by which time any claim hereunder must be received by the agent of the Guarantor in Saudi Arabia namely...(Local Bank).

(e) The Guarantor represents and warrants that the amount of this guarantee plus all other facilities granted by them to their client...in connection with their work executed in Saudi Arabia does not exceed twenty (20) percent of the total of the paid up capital and reserves of the Guarantor.

(f) This guarantee is governed by and construed in accordance with the laws and regulations of the Kingdom of Saudi Arabia.

...Authorised Signature...Bank, Head Office

It is usually better, from the exporter's point of view, for the guarantee to be issued by a bank in his own country direct to the buyer. This eliminates the risks and costs associated with a second bank in the buyer's country. In the following example, however, the exporter's bank is able to issue the guarantee but it must be translated and affirmed by a local bank in the buyer's country. In most cases, there is a single fee for this, considerably less than the cost of issuing the bond.

To: Saudi...Company
Kingdom of Saudi Arabia

We the...(the Guarantor) hereby irrevocably and unconditionally guarantee to the Saudi...Company of... Kingdom of Saudi Arabia (the Company), subject only to the monetary limitation hereinafter specified, that...a...(legal status) (the Contractor), having received from the Company an advance payment in the amount of S.R...(figures and words) with respect to the Contract dated...day of... A.H., corresponding to...day of... A.D. (the Contract) between the Company and the Contractor for the...project, shall well and truly perform and fulfil all the undertakings, covenants, terms and conditions of the Contract and of any extensions thereof that may be granted by the Company and during the term of any warranty period set forth in the Contract, and that the Contractor shall well and truly perform and fulfil all the undertakings, covenants, terms and conditions of any and all changes, modifications, additions or amendments of the Contract that may hereafter be made, and that the Contractor shall also fully indemnify, defend and hold harmless the Company from all cost, liability, and damage which they may suffer by reason of the failure of the Contractor to do so.

In the event the Company, in their absolute discretion, give written notice to us at any time of any failure of the Contractor to perform or fulfil any of the acts or obligations set forth in the preceding paragraph, we hereby unconditionally and irrevocably undertake, without any right of any defence, set off, or counterclaim whether on our behalf or on the behalf of the Contractor, to pay to...the sum of Saudi Riyals...(figures and words) being the amount equal to the aforesaid advance payment. Such written notice of the Company shall be conclusively binding on us for all purposes under this Advance Payment Guarantee.

We further agree that any changes, modifications, additions or amendments which may be made to the terms and conditions of the Contract, or to the work to be performed thereunder, or in the payments to be made on account thereof, or any extensions of the time of performance or other forbearance on the part of either the Company or the Contractor to the other shall not in any way release us from our continuing liability hereunder, and we hereby expressly waive notice to us of any such change, modification, addition, amendment, extension or forbearance.

This Advance Payment Guarantee shall be valid until the end of the...day of... A.H., corresponding to the...day of... ...A.D., and any request for payment hereunder must be received by us on or before the expiration of such period.

This Advance Payment Guarantee shall be governed by and interpreted under the laws of the Kingdom of Saudi Arabia. Signed and sealed this...day of... 14...A.H., corresponding to the...day of... 19...A.D.

...(Signature)

The following guarantee requires the buyer's written consent that the amount of the guarantee can be reduced as the contract progresses.

To: Saudi...Company
Jeddah

Since you have awarded our clients, Messrs...(the Contractor), Contract No.
...for the installation in Saudi Arabia of...(the Contract) and since you have
agreed to reimburse to the Contractor an advance payment (the Advance Payment) up to twenty percent (20%) of the value of the Contract, we...Bank whose
registered office is situated at...Jeddah (the Guarantor) hereby irrevocably and
unconditionally guarantee the payment to you of US Dollars...(figures and
words) representing the amount of the Advance Payment and accordingly covenant and agree as follows:

   (A) On the Contractor's failure to fulfil any of the conditions of the Contract,
       as determined by you, in your absolute judgment, the guarantor shall
       forthwith, on demand made by you in writing and notwithstanding any
       objection by the Contractor, pay you such amount or amounts as you shall
       require, not exceeding in aggregate the above mentioned amount of US
       Dollars...(figures and words) by transfer to an account in your name, at
       such bank in Saudi Arabia as you shall stipulate or in such other manner
       as shall be acceptable to you.
   (B) Any payment made hereunder shall be free and clear of, and without de-
       duction for or on account of, any present or future taxes, levies, imposts,
       duties, charges, fees, deductions or withholdings of any nature whatso-
       ever and by whomsoever imposed.
   (C) The covenants herein contained constitute unconditional and irrevocable
       direct obligations of the Guarantor. No alteration in the terms of the Con-
       tract or in the extent or nature of the work to be performed thereunder and
       no allowance of time by you or other forbearance or concession or any
       other act or omission by you which, but for this provision, might exoner-
       ate or discharge the Guarantor shall in any way release the Guarantor
       from any liability hereunder.
   (D) This Guarantee shall remain valid and in full force and effect until...19...
       The value of this Guarantee shall be reduced by twenty (20%) percent of
       the total value of installation work carried out on site each quarter. The
       Contractor will present a formal request for the reduction of the Guaran-
       tee in writing to the Employer who will, if in agreement with the request,
       within fourteen days, notify the Guarantor of the reduced value of the
       Guarantee.
   (E) This guarantee is governed by and shall be construed in accordance with
       the laws and regulations of the Kingdom of Saudi Arabia.

Yours faithfully
Signed...Bank, Jeddah Branch

With contracts awarded under development loans, unfair calls are often
avoided by making claims against advance payment guarantees payable
back into the loan fund. In the following example, the liability of the guarantor is reduced as claims are paid into the loan but there is no provision to
reduce the bond *pro rata* to contract performance. All claims have to be
signed by an authorised officer of the buyer, often pre-advised to the guarantor. The guarantee is silent on law and jurisdiction.

To: Sri Lankan public utility
Sri Lanka

WHEREAS...(hereinafter called the Contractor) has entered into a Contract with...(the Buyer) in connection with...project for the sum of...(figures and words) and

WHEREAS it is one of the conditions of the said Contract that the Buyer shall upon the production of a Bank Guarantee acceptable to the Buyer advance to the Contractor...(figures and words)

AND BY THIS GUARANTEE we...(the Bank) waiving all objections and defences under the aforesaid Contract hereby irrevocably and independently guarantee to pay to the Saudi Fund for Development for the account of the Government of Sri Lanka upon the Buyer's first written demand any amount claimed by the Buyer up to the extent and not exceeding in the aggregate a sum of...against the Buyer's written declaration that the Contractor has refused or failed to perform the aforementioned Contract.

Every demand hereunder shall be in writing under the hand of the authorised officer of the Buyer and addressed to the Bank. Every payment made by the Bank hereunder shall be a pro tanto discharge of our liability to the Buyer hereunder.

This guarantee shall remain in full force and until the issue of the taking over certificate.

Authorised Signatory...   Witnesses...

Advance payment guarantees do not need to be long and wordy. In a few lines the following guarantee, issued by the seller's bank, and therefore usually with the authority to debit the seller's bank account, states that it will pay on *first demand plus interest* against the beneficiary's unsubstantiated statement that the seller is in default, without any right to object. Again, the bond is silent on law and jurisdiction, recognising that under the bond there are no grounds for a dispute.

To:...
Turkey

Whereas our Bank stands as joint and several surety for the debtor for the advance payment of up to...(figures and words) which you will pay to...(the Contractor) in accordance with Contract No...covering the supply of...(the Contract) which has been signed by and exchanged between...(the Buyer) and the Contractor, we hereby undertake and state on behalf of the Bank, as responsible representatives with full power to affix our signature, that the above guaranteed amount of...(figures and words) will be paid in cash, in full, immediately and without raising any objection, to you or to your order upon your first written demand stating that the Contractor has violated the provisions of the Contract and/or has failed to perform his undertaking completely or partially, together with legal interest for the days to be elapsed between the date of such written request and the date of actual payment without the need to issue a protest or to obtain a court order or the Contractor's consent.

Signed...(Seller's bank)

An advance payment guarantee should not become effective and payable against a claim until the advance payment, *in cleared funds*, has been received. In the following example, the guarantee contains *a coming into force clause*. It is also interesting to note that the guarantee does not reduce *pro rata* to performance but, in theory, expires on a fixed date irrespective of whether the contract is completed. However, failure to complete by this date could trigger a claim for default or a request for a validity extension.

To:...
Belgrade

Dear Sirs

GUARANTEE NO...

We have been informed by our clients...(the Supplier) that they have concluded a contract with you for the amount of...(figures and words) for the supply of...for the...project.

According to that contract, an advance payment of 20% of the contract price has to be made.

In this connection we...Bank Ltd. of... undertake to pay you the maximum amount of...(figures and words) on your first written request by registered letter with indication of reason for demand, in case the Supplier should fail to perform their contractual obligations.

This Guarantee comes into force when payment of...(the advance payment) is made to the Supplier's account.

It shall remain valid until all contractual deliveries will be performed in accordance with the contract stipulation for delivery and method of payment, but in any event not later than...19...

Yours faithfully
Signed...
Countersigned...(Supplier's bank)

Conditional tender guarantee requiring independent evidence

Less one-sided is a bond that requires the buyer's claim to be supported by an independent third party. One method of avoiding unfair and capricious calls is to ensure that the buyer does not benefit from a claim. In the following example, the issuing bank is required to pay any claims moneys direct to the account of the German aid agency KfW.

To: Government Purchaser   Our Guarantee No: Philippines

We, the undersigned bank, in order to allow Messrs...(the Bidder) of... (domicile) to submit a bid for the...(goods) for the...(project) waiving all objections and defences on the part of said Bidder or any third party, hereby irrevocably and independently guarantee to pay to you without delay any amount up to a total sum of...(amount in words)...being five (5) percent of the Bid price.

We shall effect payments under this guarantee on your first written demand which must be accompanied by the Engineer's and your confirmation that you have accepted the above mentioned bid and that the Bidder is not willing to enter into a contract in accordance with the terms of the bid.

In case of any claim under this guarantee, payment will be effected to the Kreditanstalt Fuer Wiederaufbau, Frankfurt, Germany, Account No...with...Bank, in favour of...(Purchaser).

This guarantee shall expire five (5) months after bid opening date by which time we must have received any claim by registered letter or cable.

It is understood that you will return this guarantee to us on settlement of the total amount to be claimed hereunder.

Dated...19....
Signed...(Bank)

The wide variety of guarantees given above is only a cross-section of the variants available. None could be comfortably recommended as an ideal model. For this, specimen bonds such as those given in Chapter 4 would, perhaps, be a more suitable starting point.

Specimen bonds, like model contract conditions, set a valuable industry standard which attempts to eliminate an area of damaging competition. They help exporters avoid setting bad precedents in bond wording which can cause considerable erosion of contractual security for subsequent sales to the same buyer by others.

Chapter 4 gives examples of guarantees recommended by the English and European institutions. These guarantees reflect the special interests and considerations of the different industries and take into account years of practical experience in the successful conclusion of contracts to the full satisfaction of both the buyer and exporter.

It explains how the English and European case law decisions in cases of unfair calling of demand bonds have, to a great extent, followed parallel paths and come to similar conclusions as to the rights and obligations of the parties to a guarantee payable on demand.

CHAPTER 4

ANTICIPATING UNFAIR DEMANDS

Chapter 3 provided a useful insight into the complex issue of drafting bank demand guarantees. It distinguished between low-risk and high-risk texts and gave examples of guarantees capable of being called unfairly, and of exposing the exporter to serious risk and hidden costs.

It also made the point that it was easy to overlook the need to discuss guarantee wording until too late in the contract negotiation. Guarantees, biased in favour of the buyer, become difficult to avoid if not discussed before the run-up to contract signature. Inevitably disputes arise, often as a result of an unfair demand on the guarantee, which cannot be settled amicably. This has led to many cases going to litigation.

Aggrieved exporters have been quick to approach the courts to obtain injunctions to prevent banks paying claims considered unjustified and unfair. Banks, on the other hand, have been anxious to ensure that their international reputation is not prejudiced by any action which prevents them from fulfilling their obligations to the beneficiary under the guarantee.

This Chapter looks at the attitude of courts to requests to prevent unfair demands being paid. It looks at how the English and European courts have dealt with cases of alleged unfair call. (It should be noted, however, that with the exception of a very few countries, for example, the former Czecho-slovakia and the former Yugoslavia, bank guarantees are not dealt with in the law *per se* of any country.)

In addition, it shows how the publication of model guarantees by banks and various national and international institutions has brought some degree of uniformity to guarantee wordings and their interpretation.

The Attitude of Courts

United Kingdom

Case law in the English courts is limited compared with European case law. The early decisions set precedents which were so unambiguous and unequivocal that there has since been little point in exporters seeking relief through the English courts.

In the United Kingdom, bank guarantees can be drafted to be payable on admitted or proven default, or on demand.

Guarantees payable on proven default

Under English law, this form of guarantee obliges the guarantor to pay to the beneficiary the amount of any claim admitted by the exporter, or any loss proven to have been suffered by the buyer as a result of the failure of the exporter to complete the contract in accordance with its terms and conditions. The precise obligations of the guarantor depend upon the detailed wording of the guarantee in each particular case.

In the separate case of liquidated damages, it is only necessary to establish that certain specified conditions or events have occurred, whereupon the liquidated sum becomes payable.

Guarantees payable on demand

Many buyers prefer bank guarantees payable on demand, and exporters can expect little comfort from English courts if they concede to this request. Courts require the bank to meet its obligations even if the exporter objects and cites circumstances strongly supporting his contention that the buyer's demand is unjustified.

Demand guarantees procured by the exporter are intended:

(a) to protect the buyer against non-performance (*R.D. Harbottle (Mercantile) Ltd.* v. *National Westminster Bank Ltd*, [1977] 3 W.L.R. 752; *Edward Owen Engineering Ltd.* v. *Barclays Bank International Ltd.* [1977] 3 W.L.R. 764); or

(b) to secure a repayment to the buyer if part or all of the purchase price has been paid in advance of full contractual performance (*Howe Richardson Scale Co. Ltd.* v. *Polimex-Cekop and National Westminster Bank Ltd.* [1977] B.L.T. 270).

The condition on which the bank is obliged to pay is usually on the buyer's *first demand*. Banks are concerned only that the terms of their mandate and the wording of the guarantee are complied with before making payment to the beneficiary.

Under English law, such first demand guarantees amount to *indemnities*; the bank must pay on demand. There is no requirement for the beneficiary to take any form of action against the exporter before making a demand under the bank guarantee.

Bank demand guarantees are normally viewed by learned judges as *absolute undertakings* by banks to pay if the conditions of payment are satisfied. In this respect, they are similar to a banker's confirmed documentary credit and many considerations applying to the latter apply also to bank demand guarantees.

In the leading cases in the English courts, simple demand guarantees have been described by judges as being of the nature of *promissory notes, letters of credit* or a *discount on the purchase price*.

There have been a number of High Court cases concerning simple demand guarantees.

The first, *R.D. Harbottle (Mercantile) Ltd.* v. *National Westminster Bank Ltd.* [1977] 1 Q.B. 146; [1977] 2 All E.R. 862; [1977] 3 W.L.R. 752, *per* Kerr J., was decided as if the facts simply concerned a confirmed letter of credit.

Kerr J., in the course of his judgment, stated that the courts would very rarely interfere with irrevocable obligations undertaken by a bank since they were "the lifeblood of international commerce".

He cited cases dealing with confirmed letters of credit, feeling they applied equally to demand guarantees.

This precedent of equating demand guarantees with confirmed letters of credit was followed in the case of *Howe Richardson Scale Co. Ltd.* v. *Polimex-Cekop and National Westminster Bank Ltd.* [1978] 1 Ll.Rep. 161 (C.A.).

Lord Roskill stated that when involved in guarantees, a bank

"is in a position very similar to the position of a bank which has opened a confirmed irrevocable credit...The bank here is simply concerned to see whether the event has happened upon which its obligation to pay has arisen".

If a demand guarantee is called, the bank must pay the amount of the guarantee *without protest*, whether or not the exporter is in default under the contract. The bank has no duty imposed upon it to inquire whether the exporter had failed to fulfil his obligations under the contract.

Only the contracting parties are bound by the terms of the basic contract; the commitments of the guarantor and the exporter are quite independent of each other.

In another case (*Edward Owen Engineering Ltd.* v. *Barclays Bank International Ltd.* [1977] 3 W.L.R. 764), the exporter in the United Kingdom, Edward Owen Engineering Ltd., agreed to supply greenhouses to a Libyan state enterprise. The buyer undertook to open an irrevocable letter of credit in favour of the exporter. Barclays Bank International Ltd. was to add its confirmation.

Under the contract, the exporter agreed to provide a guarantee payable on demand for 10 per cent. of the contract price. They instructed Barclays Bank International to issue such a guarantee to the Umma Bank in Libya, which in turn gave its own guarantee to the Libyan buyer.

The guarantee issued by Barclays was payable "on demand without proof or conditions".

In the event, the Libyan buyer was in breach of contract by failing to open a satisfactory letter of credit, so the exporter refused to supply the greenhouses. The buyer claimed under the demand guarantee from the Umma Bank who in turn claimed against Barclays Bank International under their guarantee.

The Court of Appeal (*Edward Owen Engineering Ltd.* v. *Barclays Bank International Ltd.* [1978] 1 Q.B. 159; [1978] 1 All E.R. 976; [1978] 1 Ll.Rep. 166) refused an injunction by the exporter which attempted to prohibit Barclays Bank International from paying.

The Master of the Rolls followed precedent by placing such guarantees, as previous judges had done, on a similar footing to letters of credit in so far as they concerned the position of the bank. Lord Denning M.R. observed:

> "All this leads to the conclusion that the performance guarantee stands on a similar footing to a letter of credit. A bank which gives a performance guarantee must honour that guarantee according to its terms. It is not concerned in the least with the relations between the supplier and the customer; nor with the question whether the supplier has performed his contracted obligation or not; nor with the question whether the supplier is in default or not. The bank must pay according to its guarantee, on demand, if so stipulated, without proof or conditions. The only exception is when there is a clear fraud of which the bank has notice."

The bank could not become involved in contractual disputes between the exporter and the buyer; it was obliged to pay "on demand without proof or conditions". Lord Denning concluded that no injunction could be imposed upon the bank to restrain payment.

Under English case law the position of the exporter is, therefore, clear. He has almost no power to prevent payment by the bank, and will ultimately become liable himself because of the counter-indemnity required from him by the bank. Cases subsequent to those mentioned above have confirmed the position.

In the event of an unfair call, the exporter is left merely with a claim for breach of contract against the buyer, with all the difficulties of establishing and enforcing such a claim in the courts of the overseas buyer's country.

The only possible exception would be where the bank had clear notice of *fraud* on the part of the buyer.

In *State Trading Corporation of India Ltd.* v. *E.D.F. Man (Sugar) Ltd.* [1981] Com.L.R. 235 (C.A.), an attempt was made to extend the meaning of fraud within the context of demand guarantees when the exporter sought an injunction against the buyer to prevent him from giving the bank notice of default as required by the guarantee.

The Court of Appeal rejected the argument that the buyer had fraudulently called the guarantee by not thoroughly investigating the reasons for the exporter's non-performance, since he was not obliged to do so under the guarantee.

Where it is clearly established to the satisfaction of the bank that the buyer's demand is fraudulent, the bank should not pay. It can, however, *interplead*, i.e. apply to pay the money into court and leave it to the parties to litigate on who is entitled to it.

A number of United Kingdom banks recommend standard wording, which they try to persuade their customers to use. It has the advantage of familiarity and therefore makes assessment of claims for payment that much easier. With standardised texts, the risk of disputes due to ambiguity or misinterpretation is greatly reduced.

The following is wording published by Barclays Bank plc:

Simple demand tender guarantee
  Our Guarantee No...

We are informed that...(hereinafter called the Seller) are tendering for a contract with you for the supply of...and that a tender guarantee is required for the sum of...

On behalf of the Seller we Barclays Bank plc [branch] hereby give you our guarantee and undertake to pay to you any amount or amounts not exceeding in total a maximum of...on receipt of your first demand in writing. Any claims must bear the confirmation of your bankers that the signatures thereon are authentic.

This guarantee is valid for written demands received by us on or before...after which date our liability to you under this guarantee will cease and this guarantee will be of no further effect.

This guarantee is personal to you and not assignable.

This guarantee is governed by English law.[1]

Documentary demand tender guarantee
  Our Guarantee No...

We are informed that...(hereinafter called the Seller) are tendering for a contract with you for the supply of...and that a tender guarantee is required in the sum of...

On behalf of the Seller we Barclays Bank plc [branch] hereby give you our guarantee and undertake to pay you any amount or amounts not exceeding in total a maximum of...[amount] on receipt of your first demand in writing accompanied by your signed statement certifying either that:

(1) the Seller has without your agreement withdrawn his tender during the period of the tender validity; or
(2) the contract to which this tender relates has been awarded to the Seller on the terms of such tender or on such terms that have been specifically agreed by the Seller and that the Seller has failed to take up the contract; or
(3) the Seller has failed to provide the guarantee(s) required following the taking up of the contract.

Any claims must bear the confirmation of your bankers that the signatures thereon are authentic.

---

[1] It is desirable for sellers to try to include after para. 2 a clause to the effect that any claim must be supported by a statement that the seller is in breach of his obligation and preferably also stating the nature of such breach, *e.g.* "...on receipt of your first demand in writing which shall state the nature of the seller's breach of his obligations".

This guarantee is valid for written demands on us as set out above which are received by us on or before...[date] after which our liability to you under this guarantee will cease and this guarantee will be of no further effect. Any request for an extension of the above expiry date will only be considered by us if the request is signed by or on behalf of both yourselves and the Seller.

This guarantee is personal to you and is not assignable.

This guarantee is governed by English law.

Simple demand performance guarantee
Our Guarantee No...

We are informed that...(hereinafter called the Seller) have entered into a contract with you dated...for the supply of...and that a bank guarantee for...being...percent of the contract price is required.

On behalf of the Seller we Barclays Bank plc [branch] hereby give you our guarantee and undertake to pay you any amount or amounts not exceeding in total a maximum of...on receipt of your first demand in writing. Any claims must bear the confirmation of your bankers that the signatures thereon are authentic.

This guarantee is valid for written demands received by us on or before...after which date our liability to you under this guarantee will cease and this guarantee will be of no further effect.

This guarantee is personal to you and not assignable.

This guarantee shall be governed by English law.[2]

Documentary demand performance guarantee
Our Guarantee No...

We are informed that...(hereinafter called the Seller) have entered into a contract with you dated...for the supply of...and that a bank guarantee for...being...percent of the contract price is required.

On behalf of the Seller we Barclays Bank plc [branch] hereby give you our guarantee and undertake to pay you any amount or amounts not exceeding in total a maximum of...on receipt of your first demand in writing provided that it is countersigned by the Seller as being a demand that is agreed by both of you or that it is supported by a copy of an award relating to the above contract and to this guarantee made under the rules of reconciliation and arbitration of the International Chamber of Commerce. Any claims must bear the confirmation of your bankers that the signatures thereon are authentic.

This guarantee is valid for written demands received by us on or before...after which date our liability to you under this guarantee will cease and this guarantee will be of no further effect, provided always that neither you nor the Seller shall on or before the above date have given us written notice at our above address of an intention to resort to the arbitration procedure, since in that event this guarantee will remain in full force and effect until receipt by us of a notice of an arbitration award as provided above, or alternatively of a notice signed by or on behalf

---

[2] It is desirable for sellers to try to include after para. 2 a clause to the effect that any claim must be supported by a statement that the seller is in breach of his obligation and preferably also stating the nature of such breach, *e.g.* "...on receipt of your first demand in writing which shall state the nature of the seller's breach of his obligations".

of both you and the Seller stating that a resort to arbitration has otherwise been terminated.

This guarantee is personal to you and not assignable.

This guarantee shall be governed by English law.

Simple demand advance payment guarantee
Our Guarantee No. . .

We are informed that. . .(hereinafter called the Seller) have entered into a contract with you dated. . .for the supply of. . .and that under the terms of the contract you are to pay the Seller the sum of. . .as an advance payment being. . .percent of the contract value.

In consideration of the receipt by the Seller of the amount specified above to the credit of his account at Barclays Bank plc we Barclays Bank plc [branch] hereby give you our guarantee and undertake to pay you any amount or amounts not exceeding in total a maximum of. . .on receipt of your first demand in writing. Any claims must bear the confirmation of your bankers that the signatures thereon are authentic.

This guarantee is valid for written demands received by us on or before. . .after which date our liability to you under this guarantee will cease and this guarantee will be of no further effect.

This guarantee is personal to you and not assignable.

This guarantee shall be governed by English law.[3]

Documentary demand advance payment guarantee
Our Guarantee No. . .

We are informed that. . .(hereinafter called the Seller) have entered into a contract with you dated. . .for the supply of. . .and that under the terms of the contract you are to pay the Seller the sum of. . .as an advance payment being. . .percent of the contract value.

In consideration of the receipt by the Seller of the amount specified above to the credit of his account at Barclays Bank plc we Barclays Bank plc [branch] hereby give you our guarantee and undertake to pay you any amount or amounts not exceeding in total a maximum of. . .on receipt of your first demand in writing which shall state the nature of the Seller's breach of his obligations. Any claims must bear the confirmation of your bankers that the signatures thereon are authentic.

This guarantee is valid for written demands received by us on or before. . .after which date our liability to you under this guarantee will cease and this guarantee will be of no further effect.

This guarantee is personal to you and not assignable.

This guarantee shall be governed by English law.

---

[3] It is desirable for sellers to try to include after para. 2 a clause to the effect that any claim must be supported by a statement that the seller is in breach of his obligation and preferably also stating the nature of such breach, *e.g.* ". . .on receipt of your first demand in writing which shall state the nature of the seller's breach of his obligations".

Checking claims

Where the buyer has to make a statement of the exporter's breach of his obligations, banks will accept whatever the statement says without attempting to check that it is accurate. It is left to the exporter to pursue the buyer under the contract for recovery of any sums paid against an improper and unjustified claim.

The European Situation

In Europe, with its system of codified law, the situation is less clear-cut, and exporters and their lawyers have attempted to invoke parts of their Civil Code to protect themselves from the financial consequences of an unfair call.

France

(Source: Michael Vasseur, Professor of Commercial Law, Paris University for Law, Economics and Social Sciences, 1989.)

Up to the late 1970s, French law ignored *independent* guarantees. Now French law is exclusively case law and in line with other countries as regards guarantees independent of the contract.

At first there was a legal void to be bridged which required careful legal decisions. The international context (mainly reflecting the rapidly changing economic and cultural situation in the Middle East) led to claims in the 1970s that in other times would probably not have been referred to the courts.

The involvement of French exporters in lawsuits, many of which were due to contracts concluded with Iran, provided an opportunity to fill the gap in French law on guarantees.

Overall, more than 20 decisions of the Cour de Cassation (the French Supreme Court) were made after two major judgments of December 20, 1982 ([1983] D. 365, note Vasseur). In addition, there are over 60 known decisions of courts of first instance or courts of appeal. About 100 cases were taken to the French courts in little more than 10 years (not counting arbitral awards).

As in England, once the jurisprudential rules applicable to guarantees became established, the number of cases diminished. This was also because the disputes due to Iranian cases were settled and the big international contracts to which guarantees are related became less numerous in subsequent years.[4]

---

[4] For a doctrinal review of the law on guarantees, see presentation to the symposium in Tours in June 1980: *Les garanties bancaires dans les contrats internationaux* (collection Feduci, Editions du Moniteur, 1981), pp. 319–364.

Available French case law shows that most of the cases about guarantees were initiated by exporters trying to prevent payment by the guarantor bank. In France, first instance judges were often moved to pity by the principal, or rather his lawyers, advocating the facts rather than the law. These judges were motivated by the unspoken or unconscious urge to help the exporter in his predicament.

The Cour de Cassation, on the other hand, showed strict adherence to the law, however harsh or drastic.

In some instances, the exporter tried to ward off the impact of the guarantee by endeavouring to place the commitments undertaken by their guarantor bank outside the field of the guarantee by making judges decide that such commitments were no more than a *bond*, the grounds for this being the fact that frequently the commitment was called a "bond" in the document establishing it.

The exporters were relying on the fact that there are different types of bonds, some being in fact guarantees, with others coming closer to indemnities, the interpretation in each case depending on the exact language of the instrument used. The exporters had no other aim than to keep open this possibility.

In the event, their argument failed. When a soft-hearted Court of Appeal found a commitment which was an independent guarantee to be a collateral bond, the Cour de Cassation overruled its decision.

A bond is a collateral which allows the guarantor to use in opposition any exception which the main debtor (the exporter) might use against the beneficiary. However, the Commercial Chamber of the Cour de Cassation cut short this argument in its first two judgments on December 20, 1982 ([1983] D. 365, note Vasseur), in particular in the first of these, the *Creusot-Loire-Enterprise* case.

The exporter argued:

> "The commitment through which a third party [the bank] undertakes to pay to a creditor debts resulting from a contract to which it is not a party, subject to a possible claim against the debtor, is necessarily a collateral surety."

The Cour de Cassation disagreed:

> "Considering that the Court of Appeal, by giving back to the bank's commitment its true legal ground and noting that [the bank] had committed itself *vis-à-vis* Creusot-Loire to pay (on demand), rightly decided that such a commitment was not a *collateral* but an *autonomous* guarantee."

Even clearer than this, the judgment of the Commercial Chamber on February 2, 1988 ([1988] D.Somm. 239, obs. Vasseur) states that using the word "bond" has no importance. The criterion of an on-demand guarantee "results from the clause committing the financial institution not to delay payment when receiving the order to pay, and not to raise any objection for any reason whatsoever".

It was also ruled that stipulating joint liability does not in any way exclude qualification as an independent guarantee ([1988] D.Somm. 240, obs. Vasseur (Com.)).

A review of the Cour de Cassation's judgments reveals that the Supreme Court does not speak of independent guarantees, but rather uses the expression *autonomous guarantee, i.e.* autonomous in relation to the basic contract.

The Commercial Chamber pointed this out in its judgment of October 17, 1984 ([1985] D. 269, note Vasseur).

However, the guarantee is obviously not without a link with the basic contract. The basic contract is its very cause, as was suggested by the Commercial Chamber in its second judgment of December 30, 1982 ([1983] D. 365, note Vasseur). The guarantee, however, is nevertheless cut off from its source; it is therefore autonomous.

The exporter is wasting his time trying to make an autonomous demand bond into an ancillary undertaking by using the word *"bond"* when the wording of the guarantee agreement is otherwise sufficiently clear. A judgment rendered by the Tribunal de Commerce, in Paris, on November 30, 1988 ([1989] D.Somm. 149) provides a good example of this.

French law on autonomous guarantees would seem to have reached a plateau. The very rich and firmly rooted case law of the Commercial Chamber of the Cour de Cassation contributed to this considerably. The decisions of the courts which will continue to be taken will have no other result than to further refine this construction.

Germany

(Source: Commerzbank.)
In Germany there are two main types of guarantee:

(a) a *Garantie* which is always an abstract, autonomous undertaking, quite independent of the underlying contract between the exporter and the buyer (the beneficiary). Such a *Garantie* under English law would be the equivalent of a *"contract of indemnity"*. On the other hand, what English law understands as a "guarantee" would in Germany be;

(b) a *Bürgschaft, i.e.* a "surety". That is to say, an accessory or *"secondary"* obligation. The *Bürgschaft* is covered in section 18, Articles 765–778 of the German Civil Code, whereas the *Garantie* is not dealt with at all in German law.

Normally in international transactions, only the *Garantie* is used.
There are practically no legal constraints on a bank to establish a

Garantie other than a provision under the lending limit regulations/capital adequacy requirements, according to which banks in Germany must not lend more than 18 times their equity capital—or double that figure as far as loans in connection with *Garantien* (and *Bürgschaften*) are concerned.

The five types of guarantee most frequently used by German banks are:

(1)   Tender guarantee—*Bietungsgarantie*;
(2)   Advance payment guarantee—*Anzahlungsgarantie*;
(3)   Performance guarantee (a)—*Liefergarantie* (covering the risk that the exporter may fail to fulfil his obligation to deliver the merchandise exactly as stipulated in the contract);
(4)   Performance guarantee (b)—*Gewährleistungsgarantie* (covering the risk that the exporter may ship merchandise that is not in conformity with the terms of the contract as to its quality, condition, functioning, etc., and that he then does not fulfil his warranty obligations as specified in the contract); and
(5)   Performance guarantee (c)—*Vertragserfüllungsgarantie* (covering the risk that the exporter may not fulfil any one of his contractual obligations towards the buyer).

The following are the English language texts used by Commerzbank when neither the exporter nor the buyer have any special preferences as to the precise wording of the requested guarantee.

Tender guarantee (Bietungsgarantie)
Tender Guarantee No...

We have been informed that, responding to your invitation to Bid No...of...for the supply of..., our customer...has submitted to you an offer No...of...

According to your conditions for bidders, offers must be supported by a bank guarantee.

In consideration of the aforesaid, we, COMMERZBANK AKTIENGESELL-SCHAFT, of...hereby irrevocably undertake to pay to you any amount up to the maximum of...(say...) upon receipt of your first demand in writing wherein you declare simultaneously that...(seller) failed to meet their obligations resulting from their participation in your above Invitation to Bid.

Our liability under this guarantee will expire on...at the latest. Consequently, any claim under it must be received by us by that date.

This guarantee is to be returned to us as soon as it is no longer required, or its validity has expired, whichever is earlier.

Signed: COMMERZBANK

Advance payment guarantee (Anzahlungsgarantie)
Advance Payment Guarantee No...

We have been informed that our customer...(hereinafter called the Seller), and you, the Buyer, have entered into a contract No...dated...concerning the supply of...in the total value of...

In accordance with the payment conditions agreed upon, an advance payment amounting to...% of the total value, i.e...will be made by you to the Seller against a bank guarantee in the same sum in your favour.

In consideration of the aforesaid, we, COMMERZBANK AKTIENGESELL-SCHAFT, of... hereby irrevocably undertake to repay to you any sum you may claim from us but not exceeding the advanced amount of...(say...) upon receipt of your first demand in writing wherein you declare simultaneously that the Seller failed to deliver the above...

It is a condition for claims and payment under this guarantee to be made that the advance payment in the sum of...has been received by us in favour of the Seller.

This Guarantee will be reduced by...% of the value of each part-shipment proved by presentation to us of copies of the relevant invoice(s) and transport documents.

Our liability under this guarantee will expire upon delivery of the...(goods/ services) mentioned above, however, on...at the latest. Any claim under it must be received by us by that date.

This Guarantee is to be returned to us as soon as it is no longer required, or its validity has expired, whichever is earlier.

Signed: COMMERZBANK

Performance guarantee (Liefergarantie)
Performance Guarantee No...

We have been informed that our customer...(hereinafter called the Seller) in accordance with Contract No...entered into with you, the Buyer, on...has to deliver to you...(description of goods/services) in total value of...

We also understand that it has been agreed between you and the Seller that the latter has to provide a bank guarantee in your favour, amounting to...% of the total value, i.e...to cover the due fulfilment of his delivery obligations.

In consideration of the aforesaid, we, COMMERZBANK AKTIENGESELL-SCHAFT, of...hereby irrevocably undertake to pay to you any amount up to the maximum of...(say...) upon receipt of your first demand in writing wherein you declare simultaneously that the Seller failed to meet his delivery obligations.

Our liability under this guarantee will expire on... at the latest, by which date any claim under it must be received by us.

This guarantee is to be returned to us as soon as it is no longer required, or its validity has expired, whichever is earlier.

Signed: COMMERZBANK

Performance guarantee (Gewährleistungsgarantie)
Performance Guarantee No...

We have been informed that our customer...(hereinafter called the Seller) has entered into a Contract No...with you, the Buyer, on...concerning the supply of... (description of goods) in total value of...

We also understand that it has been agreed between you and the Seller that the latter has to provide a bank guarantee in your favour, amounting to...% of the total value, i.e...to cover the due fulfilment of his warranty obligations concerning the goods.

* quality/condition/functioning of the ...(goods) supplied;
* [Against this guarantee the retention money/last instalment of the above total value in the sum of...will be released/paid.]

In consideration of the aforesaid, we, COMMERZBANK AKTIENGESELL-SCHAFT, of...hereby irrevocably undertake to pay to you any amount up to the maximum of...(say...) upon receipt of your first demand in writing wherein you declare simultaneously that the Seller failed to meet his warranty obligations.

* [It is a condition for claims and payment under this guarantee to be made that the retention money/the last instalment amounting to...has been received by us in favour of the Seller.]

Our liability under this guarantee will expire on... at the latest, by which date any claim under it must be received by us.

This guarantee is to be returned to us as soon as it is no longer required, or its validity has expired, whichever is earlier.

Signed: COMMERZBANK
(*) delete as inapplicable

Performance guarantee (Vertragserfüllungsgarantie)
Performance Guarantee No...

We have been informed that our customer...(hereinafter called the Seller) and you, the Buyer, have entered into Contract No...on...concerning the supply of... (description of goods/services) in total value of...

We also understand that it has been agreed between you and the Seller that the latter has to provide a bank guarantee in your favour, amounting to...% of the total value, i.e...to cover the due fulfilment of his obligations resulting from the above contract.

In consideration of the aforesaid, we, COMMERZBANK AKTIENGESELL-SCHAFT, of...hereby irrevocably undertake to pay to you any amount up to the maximum of...(say...) upon receipt of your first demand in writing wherein you declare simultaneously that the Seller failed to meet his contractual obligations.

Our liability under this guarantee will expire on... at the latest, by which date any claim under it must be received by us.

This guarantee is to be returned to us as soon as it is no longer required, or its validity has expired, whichever is earlier.

Signed: COMMERZBANK

Abuses such as making improper claims under a guarantee occur, above all, because guarantees are generally issued payable "on first demand" (*cf.* Schütze, "Einstweilige Verfügungen und Arreste im internationalen Rechtsverkehr, insbesondere im Zusammenhang mit der Inanspruchnahme von Bankgarantien" [1980] W.M. 1438; Trost, "Problemlösungen bei Bankgarantiegeschäften durch Umstrukturierung des Geschäftstyp" [1981] R.I.W. 659 *et seq.*).

As with other banks, German banks will accept the documents as presented in support of a demand, and will not question the accuracy of the statements they contain unless there is an obvious fraud.

The bank is required, after being so requested by the beneficiary, to pay the guarantee sum "without any objections whatsoever", thus without consideration of the merits of the claim for payment (*cf.* Trost, *op. cit.*).

If the claim under a guarantee is manifestly improper, the guarantor, despite his waiver to raise pleas, may put in a plea of unlawful exercise of rights (section 242, German Civil Code). This is undisputed in legal writings (Liesecke, "Rechtsfragen der Bankgarantie" [1968] W.M. 22, 26, 27; Horn, "Bürgschaften und Garantien zur Zahlung auf erstes Anfordern" [1980] N.J.W. 2153–2156; Schütze, *op. cit.* See also Mülbert, "Missbräuch von Bankgarantien und einstweiliger Rechtsschütz" in *Tübinger Rechtswissenschaftliche Abhandlungen* (Tübingen, 1985), Band 60, pp. 50 *et seq.*).

By virtue of the *Geschäftsbesorgungsvertrag* (agency agreement) entered into between the bank and the exporter, the bank is under an obligation to raise a plea and will be liable to damages if it fails to do so (Pleyer, "Die Bankgarantie im Zwischenstaatlichen Handel" [1973] W.M. 18, 19; Finger, "Formen und Rechtsnatur der Bankgarantie" [1969] B.B. 206–208).

The German Federal Court applies this ruling on abusive calls under a bank guarantee. In its judgment of March 12, 1984 ([1984] D.B. 1389 *et seq.*), in a procedure where the plaintiff had to prove his claim by documents only—*Urkundenprozess*—the Federal Court held that the exporter could use the defence of abuse of rights to defeat the claim for payment if it was obvious or provable that the purported event giving rise to the obligation to pay had not happened, although the formal requirements were met (Canaris, *Grosskommentar HGBm* (3rd ed., 1981), Nos. 1139, 1140; Stumpf/ Ullrich, "Die Missbräuchliche Inanspruchnahme von Bankgarantien im internationalen Geschäftsverkehr" [1984] R.I.W. 843 *et seq.*).

The Federal Court affirmed this principle in a further decision (judgment of September 29, 1986, [1986] Z.I.P. 1450; [1986] D.B. 2594). At the same time, however, the Court made it clear that a call was not manifestly abusive if defences had to be examined by way of interpretation of the underlying main contract between exporter and beneficiary; this would defeat the purpose of a demand guarantee. (Source: *VDMA Maschinenbau-Verlag GmbH Sonderveröffentlichung* (No. 1/86, 4th ed., Order No. 11 66 01); Stumpf/Claus, *Bankgarantien (Vertragsgarantien)* (Ullrich, ISBN 3–8163–0156–8).

Injunction vs Attachment

German exporters also face the risk of an unfair demand. Their remedy is also to seek protection from their courts.

German procedural law knows two types of summary court procedure: the temporary interlocutory injunction (*Verfügung*), and the so-called attachment (*Arrest*). *Arrest* means attachment of the claim for payment that the beneficiary, or the local guarantor, has against the guarantor in the exporter's country.

These two procedures are designed to settle urgent cases provisionally where a normal, time-consuming procedure would entail serious and partly irrecoverable loss for the party concerned.

Consequently, it is the purpose of these procedures to prevent a deterioration of the factual situation until a final settlement is reached, for instance, through a normal, ordinary litigious procedure.

German judges have been of differing opinion as to whether the *Verfügung* or the *Arrest* is the right procedure to prevent abusive calls. The attachment proceedings aim at obtaining security for a claim which is expressed in money, or may be converted into a claim expressed in money.

The purpose of an injunction is either to secure the exporter's claim for a tangible item or to deal provisionally with a situation in respect of a legal relationship in dispute. In this context, the term *Sicherungs und Regelungsverfügung* (securing and dealing injunction) is used.

German courts have overwhelmingly taken the view that the *injunction* is the right procedure. This has been demonstrated by decisions in the higher regional courts of:

(a) Frankfurt am Main (Order of June 6, 1981: [1981] N.J.W. 1914; Judgment of March 3, 1983, [1983] Z.I.P. 556);
(b) Stuttgart (Judgment of February 11, 1981: [1981] Z.I.P. 497 *et seq.*);
(c) Saarbrücken (Judgment of January 23, 1981: [1981] W.M. 275 *et seq.*);

and also the regional courts of:

(d) Munich (Judgment of January 30, 1981: AZ:10 HKO 989/81);
(e) Frankfurt am Main (Judgment of December 11, 1979: [1981] N.J.W. 56; Order of February 23, 1981: AZ:3/11 0 36/81);
(f) Dortmund (Judgment of July 9, 1989: AZ:10 0 9/80);
(g) Düsseldorf (Order of July 27, 1984, mentioned in judgment of August 9, 1984, [1985] W.M. 192);
(h) Detmold (Order of January 18, 1985: AZ:8 0 8/85) (see below);
(i) Mannheim (Order of January 25, 1982: AZ:23 0 18/82);
(j) Hanover (Order of April 25, 1986: AZ:21 0 63/86; and
(k) Braunschweig (Judgment of May 22, 1980, [1981] R.I.W. 789 *et seq.*).

The regional courts of Nürnberg-Fürth (Order of April 6, 1979) and Kempten (Order of July 10, 1980: AZ:2 0 1139/80) prefer the attachment proceedings.

Even the German courts, which prefer the injunction, are not of the same opinion with regard to the contents of the application made by an exporter who wants to prevent an abusive call.

The exporter's request aims at preventing the issuing bank from paying the sum under the guarantee. Consequently, principals generally apply for an *interlocutory injunction* requiring the bank to refrain from paying a sum of money which constitutes the guarantee sum.

Some courts take a somewhat different view, namely that the guarantor cannot be restrained from paying the guarantee sum to the beneficiary, but that the exporter has a right to demand that the issuing bank refrain from debiting his bank account with the amount of the guarantee.

This view was taken by the higher regional courts of Stuttgart (Judgment of February 11, 1981, [1981] Z.I.P. 497 *et seq.*) and Frankfurt (Order of June 6, 1981, [1981] N.J.W. 1914).

The right of the exporter to restrain the guarantor from debiting the exporter's account is more restricted than the right to prevent the guarantor from honouring a manifestly improper claim.

Common sense dictates that legal protection can only be ensured for the exporter if he applies for an *interlocutory injunction* as soon as he becomes aware of the danger of the guarantee sum being paid, and not when payment has already been effected.

The question consequently arises about the right procedure the exporter should follow and the kind of application to be filed, either to prevent:

(a)   payment of the beneficiary's claim; or
(b)   debiting of the exporter's bank account in reimbursement.

As court decisions in Europe are not totally consistent, exporters faced with an unfair call need to establish through their lawyers the views of the competent court.

In some cases the answer may be to file alternative applications in case the main application fails.

When applying for an *interlocutory injunction*, the applicant should make sure that the very strict procedural provisions are followed exactly. There must be a so-called *Verfügungsgrund* (injunction ground), that is to say, the reason why an injunction should be granted.

The injunction claim is an individual or personal claim intended to restrain the guarantor from paying the amount of the guarantee, or from drawing on the exporter's bank account, and may result from the *Geschäfts-besorgungsvertrag* (agency agreement) between the exporter and the guarantor.

However, this claim may be prejudiced, that is to say, the exporter may suffer considerable loss if the order restraining the bank can no longer be enforced. For this reason, the exporter's case against the beneficiaries' actions, the so-called *Verfügungsgrund*, must be sound.

It is a requirement of German procedural law to furnish the prima facie evidence for the existence of both the injunction claim and the injunction grounds.

Prima facie evidence constitutes a lower degree of evidence: *"evidence"* means *probability bordering on certainty*, whereas *"prima facie evidence"* means *preponderant probability*.

In summary court procedures in Germany, preponderant probability will suffice. If, on the other hand, all facts had to be completely proved, summary proceedings would become impracticable and fail to achieve their purpose.

A prerequisite for furnishing prima facie evidence in respect of an injunction claim and grounds for an injunction is that all the facts which support the claim and the grounds are immediatcly put forward. This is normally done by submitting documents from which it is obvious that the guarantee is wrongfully claimed and that payment of the amount of the guarantee would entail very harmful consequences for the exporter.

The higher regional court of Frankfurt am Main (Order of June 10, 1981, [1981] N.J.W. 1914; Judgment of March 3, 1983, [1983] Z.I.P. 556) held that a mere submission of affidavits or statutory declarations in order to establish the prima facie evidence was not sufficient. Additional documents or vouchers had to be presented.

The court observed that, for instance, a statutory declaration containing an exporter's general statement that he had supplied all he was obliged to supply was insufficient.

If, on the other hand, the exporter had submitted both a list of all the items he had to supply under the supply contract and also the relevant shipping documents, he would have shown to the satisfaction of the court that the beneficiary had manifestly made an unlawful exercise of his right to claim the amount of the guarantee. The exporter had failed to do this, as the court decided in the above-mentioned case.

It is possible to hear witnesses, who must be present, provided an oral hearing is fixed. As a rule, however, interlocutory injunctions of this kind are granted without an oral hearing. Such a hearing takes place only if the opponent objects to the injunction or to the *Arrest* (attachment).

There have been many legal cases in which *injunctions* were not granted because the required credibility of the alleged facts or events was not, or at least not sufficiently, established. For example, the judgment of the higher regional courts of:

(a) Stuttgart (Judgment of February 11, 1981, [1981] Z.I.P. 497 *et seq.*);
(b) Frankfurt am Main (Judgment of March 3, 1983, [1983] Z.I.P. 556 *et seq.*); and
(c) Saarbrücken (Judgment of January 23, 1981, [1981] W.M. 275 *et seq.*);

and of the regional court of Munich I (Judgment of January 30, 1981, [1981] W.M. 416 *et seq.*).

In the judgments rendered by the higher regional court of Frankfurt am Main (Order of June 10, 1981, [1981] N.J.W. 1914) and by the regional court of Braunschweig (Judgment of May 22, 1981, [1981] R.I.W. 789 *et seq.*) the *interlocutory injunctions* applied for were refused for other factual reasons. Consequently, it is very important to draw attention once again to the fact that the legal requirements have to be met, especially if one considers the usually very large sums that are often at stake.

Attachment (Arrest) case histories

There are court judgments (Order of April 6, 1979, Regional Court of Nürnberg-Fürth, and Order of July 10, 1980, Regional Court of Kempton: AZ:2 0 1139/80) which prevented a beneficiary from making an abusive call by way of attachment (*Arrest*).

(1) In the judgment rendered by the Kempton court, the facts were the following:

A German machinery manufacturer sold a machine to a Russian purchaser. When several defects appeared in the machine, the parties agreed to have it rebuilt in the manufacturer's works where the Russian purchaser would then take delivery of the machine.

After completion of the rebuilding work, the Russian purchaser did not send representatives to the manufacturer's works to take delivery, as agreed. On the contrary, he refused to take delivery on the grounds that the rebuilding work did not show positive results.

Because of the purchaser's refusal to send representatives to the manufacturer's works to take delivery, it was feared that the purchaser might call in a performance guarantee amounting to one million Deutschmarks.

In the legal proceedings that followed, the German manufacturer, who had furnished an expert opinion, succeeded in establishing the prima facie evidence that the rebuilding work had been successful and that the Russian purchaser had no reason for refusing the machine and calling the guarantee.

The court *attached* the payment claim under the guarantee which the Russian purchaser had against the German guarantor in favour of the German manufacturer. Consequently, the Russian purchaser could no longer raise a claim for payment as this claim was *attached*.

(2) In another attachment case, a supply contract, entered into by a German manufacturer and an Iranian company, could not be performed because of political circumstances in Iran (1979).

Under the agreement made by both parties, the German manufacturer was entitled to keep the down payment in return for expenses incurred by him up to that day.

However, despite this agreement, the Iranian company claimed the down payment guarantee.

In this case too, the claim for payment by the Iranian company against the guarantor in the Federal Republic of Germany was *attached*.

(3) In another decision rendered by the higher regional court of Hamburg in 1977 (Judgment of November 4, 1977, [1978] R.I.W. 615 *et seq.*) the court held that the bank could not honour the claim if the claim was made after the expiration of the validity period of the underlying guarantee (see also Judgment of September 26, 1985, regional court of Munich II: AZ:HKO 3277/85, on guarantees of limited duration, with reference to the Judgment of November 4, 1977 of the higher regional court of Hamburg, [1978] R.I.W. 615).

This view seems to be shared by the Federal Court of Justice (Judgment of September 29, 1986, [1986] Z.I.P. 1450 *et seq.*). The facts were as follows:

The plaintiff, a German exporter, sold goods to Egypt. He had to furnish a guarantee of limited duration amounting to 5 per cent. of the selling price as an assurance for the Egyptian buyer that he would properly perform the contract.

After the expiration of the validity period, the guarantee document was not returned by the beneficiary. The bank blocked the exporter's business account in order to use the credit balance as security for an eventual claim under the guarantee.

The court held that after the expiration of the validity period the bank (the defendant) was not entitled to retain any moneys as security until return of the guarantee document.

Even in the case of a first demand guarantee, payment of the guarantee sum would be forbidden, since, as the court observed, the beneficiary's claim would be *manifestly wrongful*.

Moreover, the court took the view that after the expiration of the validity period a bank could not debit a principal with bank charges, regardless of whether the document was returned or not.

The regional court of Stuttgart shared the view taken by the higher regional court of Hamburg: a bank may not honour a beneficiary's claim for payment after the validity period of the guarantee has expired.

This judgment was affirmed by the higher regional court of Stuttgart (Judgments of June 15, 1978, [1978] W.M. 1056, and of January 25, 1979, [1979] R.I.W. 729 *et seq.*).

In some opinions, a bank may not debit the exporter with the amount of the guarantee if the bank, contrary to its obligation under the *Geschäftsbesorgensvertrag* (agency agreement), fails to inform the exporter of the beneficiary's claim for payment and thus deprives the exporter of the opportunity of proving the clearly wrongful character of this claim (Pleyer, *op. cit.*, sonderbeilage 19, n. 127).

This last point is reflected in the 458 Rules (see Chapter 10) which now make it a requirement that the bank advise the exporter without delay when it receives a demand on a guarantee.

Interlocutory injunction (Verfügung) case histories

It was through an interlocutory injunction that the regional court of Detmold (Order of January 18, 1985: AZ:8 0 8/85) enjoined a German bank from paying the amount of the guarantee. The facts are as follows:

In its supply contract with an Egyptian purchasing company, a German industrial company undertook to give a repayment guarantee as an assurance for the Egyptian company that the German company would repay the down payment in case it did not perform the supply contract.

The repayment guarantee was duly issued; however, the down payment was not made by the Egyptian company in spite of three reminders. This did not prevent the Egyptian company from claiming payment under the repayment guarantee or, alternatively, demanding an extension of its validity.

The court considered this an unlawful exercise of rights. It held that the formal requirements for claiming payments were met, but that the German bank was bound by a *Geschäftsbesorgungsvertrag* (agency contract) entered into with the German company to the effect that no payment may be made as long as the down payment was not made.

Having presented several contract documents (partly in the form of certified translations), telexes, invoices and also reminders, the German company succeeded in furnishing satisfactory evidence that the guarantee was *abusively* called.

The above examples show that German law courts are trying, within the limits of the law, to prevent guarantors from honouring abusive claims under a guarantee by preventing them from paying the guarantee sum. The view that this is permissible was shared by the higher regional court of Saarbrücken (Judgment of January 23, 1981, [1981] W.M. 275 *et seq.*).

In a case before the higher regional court of Stuttgart (Judgment of February 11, 1981, [1981] Z.I.P. 497 *et seq.*), the parties did not agree as to whether a performance guarantee of limited duration, issued in connection with a supply contract between a German exporter and an Iraqi beneficiary, was claimed within the validity period or after its expiration.

In the exporter's view, the claim was belated and therefore improper. The court, however, held that the question as to whether the claim was made during or after the validity period was of no relevance; what mattered was the impossibility of preventing a bank from honouring a claim, even if the call was *abusive*.

The judge thought that the exporter was only entitled to demand from the guarantor that he refrain from debiting the exporter's bank account with the sum under the guarantee.

International Model Texts

English and European courts are clearly unwilling to protect the exporter from errors in commercial judgment after he has effectively given a blank cheque to the buyer, in the form of a simple demand guarantee. As a result, many banks and national and international commercial institutions have developed specimen texts to help minimise the risks of unfair calls, such as:

(a) ORGALIME, the Brussels-based Organisme de Liaison des Industries Métalliques Européenes, representing the central engineering, electrical, electronic and metalworking trade associations in 15 European countries;
(b) FIDIC, the Fédération Internationale des Ingénieurs de la Construction, representing the international civil engineering industry;
(c) International Chamber of Commerce, Paris, with its links with local chambers of commerce and international representation from key sectors of finance, commerce and industry;
(d) United Nations Commission on Trade Law (UNCITRAL), which aims to assist the economic development of Third World countries; and
(e) Confederation of British Industry (CBI), London (Publication: *Contract Bonds and Guarantees* (3rd ed., March 1987)).

Such key organisations have published specimen texts of guarantees, which endeavour to reflect the reasonable interests of the parties to the guarantee. They are drafted to give neither party an unnecessary advantage over the other. Payment is conditional on the establishment of an event of default by the exporter rather than the simple demand by the buyer.

The following model texts have been published by the European representative institution ORGALIME in line with the guidelines set out in the 458 Rules (see Chapter 10):

Tender guarantee
Guarantor...

Principal...

Beneficiary (party inviting to tender)...

Tender to which the guarantee relates...

Amount of guarantor's liability...

Expiry date...

We, the undersigned, being the Guarantor under the present Guarantee, hereby undertake to pay to the above Beneficiary upon his request in writing any sum or sums up to an amount as stated above, provided,

(1) that the claim for such payment and documents is received by us not later than the above expiry date;
(2) that the claim is supported by a written declaration of the Beneficiary confirming that the Principal's tender has been accepted by the Beneficiary and that the Principal has either failed to sign a contract corresponding to his tender or to submit a performance guarantee as provided for in his tender.

We as Guarantor will effect payment without any other delay than that necessary for us to satisfy ourselves that the conditions specified in this Guarantee have been complied with, and not later than 14 working days from the receipt by us of documentation as set out above.

Any dispute between ourselves as Guarantor and the Beneficiary relating to this Guarantee or any payment thereunder shall be finally settled by arbitration under the Rules for Conciliation and Arbitration of the International Chamber of Commerce.

. . . .   Guarantor
place and date

Repayment guarantee
Guarantor. . .

Principal (supplier-contractor). . .

Beneficiary (purchaser-employer). . .

Contract to which guarantee relates. . .

Aggregate, maximum amount of guarantor's liability. . .

Expiry date. . .

We, the undersigned, being the Guarantor under the present Guarantee, hereby undertake, subject to no other conditions than those specified in this document, to pay to the above Beneficiary upon his request in writing any sum or sums up to an aggregate, maximum amount as stated above, provided

  (1)   that the claim for such payment and documents are received by us not later than on the above expiry date;
  (2)   that the claim is supported by a written declaration of the Beneficiary that the Principal has failed to deliver the goods in respect to which advance payment was made, and that as a result thereof the Beneficiary, under the terms of the said contract, has become entitled to repayment of advances made by him.

We as Guarantor will effect payment without any other delay than that necessary for us to satisfy ourselves that the conditions specified in this Guarantee have been complied with, and not later than 14 working days from the receipt by us of documentation as set out above.

Any dispute between ourselves as Guarantor and the Beneficiary relating to this Guarantee or any payment thereunder shall be finally settled by arbitration under the Rules of Conciliation and Arbitration of the International Chamber of Commerce.

. . . .   Guarantor
place and date

Performance guarantee
Guarantor. . .

Principal (supplier-contractor). . .

Beneficiary (purchaser-employer). . .

Contract to which guarantee relates. . .

Aggregate, maximum amount of guarantor's liability...

Expiry date...

We, the undersigned, being the Guarantor under the present Guarantee, hereby undertake, subject to no other conditions than those specified in this document, to pay to the above Beneficiary upon his request in writing any sum or sums up to the aggregate, maximum amount as stated above, provided

    (1)   that the claim for such payment is received by us not later than on the above expiry date;

    (2)   that the claim is supported by a written declaration of the Beneficiary confirming that the Principal has failed to perform his obligations under the contract, specifying in what respect(s) the Principal has so failed and that as a result thereof the Beneficiary, under the terms of the said contract, has become entitled to payment of the amount claimed by him.

We as Guarantor will effect payment without any other delay than that necessary for us to satisfy ourselves that the conditions specified in this Guarantee have been complied with, and not later than 14 working days from the receipt by us of documentation as set out above.

Any dispute between ourselves as Guarantor and the Beneficiary relating to this Guarantee or any payment thereunder shall be finally settled by arbitration under the Rules of Conciliation and Arbitration of the International Chamber of Commerce.

.... Guarantor
place and date

The following model texts permit payment by the bank against a written demand plus the beneficiary's declaration that the exporter is in default. There is no arbitration clause.

Tender guarantee
(Payable on first demand.)

    Tender guarantee given by...Bank (Guarantor) to...(Beneficiary) in the event of default by...(Principal) in the obligations resulting from the Tender, dated...for...(exact description of the object of the tender).

    The Guarantor hereby undertakes irrevocably to pay to the Beneficiary, within a period of 14 working days from the date of receipt by him of the beneficiary's first request in writing, any sum claimed, up to the amount of...provided this request is received not later than...(expiry date).

    The request must be accompanied by a certified copy of the document concerning the award of the Contract to the Principal (or by a relevant statement in writing of the Beneficiary), as well as by a written statement of the Beneficiary indicating the default of the Principal in the obligations resulting from the above-mentioned Tender.

    .... Guarantor
place and date

Repayment guarantee
(Payable on first demand.)

> Repayment Guarantee given by...Bank (Guarantor) to...(Beneficiary) in the event of default by...(Principal) in the obligations resulting from the Contract, dated...for...(exact description of the subject-matter of the contract).
>
> The Guarantor hereby undertakes irrevocably to pay to the Beneficiary, within a period of 14 working days from the date of receipt by him of the Beneficiary's first request in writing, any sum claimed, up to the amount of... provided this request is received not later than...(expiry date).
>
> The request must be accompanied by a written statement of the Beneficiary indicating the default of the Principal in the obligations resulting from the Contract.
>
> .... Guarantor
> place and date

Performance guarantee
(Payable on first demand.)

> Performance Guarantee given by...Bank (Guarantor) to ...(Beneficiary) in the event of default by...(Principal) in the obligations resulting from the Contract, dated...for...(exact description of the subject-matter of the Contract).
>
> The Guarantor hereby undertakes irrevocably to pay to the Beneficiary, within a period of 14 days from the date of receipt by him of the Beneficiary's first request in writing, any sum claimed, up to the amount of...provided this request is received not later than...(expiry date).
>
> The request must be accompanied by a written statement of the Beneficiary indicating the default of the Principal in the obligations resulting from the Contract.
>
> .... Guarantor
> place and date

(Reproduced by kind permission of ORGALIME, from *Guide on Bank Guarantees*, July 1987.)

Other trade organisations and industrial associations have also published texts which avoid the risk of an unfair call. Often these represent the interests of the exporter, for example:

(a) the Frankfurt-based machine and plant builders association VDMA—Verband Deutscher Maschinen und Anlagenbau e.V.;
(b) the United Kingdom's Process Plant Association;
(c) the Engineering Industries Association; and
(d) the Chemical Industries Association, etc.

and their United States and Japanese equivalents.

Occasionally the well-intentioned attempts to encourage the international business community to adopt a standard guarantee format with a high moral content meets with rejection by all parties.

For example, the following specimen guarantees were published and recommended by the International Chamber of Commerce. However, since their introduction following the publication of the 325 Rules (see Chapter 10) they have been little used by most banks, nor asked for, nor accepted. This is because they are biased against the beneficiary, and completely opposed to the trend of international guarantee practice and usage.

Tender guarantee
(Issued subject to the Uniform Rules of Contract Guarantees of the International Chamber of Commerce (ICC Publication No. 325).)

Guarantor. . .

Principal (tenderer). . .

Beneficiary (party inviting to tender) . . .

Tender to which guarantee relates. . .

Aggregate amount of guarantor's liability. . .
(amount and currency to be specified or % of the tender price)

Documentation to support any claim (as set out below). . .

Expiry date. . .
(to be specified; or otherwise determined as mentioned in Art. 4(a) of the Rules.)

We, the undersigned, being the Guarantor under the present Guarantee, hereby undertake, subject to no other conditions than those specified in this document and the above-mentioned Rules, to pay to the above Beneficiary upon his request in writing or by cable, telegram or telex any sum or sums up to an aggregate, maximum amount as stated above, provided

(1)   that the claim for such payment is received by us as set out in Art. 8 of the Rules not later than on the above expiry date;
(2)   that the claim incorporates a declaration of the Beneficiary that the amount claimed has not otherwise been paid to him, whether directly or indirectly, by or on behalf of the Principal;
(3)   that the claim is supported by a declaration of the Beneficiary that the Principal's tender has been accepted by the Beneficiary and that the Principal has then either failed to sign a contract corresponding to the tender or to submit a performance guarantee as provided for in the tender;
(4)   that the claim is accompanied by a declaration of the Beneficiary addressed to the Principal agreeing to have any dispute on any claim by the Principal for payment to him by the Beneficiary of all or part of the amount paid under the guarantee settled by a judicial or arbitral tribunal specified or agreed as set out in Art. 9(a) of the Rules.
(5)   that. . .(insert any other documentation specified as a prerequisite for honouring a claim for payment).

Any dispute between ourselves as Guarantor and the Beneficiary relating to this Guarantee or any payment thereunder shall be finally settled by Arbitration under the Rules of Conciliation and Arbitration of the International Chamber of Commerce. (If a different arbitration system is chosen, mention it here instead of ICC Arbitration.)

(If the arbitration clause above has been deleted, the court having exclusive competence is defined in Art. 11.3 of the Rules.)

Signed...............   Guarantor
          place and date

Repayment guarantee
(Issued subject to the Uniform Rules of Contract Guarantees of the International Chamber of Commerce (ICC Publication No. 325).)

Guarantor...

Principal (supplier-contractor)...

Beneficiary (buyer-employer)...

Contract to which guarantee relates...

Aggregate maximum amount of guarantor's liability...
(amount and currency to be specified or % of the contract price)

Documentation to support any claim (as set out below)...[5]

Expiry date...
(to be specified; or otherwise determined as mentioned in Art. 4(c) of the Rules)

Other conditions (if any)...

We, the undersigned, being the Guarantor under the present Guarantee, hereby undertake, subject to no other conditions than those specified in this document and the above-mentioned Rules, to pay to the above Beneficiary upon his request in writing or by cable, telegram or telex any sum or sums up to an aggregate, maximum amount as stated above, provided

(1)   that the claim for such payment is received by us as set out in Art. 8 of the Rules not later than on the above expiry date;
(2)   that the claim incorporates a declaration of the Beneficiary that the amount claimed has not otherwise been paid to him, whether directly or indirectly, by or on behalf of the Principal;
(3)   that the claim is supported by a declaration of the Beneficiary that the Principal has failed to perform his obligations under the contract, specifying in what respects the principal has so failed, and that as a result thereof the Beneficiary, under the terms of the said contract, has become entitled to repayment of advance payments made by him;
(4)   that the claim is supported by:
    (a)   a decision of a court of first instance;
    (b)   an arbitral award justifying the claim;
    (c)   the approval of the Principal in writing to the claim and the amount to be paid;
    (d)   ...(delete as applicable, or insert under (d) any other document specified as a prerequisite for honouring a claim for payment).

We as Guarantor will effect payment without any delay other than that necessary for us to satisfy ourselves that the conditions specified in the Rules and in this

---

[5] It may be appropriate in some cases to insert a clause providing for reduction of the guarantee sum in step with performance of the contract.

guarantee have been complied with, and not later than (...) working days from receipt by us of documentation as set out above.

Any dispute between ourselves as Guarantor and the Beneficiary relating to this Guarantee or any payment thereunder shall be finally settled by Arbitration under the Rules of Conciliation and Arbitration of the International Chamber of Commerce. (If a different arbitration system is chosen, mention it here instead of ICC Arbitration.)

(If the arbitration clause above has been deleted, the court having exclusive competence is defined in Art. 11.3 of the Rules.)

Signed...............   Guarantor
      place and date

Performance guarantee
(Issued subject to the Uniform Rules of Contract Guarantees of the International Chamber of Commerce (ICC Publication No. 325).)

Guarantor...

Principal (supplier-contractor)...

Beneficiary (buyer-employer)...

Contract to which guarantee relates...

Aggregate maximum amount of guarantor's liability...
(amount and currency to be specified or % of the contract price)

Documentation to support any claim (as set out below)...[6]

Expiry date...
(to be specified; or otherwise determined as mentioned in Art. 4(b) of the Rules)

Other conditions (if any)...

We, the undersigned, being the Guarantor under the present Guarantee, hereby undertake, subject to no other conditions than those specified in this document and the above-mentioned Rules, to pay to the above Beneficiary upon his request in writing or by cable, telegram or telex any sum or sums up to an aggregate, maximum amount as stated above, provided

(1)   that the claim for such payment is received by us as set out in Art. 8 of the Rules not later than on the above expiry date;

(2)   that the claim incorporates a declaration of the Beneficiary that the amount claimed has not otherwise been paid to him, whether directly or indirectly, by or on behalf of the Principal;

(3)   that the claim is supported by a declaration of the Beneficiary that the Principal has failed to perform his obligations under the contract, specifying in what respects the Principal has so failed, and that as a result thereof the Beneficiary, under the terms of the said contract, has become entitled to payment of the amount claimed by him;

(4)   that the claim is supported by:

  (a)   a decision of a court of first instance;

  (b)   an arbitral award justifying the claim;

---

[6] It may be appropriate in some cases to insert a clause providing for reduction of the guarantee sum in step with performance of the contract.

(c)   the approval of the Principal in writing to the claim and the amount to be paid;

(d)   ...(delete as applicable, or insert under (d) any other document specified as a prerequisite for honouring a claim for payment).

We as Guarantor will effect payment without any delay other than that necessary for us to satisfy ourselves that the conditions specified in the Rules and in this guarantee have been complied with, and not later than (...) working days from receipt by us of documentation as set out above.

Any dispute between ourselves as Guarantor and the Beneficiary relating to this Guarantee or any payment thereunder shall be finally settled by Arbitration under the Rules of Conciliation and Arbitration of the International Chamber of Commerce. (If a different arbitration system is chosen, mention it here instead of ICC Arbitration.)

(If the arbitration clause above has been deleted, the court having exclusive competence is defined in Art. 11.3 of the Rules.)

Signed...............   Guarantor
    place and date

The ICC have subsequently come into line with the general practice of the international market and provide specimen guarantees which correspond to the guidelines stated in their 458 Rules (see Chapter 10).

To assist their exporters, the German VDMA Maschinenbau-Verlag GmbH in its publication *Sonderveröffentlichung* (No. 1/86, 4th ed., Order No. 11 66 01) has prepared its own model forms of demand guarantees:

Tender guarantee
(Payable on first demand in the event of default.)

Tender Guarantee given by...Bank (Guarantor) to...(Beneficiary) in the event of default by...(Principal) in the obligations resulting from the Tender dated...for...(exact description of the object of the Tender).

The Guarantor hereby undertakes irrevocably to pay to the Beneficiary, within a period of 14 working days from the date of receipt by him of the beneficiary's first request in writing, any sum claimed, up to the amount of...DM, provided this request is received not later than...(expiry date).

The request must be accompanied by a certified copy of the document concerning the award of the Contract to the Principal (or by a relevant statement in writing of the Beneficiary), as well as by a written statement of the Beneficiary indicating the default of the Principal in the obligations resulting from the above-mentioned Tender.

After the lapse of the Guarantee, the Beneficiary shall, without delay, return the guarantee document to the Principal. Where the Guarantee has been paid out to the Beneficiary, it shall be the Guarantor's duty to return the guarantee document to the Principal.

German law shall apply to all disputes arising out of or in connection with this Guarantee.

The German text of this Guarantee shall be the original text.

Repayment guarantee
(Payable on first demand in the event of default.)

Repayment Guarantee given by...Bank (Guarantor) to...(Beneficiary) in the event of default by...(Principal) in the obligations resulting from the Contract dated...for...(exact description of the subject-matter of the Contract).

The Guarantor hereby undertakes irrevocably to pay to the Beneficiary, within a period of 14 working days from the date of receipt by him of the beneficiary's first request in writing, any sum claimed, up to the amount of...DM, provided this request is received not later than...(expiry date).

The request must be accompanied by a written statement of the Beneficiary indicating the default of the Principal in the obligations resulting from the Contract.

After the lapse of the Guarantee, the Beneficiary shall, without delay, return the guarantee document to the Principal. Where the Guarantee has been paid out to the Beneficiary, it shall be the Guarantor's duty to return the guarantee document to the Principal.

German law shall apply to all disputes arising out of or in connection with this Guarantee.

The German text of this Guarantee shall be the original text.

Performance guarantee
(Payable on first demand in the event of default.)

Performance Guarantee given by...Bank (Guarantor) to...(Beneficiary) in the event of default by...(Principal) in the obligations resulting from the Contract dated...for...(exact description of the object of the Contract).

The Guarantor hereby undertakes irrevocably to pay to the Beneficiary, within a period of 14 working days from the date of receipt by him of the beneficiary's first request in writing, any sum claimed, up to the amount of...DM, provided this request is received not later than...(expiry date).

The request must be accompanied by a written statement of the Beneficiary indicating the default of the Principal in the obligations resulting from the Contract.

After the lapse of the Guarantee, the Beneficiary shall, without delay, return the guarantee document to the Principal. Where the Guarantee has been paid out to the Beneficiary, it shall be the Guarantor's duty to return the guarantee document to the Principal.

German law shall apply to all disputes arising out of or in connection with this Guarantee.

The German text of this Guarantee shall be the original text.

As in the case of the 325 Rules, these model texts have not been wholeheartedly adopted by German banks, nor asked for as a matter of course by exporters.

The main reason for this is that the specimen guarantees are not drafted in accordance with the usual international practice and, ironically, fail to give protection to those for whose benefit they were intended, *i.e.* the beneficiary. In every instance there is a requirement on the beneficiary to show, and on the bank to judge, that there has been a default by the exporter.

In all these examples the bank promises to pay upon receipt of the beneficiary's *first demand in writing*, incorporating the statement that the exporter has failed to fulfil his obligations.

No proof that this is in fact the case is needed. This what makes a guarantee a highly valuable instrument in the hands of the beneficiary, granting him immediate access to the exporter's funds should he decide that the exporter did not, in his opinion, meet his contractual obligations.

If they are acceptable to the buyer, standard texts have a clear advantage over attempts to tailor-make a demand guarantee. Banks know when a claim is valid and can be accepted. There is no imprecision regarding validity dates, the amount to pay and when. They know how the courts will interpret the wording.

A key advantage from the exporter's point of view is that they are able to issue standard specimens faster and more efficiently than those that have been specially drafted, which have to be double-checked by lawyers to avoid mistakes and ambiguity.

Attitude of Banks

Banks have been developing standard specimen guarantees over the years, constantly improving on them as commercial, financial and legal experience is gained. For this reason, drafts will vary from country to country based on their local experience and legal system.

Banks resist guarantees which give the exporter an opportunity to request the bank not to pay *because all obligations have in fact been fulfilled* (which the bank is in no position to verify), or which would encourage the exporter to attempt having a court prohibit payment by the bank by means of preliminary injunctions and the like.

Such attempts to prevent payment can seriously undermine the international reputation and standing of a bank. Banks, in most cases, have no other choice than to take legal steps themselves in order to have such injunctions withdrawn.

From the bank's point of view, it is a question of *Pay first, litigate later*!

In the United States of America, the contract guarantee mechanism is quite different.

United States of America

In the United States, contract bonding is predominantly in the hands of the surety companies. The extent, amount and nature of the bonds provided by surety companies often go far beyond those provided by, say,

European banks, and can include a main contractor's payment to sub-contractors, performance bonds in excess of 100 per cent. to buyers, etc.

To the extent that United States banks compete with the surety companies they must use a totally different guarantee instrument. United States banks use *stand-by letters of credit* as opposed to surety bonds or bank demand guarantees. This is because historically United States banks have been faced with lawsuits in the United States from shareholders claiming that it is not within the powers of banks (as opposed to surety companies) to provide commitments in the nature of guarantees.

Case law in the United States is therefore associated with surety bonds and letters of credit and is beyond the scope of this book (for exceptional cases, see Stumpf/Ullrich, *op. cit.*, pp. 843 *et seq.*).

Typically, stand-by letters of credit can be drafted as follows:

Example 1: Specimen stand-by letter of credit
  To...(Beneficiary)

            IRREVOCABLE STAND-BY LETTER OF CREDIT NO...

Dear Sir(s)

In accordance with instructions received from...we hereby issue in your favour our stand-by letter of credit for...(amount) available by your drafts drawn on us at sight accompanied by:

...

together with your signed statement that the sellers have failed to perform their obligations under the terms of the contract number...dated...

Any Claims must bear the confirmation of your bankers that the signatures thereon are authentic.

This stand-by letter of credit is available for presentation of documents to us until...

We undertake that drafts and documents drawn under and in strict conformity with the terms of this credit will be honoured on presentation.

Subject to Uniform Customs and Practice for Documentary Credits 1983 Revision, ICC Publication No. 400.

Example 2: Stand-by letter of credit
  To... (Beneficiary)

Gentlemen

We hereby establish our irrevocable stand-by letter of credit for account of...(the Sellers) in your favour in the amount of...available by your drafts drawn at sight on...(bank) and accompanied by the following document:

—your signed statement that the Sellers have failed to perform their obligations under the terms of the contract dated...

This credit is available for presentation of documents to us until...

We undertake that drafts and documents drawn under and in strict conformity with the terms of this credit will be honoured upon presentation.

This credit is subject to Uniform Customs and Practice for Documentary Credits 1983 Revision, ICC Publication No. 400.

(Source: CBI publication, *Contract Bonds and Guarantees* (3rd ed.)

In the United States, stand-by letters of credit offer, in law, similar security to the buyer as demand guarantees. They are normally issued subject to the guidelines in the Uniform Customs and Practice for Documentary Credits 1983 Revision (ICC Publication No. 400 (No. 500 from January 1, 1994), "UCP").

Non-United States banks can sometimes use stand-by letters of credit if so instructed, and if buyers are prepared to accept them. However, this does not apply in all cases; for example, they are rejected in Thailand.

The advantage to exporters is that stand-by letters of credit governed by the UCP incorporate disciplines concerning claims and expiry dates which appear in this code of practice, which help reduce the risk of payment of unfair demands. However, there have been cases of unfair claims and exporters have instituted legal proceedings to prevent banks from paying abusive claims ((1980) 93 *Harvard Law Review* 992 *et seq.*).

Annex—Schedule of Legal Cases in Europe Relating to Unfair Calls of Contract Demand Bonds

In each of the following countries, judicial measures have been taken to prevent guarantors from honouring abusive calls.

Italy

- Bologna: *Lenzi c. Credito Romagnolo* (unreported, 1981);
- Padua: *Eurofur* c. *Banca Commerciale Italiana* (unreported, November 24, 1977);
- Reggio Emilia: *Foro Pad.* (unreported, October 10, 1978);
- Pretura di Milano: *Godwana Spa c. Instituto San Paolo di Torino* [1985] II B.B.T.C. 84;
- Pretura di Milano: *Safimi Babcock* c. *Banca Commerciale Italiana* [1985] II B.B.T.C. 87.

Belgium

- Bruxelles, [1982] J.T. 358; [1982] *Revue Banque* 99;
- Cour d'Appel de Bruxelles, [1982] J.C.B. 349;
- Trib. de Commerce de Bruxelles (référés), [1985] R.D.C. 569;
- Trib. de Commerce de Liège (référés), [1984] J.L. 512;
- Trib. de Commerce de Bruxelles, [1985] R.D.C. 567;
- Trib. de Commerce de Charleroi (référés), [1985] R.R.D. 73;
- Trib. de Commerce de Bruxelles (référés), [1986] *Recueil Dalloz* 162.

Luxembourg

- Trib. de Commerce, [1981] *Dalloz* 504;
- Cour d'Appel, [1983] *Dalloz* 299.

France

- Trib. Com. Paris (unreported, March 24, 1981);
- Cour d'Appel, Paris (unreported, January 29, 1981);
- Trib. Com. Paris, [1984] *Recueil Dalloz* 92;
- Paris, 14e Ch.C., *Aff. Union des Banques Suisses* c. *Socit. O.I.P., Socit. Gondwana* (unreported, January 7, 1983);
- Paris, 1e Ch.A., *Aff. Banque Maskan* c. *Socit. Auxiliaire d'Entreprises et Credit Lyonnais* (unreported, May 25, 1983);
- Paris, 1e Ch.A., [1985] *Banque* 92;
- Paris, 1e Ch.A., [1983] D. 437;
- Trib. Com. Paris, 13e Ch. (unreported, July 8, 1983);
- Cour de Cassation, Chambre Commerciale, *Bank Tejarat* c. *Société Auxiliaire d'Entreprises et Crédit Lyonnais* [1986] *Recueil Dalloz* 213;

- Cour de Cassation, Chambre Commerciale, *Bank Tejarat* c. *Pipe Line Service et Paribas* (source unknown, June 10,1986);
- Trib. de Commerce de Melun, *BNCP* c. *Soc. Anon. Granit* [1986] *Recueil Dalloz* 159.

The Netherlands

- Amsterdam, *Trengrouse* v. *Bank of America* [1982] N.J. 32;
- Leeuwarden, [1973] N.J. 188 (75);
- Amsterdam, *Tasmac* v. *Stevin Bahareth* [1981] K.G. 74;
- Arnhem, *Globogal* v. *Bax* [1983] N.J. 750.

Switzerland

- Cour de Justice de Genève, *Union Bank of Switzerland* v. *I.P.I. Trade International and Banque Melli Iran* [1984] *Dalloz* 94;
- Cour de Justice de Genève, [1984] *Recueil Dalloz* 94;
- Cour de Justice de Genève, *Union Bank of Switzerland and General Establishment for Cereal Processing and Trade* v. *Miranos International Trading Corporation Inc. S.A.* (unreported, September 12, 1985);
- Cour de Justice de Genève, *Iranian Government Trading Corporation and Banque Melli Iran* v. *Segogest S.A.* [1986] *Recueil Dalloz* 164 at 165;
- Züricher Obergericht, *Blatt für Züricher Rechtsprechung* [1985] Bd. 44.

(See also Mülbert, *op. cit.*, p. 16 and further references.)

Greece

An Athens court required a beneficiary to refrain from making a claim under a guarantee where this could constitute an unlawful exercise of rights.

India

A decision of the High Court of Calcutta, made on 7 March, 1984, enjoined payment of a warranty guarantee although the guarantee was not even called (Stumpf/Ullrich, *op. cit.*, pp. 843 *et seq.*) although in the view of Stumpf and Ullrich this decision probably goes too far.

Spain

In Spain, guarantees as such are not valid.

England

Up to now, English courts do not admit the general defence of abuse of rights (Graupner, "Die Vertragpraxis der britischen Industrie im Auslandsgeschäft" [1984] R.I.W. 843 *et seq*.).

Thus a bank may reject a beneficiary's claim only if there is a clear case of fraud of which the bank has notice (*Edward Owen* v. *Barclays Bank* [1979] All E.R. 978; [1978] Q.B. 159 (C.A.); see also *Boliventer Oil S.A.* v. *Chase Manhattan Bank N.A.* [1984] 1 W.L.R. 392 (C.A.); *Pottom Homes Ltd.* v. *Coleman Contractors Overseas* (unreported, Court of Appeal, February 28, 1984); as well as *United Trading Corporation* v. *Allied Arab Bank Ltd.* (unreported, Court of Appeal, July 17, 1984); and *Murray Clayton Ltd.* v. *Rafidain Bank* [1984] *International Banking Law* 48; [1986] *Recueil Dalloz* 162 at 163).

CHAPTER 5

PROJECT GUARANTEES

So far, we have only considered bank demand guarantees from the point of view of a buyer and single seller. However, many major contracts, too large for one supplier or contractor, also require bonds to provide the buyer with an acceptable level of comfort over the contractor's ability to perform.

Projects often involve complex bonding arrangements if the contractor is to satisfy the needs of the buyer and ensure that the contractor does not carry on his own balance sheet the full financial impact of issue. It is also important in multi-disciplined projects that the risk of a demand falls on the party responsible for default.

Project guarantees require careful consideration in respect not only of their text, but also when they are given, by whom, to whom, by which bank and against what security and recourse.

Project bonding should meet the needs of the buyer who seeks security of overall contract performance when there is more than one contractor on the job. It must also assure the buyer that he can recover unearned advance payments when most of the advance payment has been passed back to other suppliers and contractors.

With large projects, much of the work is likely to be sub-contracted to companies in countries different to that of the main contractor.

This cross-border nature of bonding increases its complexity and risks. Guarantees from several banking and financial systems, subject to a variety of banking practices, taxes and laws, may be issued. The cost structures for issue and maintenance and the treatment of claims can, and do, often differ.

Limiting the Financial Exposure

Many projects are too large for the balance sheet of a single contractor to support. It could be commercially and financially imprudent for a main contractor to expose too much of his balance sheet to one project, buyer or country.

Even the very largest contractors would not willingly choose to bear the burden of full contractual bonding, even if their balance sheets could carry

117

the exposure, when there is an alternative way of spreading the risk and cost.

Many main contractors will therefore usually want to ensure back-to-back security from sub-contractors and key suppliers, etc., for example, the bonding of distinct individual elements of work to be done by each sub-contractor.

With other projects, where there is no clear interface between the responsibilities of the various contractors and subcontractors, a less specific form of security may be more suitable.

Guarantors are concerned to satisfy their own recourse requirements when the level of bonding is too great for a single contractor. They will seek to ensure that in the event of a claim on a guarantee their obligation to pay is fully indemnified by recourse-worthy parties.

The bank's risk is whether their client, the contractor, is capable of withstanding the level of recourse the bank will be obliged to take under their counter-indemnity at the time of a claim.

Project Structures

The actual structure of a project is rarely decided by the bonding requirement itself. On the contrary, it is the project structure which dictates who the project partners are and how best the burden of bonding is to be shared.

There are a number of alternative structures that can be uniquely tailored to the nature and scope of the project, and the requirements of the buyer and guarantor. Subject to the final project structure being acceptable to the buyer, the skills and abilities of the main contractor will greatly influence the extent to which he uses speciality supplies and management expertise of other parties. For example, the main contractor may wish to:

(a) take advantage of a particular supplier's or country's competitive technical expertise;
(b) maximise tax efficiency;
(c) bring in the lowest cost countries;
(d) bring in those countries known for quality and reliable performance; or
(e) bring in those countries which have access to preferential financing.

It could be a combination of these or other factors.

With project structures, there is often a conflict of interest between the contractor and the buyer. The contractor prefers to dilute his bonding exposure by structuring the project so that more of the participants share the costs and burden of recourse; whereas the buyer usually prefers only one party to be responsible to him (preferably the one with the most substantial asset base).

The most common project structure is where the main contractor sub-

contracts some, or most, of the work. It is therefore possible, and convenient, to discuss first the major issues relating to contract bonding concerning
sub-contracts. The key issues associated with other structures, such as joint
ventures and consortia, are discussed later in this Chapter.

Sub-contracts

A *sub-contractor* normally has no direct relationship with the buyer. His
contract is solely with the main contractor. In many cases, the buyer does
not even know of the existence of a sub-contractor, let alone his name. The
buyer looks to the *main contractor* for full and satisfactory performance.
How this is achieved is the main contractor's responsibility, and he has to
provide bonds accordingly.

Ideally, the main contractor will try and get the buyer to accept a surety
bond. This does not impact directly on the main contractor's banking lines
and, if a claim is made, is not likely to result in a precipitous exodus of cash.

On the other hand, if the buyer insists on bank demand guarantees, the
main contractor can find himself in a seriously exposed situation if the
buyer makes a sudden unexpected claim.

The vulnerability of the main contractor can be readily appreciated. His
role is to bring in one or several sub-contractors to provide, in many cases,
inter-dependent specialist goods or services. He has full contractual responsibility for the project, but is dependent on each of the sub-contractors
to perform his contract properly. The value of the main contractor's own
contribution to the project in performance terms may only be small, but his
management responsibility can be total and has to be bonded accordingly.

The failure of a key sub-contractor to perform his contract satisfactorily
due to default or insolvency can delay the whole project and the main contractor will suffer the risk and stress of a possible demand on his bond.

In addition, the buyer may also invoke the penalty or liquidated damages clause, which can result in a further outflow of cash.

Fortunately, there are ways for the main contractor to mitigate this serious, even potentially dangerous, exposure. However, rarely do any of the
techniques give total protection. For example:

(a)   in the event of default, the main contractor could terminate the sub-
      contract and bring in another sub-contractor to complete the work,
      and so avoid a call on the main contract bonds; or
(b)   where the risk is identified in advance, the main contractor can in
      certain circumstances insure against default or insolvency of a key
      sub-contractor.

Alternatively,

(c)   he could ask the sub-contractor to provide a *performance guarantee*.

Sub-contractors who contribute substantially to a main contract are often put under pressure by main contractors to share the financial and risk burden of the bonding requirements under the main contract. They may be asked to provide, either directly or through their bank, part of the total counter-indemnity requirement of the bank providing the bond for the main contractor.

The problem for a sub-contractor agreeing to this request is that he could become *exposed to main contract risks* (and the risk of the main contract bond being called by the end-buyer *unfairly*), without being a party to the main contract and therefore without any recourse to the rights and remedies embodied in the main contract.

The same exposure arises when the main contractor requires from the sub-contractor a bond that is capable of being called not only in the event of the sub-contractor's failure to perform, but also simply when the main contractor's bond is called *fairly*.

Any *simple demand bond* given by the sub-contractor to a main contractor exposes the former to the risk of *unfair call*.

When looking at sub-contract bonding, there are a number of considerations to be taken into account. These would include:

    (i)   the suitability of the guarantor;
    (ii) the beneficiary of the guarantee;
   (iii) the guarantee value;
   (iv) the currency of the guarantee;
    (v) the text;
   (vi) the domicile and law;
  (vii) the effect of a claim; and
 (viii) the validity.

Suitability of the Guarantor

The proposed guarantor, selected by the sub-contractor, may not be satisfactory to the main contractor.

For example, if the main contractor has been required to issue a bank demand guarantee, a sub-contractor's surety bond does not necessarily protect his cashflow. The quality of security is similar in respect of a *fair* claim arising from an admitted default, but the financial risks are quite different where a demand is made *unfairly* by the end buyer. The main contractor is caught in the middle.

(a) Bank

From the main contractor's point of view, a bank demand guarantee is

more flexible than a surety bond, as a successful claim can give him immediate cash in hand.

However, whilst many banks are able to provide bank guarantees, the
prudent main contractor should satisfy himself that the guarantee as provided is acceptable and in practice enforceable. Not all financial institutions that call themselves banks are necessarily financially sound and some
banks are located in the distant country of a sub-contractor.

Some may issue a tender guarantee but refuse to issue the performance
guarantee once the contract has been awarded, because the sub-contractor
does not have the assets to support it. This can place the main contractor in
an exposed position *vis-à-vis* his own tender guarantee, especially if his
bank refuses to provide main contract guarantees without the support of
sub-contract guarantees.

Bank performance guarantees, issued by a first-class bank, should indicate to the main contractor that the issuing bank considers the sub-
contractor financially viable for the size and duration of the contract in
hand. It must be assumed that a bank would not issue a guarantee if it
thought the sub-contractor would not be recourse-worthy for the whole of
the contract period and the validity of the guarantee. Banks are not always
right. The economic recession of the early 1990s saw many insolvencies
and liquidations of companies with outstanding counter-indemnities with
their banks.

To counter this problem sub-contractors could provide an indemnity
supported by an insurance policy from the private insurance market which
indemnifies the main contractor against the financial loss consequent upon
the sub-contractor's *insolvency*. However, limitations of the insurance policy may make it unattractive to the main contractor.

(b) Surety company

From the sub-contractor's point of view, the main contractor should preferably accept a surety bond. With surety bonds there is normally no direct
cash payment. Unlike banks, surety companies will only issue a bond after
satisfying themselves that the sub-contractor has the technical ability and
financial, productive and human resources to complete his contract.

This involves them in checking the scope of the work and terms of the
contract, and satisfying themselves on the cashflow of the contract and its
financial impact on the sub-contractor. This vetting process can often highlight areas of potential vulnerability that they would advise the sub-
contractor to eliminate or manage and control actively.

If the surety bond is called by the main contractor, the surety company
would normally work to see that the sub-contract is completed rather than
pay cash against a claim.

The main contractor should normally be happy for a surety company to
step in to ensure that the sub-contract is completed. However, if his own
bank guarantees are at risk of being called because of failure of the sub-

contractor, then cashflow considerations in the short term will often dictate that a bank demand guarantee is of greater value than a surety bond.

Conversely, if the main contractor has been required to give surety bonds under his main contract, then there is very good reason to accept surety bonds under the sub-contract rather than bank demand guarantees. They achieve the objective of getting the contract completed. The main contractor would normally rather have the sub-contract completed than a finite sum paid into his bank account from which he has to pay another sub-contractor.

It must be appreciated that, when approached to replace a defaulting sub-contractor, no commercially-minded company is likely to quote rock-bottom prices to finish the sub-contract. The main contractor will most likely find himself paying premium prices to any substitute sub-contractor.

For this reason, a surety company helping the original sub-contractor to complete the contract at the original prices can often be a better proposition for the main contractor than a fixed sum of money from a bank demand guarantee.

Beneficiary of the Guarantee

(a) Main contractor

The type of guarantee given in support of a sub-contract often depends on the relative negotiating strength of the main contractor (the beneficiary of the sub-contractor's guarantee).

If the main contractor is a *"man of straw"* with no tangible assets of his own, a financially strong, prudent sub-contractor would be unwilling to put in his hands a bank guarantee that could be called on demand, if he thought for one moment that there was a risk of an *unfair* claim.

Many specialist consultancies acting as main contractor are in this position. They have the technical expertise to take on the main contractor role, but not the financial resources. To set up the main contract guarantees, their bankers may need to have the security of sub-contract guarantees issued on a *back-to-back* basis with the main contract.

There is a very good case for arguing that substantial sub-contractors should either negotiate on the basis that they become full *joint venture* partners and thereby parties to the main contract, or that they give bonds to the main contractor which are expressed to be in relation to their performance of their specific sub-contract only, and can only be called on *proven default*.

On the other hand, if the sub-contractor is the key supplier of a unique product or service, then even a financially strong and commercially powerful main contractor could find it difficult to persuade them to provide a bank guarantee payable on first demand.

Where the main contractor is in a strong position to insist on a demand guarantee, then the sub-contractor must look very carefully at the worst possible scenario and decide how best to protect himself from a claim, justified or unjustified, from the main contractor.

A justified claim normally occurs when the sub-contractor has defaulted under his contract. However, a default under some sub-contracts does not necessarily have any significant impact on the performance of the main contract, and therefore does not put the main contract guarantees at risk.

Under these circumstances, some main contractors may be persuaded either not to insist on bank guarantees, or to call them only in the event of main contract guarantees being called as a result, direct or otherwise, of the sub-contractor's default.

Unfortunately, many main contractors do not have the time or the capability to work out the potential knock-on effect of a sub-contractor's default and insist, where they can, on *back-to-back* bank demand guarantees.

Back-to-back bonding

Some main contractors consider that getting *back-to-back* demand bonds from a sub-contractor helps *reduce* the exposure on the main contract. This implies that the sub-contractor is at risk of a call on the main contract bonds, triggering an unjustified back-to-back call on the sub-contract bonds, *i.e.* a claim is made that is not as a result of the sub-contractor's default under his contract. Morally, a back-to-back demand should only occur where the sub-contractor's default is the reason why the main contract bond was called in the first place.

Should the main contractor be able to call the sub-contractor's bond if there was an unfair call on the main contract bond, and the sub-contractor was not in default? What does the main contractor do if there are several sub-contractors? Call all their bonds or just the biggest; or just the bonds of those weaker sub-contractors less likely to retaliate?

An additional risk to the sub-contractor arises where the main contract bonds are *insured*. Some insurance companies which insure main contractors against the unfair call of their own bonds require that all steps are taken to *mitigate the loss*. This can include a requirement to call the bonds of any sub-contractor to the main contract in question. But what happens if there is a *dispute* about whose fault it was that a bond was called? Whose cashflow is going to suffer until the dispute is resolved?

The best a sub-contractor can do is to try and agree contract clauses which restrict the circumstances in which the main contractor can make a valid claim, and get these reflected in the bond wording.

Back-to-back bonds are bad practice, unless the sub-contract specifically recognises that the sub-contract bonds can be called as a result of a call on the main contract bonds and the sub-contractor is in a position to insure them against unfair demand.

However, not all sub-contractors have access to unfair calling cover. It is normally only available when the insured has direct contractual responsibility to an overseas public buyer. This can be achieved by a main contractor passing back the bonding risks to his sub-contractor through the sub-contract, or when an exporter is sub-contracted to an overseas main contractor.

It would also be possible for the sub-contractor to qualify for cover if he were associated with the main contractor as a *joint policy-holder* under the credit insurance policy on the main contract, or the main contractor took out cover on the totality of the bonding and agreed to pay the appropriate portion of any claims to his sub-contractor.

One drawback is that it can be more difficult to *prove* an unfair call by a main contractor in a purely *commercial* situation. Many unfair calls are *politically motivated*, and such claims on the insurance cover are much easier to substantiate because the event triggering an unfair demand is usually well publicised.

Another risk to the sub-contractor is when a strong main contractor has a reputation for keeping its sub-contractors in line by threatening to call his bonds. This can cause the sub-contractor to incur additional costs and absorb valuable management time to ensure that there is absolutely no cause for the guarantee to be called.

(b) Buyer-nominated sub-contractor

Should a main contractor suffer a bond call where a defaulting sub-contractor was *nominated by the customer*? There are some circumstances in which a nominated sub-contractor provides guarantees direct to the buyer, bypassing the main contractor.

The various risks and considerations need to be identified and controlled early in the contract negotiations, especially if the sub-contract is with a company in a country different to that of the main contractor, as the value of techniques available to control the risk, *e.g.* through insurance, becomes less certain.

Nomination of the sub-contractor by the buyer can be done either in the main contract or by a side agreement. The main contractor is contractually bound to the nominated sub-contractor even though the nominated sub-contractor is not his choice. He may never have heard of the nominated sub-contractor before he was mentioned by the buyer.

Normally the main contractor's responsibilities to the sub-contractor are restricted to those issues that he can control, and the buyer assumes responsibility for the rest, taking a performance guarantee direct from the sub-contractor accordingly.

Only if the main contractor accepted full responsibility for the nominated sub-contractor's performance would he ask for bank demand guarantees from him. The buyer in these circumstances would require the main contract to be fully guaranteed.

However, there can be complications. The nominated sub-contractor may not be experienced in overseas contract negotiation, nor be happy with the costs and risks associated with dealing direct with the overseas buyer. The main contractor may therefore be required to *shelter* the nominated sub-contractor from risks associated with international contracts such as inspection, payment, and currency, as well as helping in the negotiation of bank demand guarantees to be provided by the nominated sub-contractor to the buyer.

Guarantee Value

A main contractor will usually prefer that the sub-contractor carries, as far as possible, the main contract risks that relate to the sub-contract.

A key consideration, and often a difficult problem to resolve in these circumstances, is the value of the bank guarantee to be issued. Should it be based on the sub-contract value, or the main contract value? A performance guarantee for 10 per cent. of the main contract price is going to be of a greater amount than a 10 per cent. guarantee on a sub-contract price. Normally, the main contractor has to carry any shortfall.

To some extent, the exposure can be mitigated by requiring a higher-value bond from the sub-contractor, but this increases his risks and puts up the price: for example, a 10 per cent. main contract performance guarantee could be reflected in the sub-contract as a 15 per cent. guarantee. It also depends on how much price information the main contractor is prepared to reveal to the sub-contractor.

Alternatively, the main contractor can insist on a more favourable guarantee wording from the sub-contractor than he has to concede under the main contract. For example, if the main contractor agreed with the buyer to provide a surety bond he knows that, in the event of a claim, the surety company will usually only incur the costs of rectifying the contractual default *as and when those costs arise*. On the other hand, if the main contractor secures a demand guarantee from his sub-contractor, then he can call the *full amount of that guarantee on demand* and bank the cash. This will help fund the cost of rectifying the default. In these circumstances it is purely a question of cashflow and interest earnings.

Having a shortfall in the values of the back-to-back guarantees may not therefore be a problem if the *quality* of the guarantees is in the main contractor's favour.

However, if the main contractor has to provide bank demand guarantees and is only able to secure surety bonds from his sub-contractor, then he has the worst of both worlds.

Currency of the Guarantee

Currency risk also has an impact, sometimes quite significant, on the realisable value of a bank demand guarantee. With *exchange rate volatility*, even a successful claim on a sub-contractor's guarantee can result in a shortfall of cash.

For example, a sub-contractor's guarantee denominated in United States dollars issued at the end of 1989 could have been converted to pounds sterling at US\$1.60/£1, whereas one year later the rate was US\$1.95/£1. That is to say, a guarantee valued at US\$160,000 in 1989 was worth only £82,000 to a United Kingdom main contractor at the end of 1990. This represents a movement of over 20 per cent. On the other hand, if he had to provide a guarantee at the same time to his buyer, it would have cost him nearly £105,000 at the end of 1992 when the rate was US\$1.53/£1 in the event of a claim.

Not only can exchange rate fluctuations increase the main contractor's exposure to the buyer if his bank guarantees are expressed in a currency which has strengthened against the main contractor's own currency, but, as has been demonstrated, they can also *reduce* the level of back-to-back protection from sub-contractor's guarantees, even if expressed in the same currency, because of the *timing differences* between claims on the respective sub- and main contracts.

Whilst hedging techniques do exist, there is no cheap and effective method available because of the *uncertainty* when a bond will be called. In practice, few main contractors actually proceed with hedging currency risks associated with bank demand guarantees unless they believe there is a serious, unacceptable exposure which justifies the cost.

Text

The sub-contractor should ensure that his bond is worded so as only to permit a claim if he is in default under his sub-contract.

His bond should not be callable simply because the main contract bonds have been called, or because an insurer requires the main contractor to mitigate the loss of an unfair call on the main contract bonds.

There is often no justification for the main contractor to require the same wording for sub-contract bonds as he has had to concede on the main contract.

The wording should reflect the obligations of the sub-contractor, taking into account:

(a)   the financial and commercial strength of the sub-contractor;
(b)   the long-term relationship of the main and sub-contractor;
(c)   the governing law and jurisdiction; and
(d)   the business morals of the region.

It makes sense that the opening negotiating positions of the main contractor and sub-contractor should be that:

(a)   the main contractor will try to have tight, preferably "on-demand", terms in the sub-contractor's bond provided by a first-class bank;
(b)   the sub-contractor will be seeking to minimise the cost of bonds and the risk of a claim by either:
   (i)   refusing to give a bond;
  (ii)   offering a bond that can only be cashed against admitted or proven default;
 (iii)   using a bank that has no direct access to his assets in the event of recourse being taken; or
 (iv)   arranging a surety company bond.

Often the sub-contractor is negotiating without knowing what bonds the main contractor has or may have to concede in the main contract.

Knowing the type of main contract bonds and the circumstances in which they can be called is important information, and helpful in the negotiation of the sub-contract and related bonds.

Agreement of the type and general format of the bond wording early in the negotiations between the main contractor and sub-contractor brings into clear focus the financial risk of failing to fulfil some of the conditions of the sub-contract. Knowing the consequences of default helps make sub-contractors more conscious of onerous contract clauses passed on to them by the main contractor.

When the draft text is tabled early in negotiations there is time and room to negotiate the details. Safeguards and provisos can sometimes be written into the bond to prevent a precipitous or capricious demand. The bond can be drafted to reflect more accurately and precisely those key concerns of the main contractor, for example, the types of default under the sub-contract which can have a *serious knock-on effect* in the main contract.

When a claim has to be made, there is no reason why it cannot be payable on first demand as long as the beneficiary produces *documentary evidence* of default. What such documents should be will need to be stated in the bank guarantee.

Requiring the sub-contractor to provide a guarantee payable on first simple demand can rarely be justified and should, wherever possible, be resisted and rejected.

Where such safeguards cannot be incorporated in the bond itself it may be possible to reflect them in the sub-contract. This, however, is only *secondary protection*, *i.e.* at best it helps in the effort to make a stronger case to recover through the courts, under the sub-contract, money claimed under a bank demand guarantee when there was no contractual default justifying such a call.

Domicile and Law

The question of bond text and the enforcement of claims becomes more complicated when sub-contracts are placed with suppliers in overseas countries, where bank demand guarantee practices and procedures have developed differently, as have the legal systems that govern them.

In the United Kingdom, for example, if the guarantee is payable unconditionally on demand, the bank will pay and even go to the courts to stop their client, the exporter, from preventing them from paying. As there are currently no exchange control regulations, overseas main contractors have little difficulty in enforcing claims on United Kingdom sub-contractors.

Similarly in France, Belgium and Germany, whilst there is a system of codified law covering guarantees, this was not originally intended to cover bank demand guarantees, and only to some small extent does it influence the text of guarantees. There have been a number of judgments based on the experience and trading pattern of those countries, which have set legal precedents. These are similar to those in the United Kingdom. Likewise, most European exchange control regulations do not cause problems in getting claims paid.

Therefore, from a practical point of view, any minor differences in procedures, jurisdiction and choice of law are of no serious consequence to the main contractor.

However, the situation is not the same for sub-contracts let to, say, Indian, Philippino or South Korean sub-contractors or those in Turkey, Eastern Europe or South America. Demand guarantees issued by their local banks may have less value possibly because of the perceived financial standing of the bank, currency shortages and delays in transferring cash generally.

The main contractor needs to satisfy himself that there is *no risk of payment being blocked* by local laws, exchange controls or the regulations of financial authorities controlling the issuing bank in the sub-contractor's country. Special factors need to be taken into account, for example, the relationship the issuing bank may have with the sub-contractor as a result of heavy loans or financial stakeholding.

The main contractor must decide whether to take a bond directly from his sub-contractor's own local bank, or to require the bond to be given by another bank in the sub-contractor's country, or a first-class bank in the main contractor's own country, or a neutral third country.

The obligation of the sub-contractor's bank to pay a valid claim is commercial, legal and moral. The success of enforcing a claim both commercially and legally could depend on accepting the right bank in the circumstances.

Effect of a Claim

A claim on the sub-contractor should be the *last resort* of the main contractor. His first priority should be to get the sub-contract completed in accordance with its agreed terms.

Once a claim has been made on a sub-contractor's bank guarantee, any remaining goodwill will evaporate and future relationships will be soured, especially if the reason for the call is disputed.

For this reason, a main contractor is better off with surety bonds than bank demand guarantees. They encourage close co-operation between those parties with a vested interest. The financial impact on the sub-contractor is not immediate or terminal and, with the help of the surety company, he can put right any defaults or breaches.

Calls on bank demand guarantees can destroy relationships because of their harsh financial impact. Working capital is suddenly lost, perhaps forcing defaults on other contracts.

Sub-contractors can, and do, become insolvent as a result. This still leaves the main contractor with a contract to complete and therefore the need to look for another sub-contractor to finish the job. The price they will charge will inevitably be higher than the original contractor because of the circumstances.

Even if bank guarantees have to be provided which are payable on first demand, it is reasonable that the main contractor should give the sub-contractor *due notice* to put right any default or breach.

Only if the sub-contractor fails to make progress within a reasonable time, and any negotiation and dialogue has come to an end, should the main contractor call the guarantee, and only then as a last resort.

The act of calling the bond should be carried out at the same time as terminating the sub-contract. *If the main contractor does not want to terminate the sub-contract, then he should not call the bond. It is the threat of a call that is persuasive. It is even more coercive than the call itself.*

Once a bond has been called, the main contractor has only the terms, law and jurisdiction of the sub-contract to turn to for additional compensation. This can be a slow and expensive legal process.

Validity

It is reasonable that bank demand guarantees should have an expiry date as much as it is unreasonable that the main contractor should require an open-ended commitment from the sub-contractor.

The question is how the validity date should be determined, whether by an actual date or an event determined by the progress of the sub-contract. This depends on the nature of the main and sub-contracts.

The quality of some sub-contract work sometimes cannot be determined until further work under the main contract has been completed, or until tests are made on the works under construction. In these circumstances, the main contractor would be seeking bank demand guarantees which do not expire until the buyer has accepted the section of the works incorporating the sub-contractor's input.

On the other hand, the sub-contractor would be seeking an expiry date relating to the completion date of his sub-contract. The complication is that some sub-contractors' work can be held up pending the completion of work by other sub-contractors.

The actual date will, therefore, be a matter of negotiation between the two parties depending on the circumstances. Occasionally the main contract conditions may stipulate when the sub-contract guarantees may be returned for cancellation.

The freedom to agree may be influenced by laws or banking regulations in the buyer's country. In some countries, they stipulate that bank guarantees are still enforceable after their expiry date. Until there is an acceptable code of practice to which all countries adhere, making the date or event of expiry subject to uniform rules, a bank demand guarantee should be considered enforceable until it is returned to the issuing bank and cancelled. The 458 Rules are a step in this direction, but have still to be adopted internationally (see Chapter 10).

Other Project Structures

Although sub-contracting is a very common form of project structure, there are two other, more complex forms, which need to be mentioned. These are:

(a)   joint ventures; and
(b)   consortia.

Many of the issues raised above apply also to these more complex project structures.

Joint Ventures

A joint venture (JV) can be:

(a)   a loose working arrangement between two companies set up to bid for a single project, with each company either:
  (i)   arranging its own bank guarantees direct to the buyer; or
  (ii) arranging for a bank to provide a joint guarantee on behalf of the JV; or
(b)   a formally incorporated company set up to exploit the longer-term market potential of two partners with specific compatible skills, for example, electrical and mechanical.

The key feature in the first alternative in (a) above is that although the two parties appear to be working together, this is purely to put up a strong united front in order to win a major project.

Where the technical responsibilities of the individual JV partners can be easily distinguished, a single contract could be awarded to the JV and the work allocated within the JV to each partner, or alternatively two separate contracts signed with the buyer reflecting the two different scopes of work and appropriate contract conditions.

Either way, each party can:

(a)   arrange his own guarantees;
(b)   provide individual counter-indemnities to the bank;
(c)   perform his clearly-defined specialist activities; and
(d)   get paid direct by the buyer.

When a single contract JV takes on a project with a buyer, the parties to the JV have *joint and several liability* to the buyer.

This means that in the situation of a contractual default, the buyer can claim *against both parties jointly*, or *against either party severally*. To save time and expense, most buyers pursue the JV partner with the greatest tangible assets.

When each contractor arranges his own bank guarantees under a JV, his risks and costs are similar to those of a main contractor (except there is often the possibility that in the event of one JV partner getting into trouble with his work or finances, the other partner could step in to keep the project progressing, and thus avoid the risk of a demand on a guarantee).

Where a JV partner has clearly-defined work and contractual responsibilities which have no impact on the other parties, he may prefer to provide a *several counter-indemnity*, with his liability restricted to his share in the JV, if the issuing bank agrees. This limits the use of his banking lines and the contingent liability on his balance sheet.

In a(ii) above, the division of responsibilities is not so clear (for example, a single contract for interior fixtures and fittings). A bank issues guarantees on behalf of the JV and each participant in the project picks up the counter-indemnity and costs *pro rata* to the extent of its participation, usually on a joint and several liability basis.

Should the bank not be prepared to accept the risk of a counter-indemnity of either partner not being enforceable in the event of a claim, the weak partner's share would need to be covered by the other partner, or by another bank on behalf of the weaker partner.

If a guarantee can be called for reasons difficult to attribute to one party, then the bank will take recourse on both parties. There therefore needs to be an agreement how to share the risks and costs. Usually joint venture partners give each other *cross-indemnities*. These enable a non-defaulting party to recover bond payments and costs from a defaulting party.

The text of a guarantee issued under a JV arrangement has to be very carefully worded to ensure that the whole amount cannot be called because of a default on one section of the work which does not impact on the success of the project as a whole.

In joint ventures with overseas partners, it is worth investigating the benefits of issuing bonds through the project partner's country. His local legal system may be more sympathetic to cases of unfair calls.

Consortia

There are several kinds of consortium structure involving three or more parties, each of which creates its own bank guarantee risks. The actual structure of the consortium will determine how the bank guarantees should be issued and the risks controlled. For example:

(a) it can be in the form of a *loose association of companies*, each providing its own bank guarantee to the buyer with the bank taking recourse severally to each member;

(b) it could involve *each partner indemnifying the guarantor direct, pro rata* to its share of the value of the main contract, jointly and severally for a percentage of the bank guarantees issued on behalf of the consortium as a whole; or

(c) it could be an integrated structure with a lead company or management company, consisting of representatives of each party. This instructs the guarantor to issue the bank guarantees jointly and severally on behalf of the consortium, which gives its own counter-indemnity. This has value because the consortium is either well capitalised or is guaranteed severally, or jointly and severally, by the respective parent companies of the consortium partners.

Recourse can be to the consortium company's assets in the first instance, which in turn are guaranteed by the respective parent companies *pro rata* to their participation. If the consortium company, *i.e.* the project, has assets, there may not be immediate impact on the parent companies' balance sheets, but a claim could starve the project of funds. This could call a stop to the project with the risk of other penalties.

If the consortium lead company does not wish to carry the full joint and several liability on his own balance sheet, it would usually try and use a bank that is prepared to accept counter-indemnities directly or indirectly from each of the consortium partners for their share of the consortium's interest in the main contract.

Should the bank not be prepared to accept the counter-indemnity of any single partner, that partner's share could be covered by another partner, or another bank or surety on behalf of the weaker partner.

To hedge exposure to a demand being made on the bank guarantee as a result of one of the partners being in default, consortium members usually provide each other with *cross-indemnities*.

The problems become more complicated with international cross-frontier joint ventures and consortia, and professional commercial and legal advice is recommended.

CHAPTER 6

COST OF ISSUING DEMAND GUARANTEES

One problem facing the exporter is the evaluation of the expected cost of putting up and maintaining the required demand guarantees.

Throughout this Chapter only bank demand guarantees are addressed. The risks and costs of surety bonds are generally more forecastable and controllable. This is not the case with bank demand guarantees.

There are three costs to be considered:

(a)   the direct cost of providing a bank guarantee;
(b)   the unforeseen or hidden costs that inevitably arise as a result of delays and changes affecting the guarantee; and
(c)   the opportunity cost of tying up banking lines and the balance sheet with the contingent liability.

The opportunity cost of tying up banking lines and committing the balance sheet is individual to each exporter and outside the scope of a book of this nature. We can, however, look at what influences the direct and less obvious costs of providing bank guarantees.

Influences on Direct Costs

Quoting precise figures for the direct cost of issuing and maintaining bank demand guarantees is somewhat meaningless as there are so many variables. The cost of issuing a guarantee has been known to vary from 0.06 per cent. to 5 per cent. of its value, with taxes on top of that in some countries. In Turkey, for example, the cost of issuing can be re-incurred with each amendment, even of a minor nature.

The variables affecting the cost include:

(a)   length of validity of the guarantee;
(b)   negotiating strength and ability of the exporter *vis-à-vis* his bank;
(c)   whether the exporter has access to competing banks;
(d)   number of banks involved in the issue and their domicile;
(e)   country of the beneficiary, its taxation and levy requirements; and

(f)   cost of any insurance against the risk of unfair call (see Chapter 8: "Controlling the Risk of an Unfair Demand").

An often overlooked cost is that of legal fees where a lawyer is used to help in the drafting and vetting of the guarantee text. For the simpler documents, many banks will provide this service free of charge, but for project bonding this can be a false economy. The complexity of the guarantee wording, the amounts involved and risks and consequences of getting the wording wrong, or using inappropriate wording not reflecting accurately the contractual responsibilities, justify the use of an experienced lawyer.

Where Direct Costs Arise

It is important to understand just where and how the direct costs arise and how they can be controlled.

Many banks have set tariffs or have negotiated pre-agreed ranges of charges for individual exporters, for the issue of low-value routine bank guarantees. Bond charges are also usually negotiable on a one-off basis if the overall level of bonding on the contract justifies it, or if the longer-term prospect of more business is sufficiently attractive.

To enable a bank to ascertain what rate to charge, the exporter needs to provide some key information, consisting of:

The amount of the guarantee

The bank needs to know its maximum exposure to the exporter and its liability under the guarantee.

Fees are usually calculated on the outstanding value of the guarantee, therefore, the bank will be interested in whether its value will reduce as a result of reduction clauses following part shipments and/or part payments. This directly affects the bank's exposure and income.

Provision for reduction of the guarantee amount is quite common, but a complication that arises and has to be resolved is the question of how and when the reduction becomes effective. Sometimes the reduction can only take place when the beneficiary says so in writing to the issuing bank. In other situations, the reduction is automatic through a mechanism clearly stated in the text of the guarantee.

The issuing bank as guarantor usually does not mind which system of reduction is agreed, so long as it is clearly stated in writing in terms that the bank can understand and accept. Normally they would want the reduction mechanism included in the text of the guarantee.

The exporter's costs are directly affected by his ability to reduce the amount of the guarantee.

Effect of text of guarantee on costs

It is important for the exporter and the bank to satisfy themselves that the guarantee is clear and unambiguous as to the amount that the bank must pay and when.

Reducing the outstanding value of a guarantee and minimising the validity period are effective methods of controlling risk and costs. The lower the cost of maintaining a bank guarantee and protecting it against the risk of unfair call, the more profitable the contract.

The bank guarantee text must ensure that:

(a)   any reduction mechanism is workable;
(b)   the procedure for claiming is understood;
(c)   interest for delays in paying a claim should be kept to a minimum; and
(d)   there are no express conditions which compel the exporter to "*top up*" the value after a demand, or otherwise make the amount due under the guarantee open-ended.

Expiry, reductions and cancellation

Banks need to know the length of their commitment. However, bank demand guarantees are at a disadvantage compared with surety bonds. When a bank guarantee has demonstrably reached a point where it should expire or reduce, in many cases permission has to be sought for cancellation or reduction. There could be considerable delay in obtaining this.

There are often serious problems in respect of establishing the effective date of expiry because of:

(a)   automatic validity extension clauses;
(b)   extension at beneficiary's sole request;
(c)   statutes of limitation providing up to 60 years' validity;
(d)   release of liability dependent on return of guarantee;
(e)   liability continuing until beneficiary agrees to cancel; and
(f)   *extend or pay* demands.

Automatic and unilateral extension

Automatic extension of a validity date is a provision to be avoided wherever possible. Also to be avoided is the requirement that an extension of the validity can be obtained at the beneficiary's sole request without reference to the exporter, and possibly after the stated or apparent expiry of the guarantee. Banks do not like such bonds as they like to be able to decide whether or not to extend their committment in the light of the exporter's current credit-worthiness.

Statutory expiry dates

Many overseas countries have laws and banking practices which interpret expiry dates differently to the laws of many OECD countries. Local laws or regulations such as in India and Thailand may permit claims to be made up to 60 years after the expiry date stated in the guarantee.

Cancellation on physical return

In other countries, release of liability depends on the physical return of the guarantee document itself—in other words, the piece of paper on which the guarantee wording is written assumes some sort of importance. However, this piece of paper is merely evidence of the guarantee and should not be seen as anything more. It is not like a bearer bond, or a Bank of England promise to pay written on a five-pound note.

For example, if the beneficiary lost the guarantee document or if it were destroyed in a fire, this would not mean that the guarantor's obligations ceased to exist. The guarantor bank would still be liable under his guarantee even though the physical piece of paper had been destroyed or misplaced.

This being the case, it seems wrong that the bank's liability should continue beyond expiry simply because the beneficiary does not return a piece of paper. Comparison can be drawn with documentary credits. Here the expiry question, covered by Articles 46, 47, 48 and 49 of the Uniform Customs and Practice for Documentary Credits 1983 Revision (ICC Publication No. 400 (No. 500 from January 1, 1994) "UCP"), seems to be virtually universally accepted by all banks throughout the world.

Failure to return a letter of credit on expiry does not extend its validity or cause the issuer to continue to be liable. However, unfortunately this has not been the case with bank demand guarantees. With these, some banks still consider themselves at risk and go on charging fees until they have a letter from the beneficiary stating that they no longer hold the issuing bank liable under their guarantee.

This is a real problem and exporters need to be aware that if the bank continues to be liable, then so does the exporter. The bank will not put the exporter in a better position than the bank itself is in. It will usually continue charging fees.

Extend or pay

The worst problem is the *"extend or pay"* demand. Buyers are sometimes inclined to demand payment if the exporter refuses to agree to extend the validity. Banks are less concerned about such demands as long as the exporter is credit-worthy and continues to be able to withstand a claim during the revised validity period.

However, if the exporter concedes and extends, he may well *prejudice* any bond unfair calling cover he has. Agreement to extend, therefore, should be given only with the *express approval* of the guarantor and the bond insurer (see Chapter 8).

Extend or pay demands can keep bank guarantees valid until such times as the exporter, his bank and insurer agree to refuse to extend the guarantee further. The bank would be obliged to pay a demand, except in the case of *manifest fraud* by the beneficiary, and take recourse on the exporter. It would then be necessary for the exporter to show that the guarantee was called unfairly.

If he was insured against an unfair call, then the exporter would have a claim on his bond unfair calling policy.

The longer a bank guarantee remains extant, the higher the level of bank and insurance charges. Some banks may waive their charges if it is clear that the exporter has completed his contract and that there is no outstanding dispute with the buyer.

Bank charges

A key element in the cost of bonding is the cost of issuing the guarantee in the first place, particularly if a local bank in the buyer's country is used.

The cost of providing and maintaining bank guarantees needs to be investigated at the same time as preparing contract prices to avoid last-minute surprises, particularly in respect of the cost of guarantees issued by a bank in the buyer's country. Often local banks quote excessive, sometimes *cartel*, rates.

An exporter needs to make full inquiries and ascertain from his own bank the level of foreign costs arising from the issue of bank guarantees. He should show preference for banks with local branches which can endorse the exporter's bank's guarantee without additional fees and so obtain an *all-in-one price*.

For a high-value bank guarantee, it may be possible for the exporter, either directly or through his own bank, to negotiate a special rate from the overseas correspondent bank.

It is important for the exporter to contact his bank or banks as soon as possible, as time must be allowed for this negotiation. He is far less likely to succeed in obtaining low rates for urgent requirements.

Some buyers who insist on certain bank guarantees are prepared to pay for these in full or in part as an extra cost on the contract. This is especially the case if the beneficiary has requested the involvement of a local bank. He may have done this to save the hard currency cost of an offshore bank. It can also be cheaper because profit is not added in the price build up.

Exporter's bank's cost
The cost of the exporter's bank issuing the guarantee is based on a number of factors:

(a)   *actual costs* such as:
    (i)   the cost to the bank of adding to its balance sheet the contingent liability of a guarantee being issued;
    (ii)   the bank's direct and indirect overheads and profit; and

     (iii) legal fees. In some situations the bank has to incur legal costs at the time of drafting and issuing guarantees, and also in the possible event of disputed claims;

  (b)   *risk factors* such as:

     (i)   the risk of the bank's inability to take recourse in the event of a claim, *e.g.* if the exporter becomes insolvent; and

    (ii) having issued a tender bond, the moral and sometimes legal commitment to issue subsequent contract performance and advance payment guarantees. The risk is the exporter's recourse-worthiness reducing after issue of the tender bond;

  (c)   *commercial factors* such as:

     (i)   competition from other banks;

    (ii) the desire to establish a commercial relationship with the exporter.

In setting the charges, the exporter's bank also has to take into account that there are several other banks capable of providing bank guarantees for the exporter and that to lose the business to them may be opening the door to competition for other aspects of the exporter's business. Therefore, in practice, banks are not always able to charge all their customers as much as they would like, particularly where the exporter is experienced and well-informed.

Competing foreign banks

In the United Kingdom, a distinction must also be made between banks subject to the financial regulations and controls of the Bank of England and those under the auspices of other central banks.

Foreign banks subject to more flexible controls of overseas central banks may be able to avoid the strict *reserve asset* requirements of the Bank of England (see p.24). This central bank requirement gives rise to a balance sheet cost for a bank when it issues a bank guarantee, which it will seek to recover in its charges. The cost will vary according to the nationality of the bank.

However, many exporters do not have sufficient export business to enable them to gain the necessary wider experience in contract bonding. As a result, they may not appreciate that it is possible to go outside routine banking relations to seek competitive pricing. Those that do may find that some banks may only give them competitive pricing on bank guarantees if the exporter offers them some of their other valuable business such as letters of credit, currency transactions, corporate finance, etc. This can upset established banking relationships.

Foreign banks subject to less stringent requirements than those imposed by the Bank of England and seeking to establish stronger financial roots in the United Kingdom and closer relationships with the exporters can be very competitive in their pricing.

With some banks, the provision of bank guarantees is often the easiest effective method of building up a banking relationship with an exporter, and some may even adopt a loss-leading pricing policy to establish initial business in the hope, rather than as a condition, of being able to sell additional products and services at a future date. Those exporters are often identified as medium-sized and in growth sectors.

Price is very much a matter for negotiation by the individual exporter; obviously, the sooner the exporter approaches the guarantor bank, the more time there is for negotiation.

Correspondent bank's charges

In addition to the charges of the exporter's bank, there can be charges from the exporter's bank's correspondent bank.

Where a bank in the buyer's country has to be used, either because of the buyer's insistence or local regulations, there are likely to be additional costs. In some countries these costs can be high because:

(a)   they are a source of foreign currency earnings;
(b)   there is less competition;
(c)   a local cartel can keep the charges high; and
(d)   there are local taxes, charges and levies.

In some cases, charges as high as 1 to 2 per cent. per annum of the guarantee value, charged in advance, can be asked.

Local charges can be incurred up to the guarantee's formal cancellation, as defined under local law, and not just the original, or extended, expiry date.

These costs are charged to the exporter's bank which then passes them back to the exporter, usually without mark-up, but this cannot be guarantees in all cases.

Local taxation

A further cost to be considered is local taxation. In some countries, such as Turkey, it can be very high. It may only be levied once when the guarantee is issued or, as in the case of Turkey, each time it is amended for whatever minor reason. In this case, regular reduction in the value of the guarantee can turn out to be very expensive and a compromise needs to be worked out between cost and exposure.

The influence of banking relationships

However, pricing should not be the only consideration. The risk of a demand on a guarantee and the exporter's ability to avoid the immediate financial impact has to be taken into account.

It is often better to be dealing with a bank that values its long-term relationship with the exporter than a bank that will *"cut and run"* when the going becomes difficult. Banks sympathetic to an exporter's cause have been known to question the validity of an on-demand claim on a guarantee, especially where the exporter has shown it to be, prima facie, an unjustified claim.

The relationship between the exporter's bank and the bank in the buyer's country can greatly influence the level of costs. The relationship with the local bank can be on five levels:

(i)   no regular correspondent banking relationship;
(ii) regular correspondent banking relationship;
(iii) overseas joint venture bank;
(iv) overseas subsidiary; or
(v)   overseas branch.

The ability of an exporter to get competitive rates from the overseas issuing bank depends a great deal on this *relationship* and on the *local competitive position*.

In some countries, although there are competing banks, the cost of issuing bank guarantees is often controlled by *formal or informal cartels*. In other countries, banks are government-owned or para-statal and the standard tariffs are often not negotiable for most business. Exceptions may sometimes be obtained for priority projects with high-value bonding requirements.

No regular relationship

Where the instructing bank has no regular correspondent banking relationship with the local bank, for example, where the buyer has specified the local bank to issue the guarantees, agreeing discounts to the standard tariff can be difficult, unless the bonding requirement is particularly attractive to the local bank.

Buyers often insist on locally-issued guarantees because this makes the enforcement of claims that much easier. Generally speaking, guarantees issued in overseas countries are subject to local law.

The exporter's bank is unlikely to be able to influence the level of fees charged, as usually it has no negotiating position. This is especially the case where the local bank knows it has been selected by the buyer, and does not have to nurture and protect a long-term banking relationship.

However, if the fees are unreasonably high, the exporter can raise this with the buyer and propose an alternative, cheaper, local bank. Or he could ask the buyer to intervene to try and get the local fees reduced.

The success of such a strategy depends on the size of the bonding requirement, the relationship of the exporter to the buyer, the buyer's business and personal relationship with the issuing bank and the possibility of the buyer getting a lower price on the contract.

Regular relationship

Where the exporter's bank has a regular correspondent banking relationship with the local issuing bank, there is the possibility, for higher-value guarantees, for the instructing bank to negotiate special pricing itself. Not only does it have the working relationship with the local bank, but the local bank will also respect the other's need to maintain a valuable and competitive service to its customer.

The local bank's longer-term considerations will be a powerful argument for compromising on the level of local bank guarantee fees. The only obvious constraint, apart from its direct and indirect costs, and desired level of profit, will be the recourse-worthiness of the instructing bank, which will need to be assessed and built into the fee structure.

In Saudi Arabia, it is possible for a large part of the local bank's fee to be avoided by having it *endorse and validate* the exporter's bank's guarantee bond rather than issue a separate local guarantee.

Overseas joint venture

With a joint venture bank there is an apparent conflict of interest over the pricing of bank demand guarantees. The instructing bank has a vested interest in the profitability of the overseas joint venture bank and, in principle, would be keen for that bank to maximise profitability on every business opportunity.

On the other hand, it is also interested in the profitability and growth of its customer, the exporter.

In practice, the latter consideration usually takes priority as far as the instructing bank is concerned. Its loyalty is often greater to its customer than to some remote part of its corporate structure.

However, such is the nature of joint venture banks that there is a local shareholder also wishing to maximise profitability on every business transaction. He does not have the same interest in the growth and profitability of the exporter. As a result, the management of the joint venture bank, having to satisfy two masters so to speak, needs to weigh up the commercial considerations very carefully before reducing bank guarantee fees.

They can leave themselves open to criticism by their local shareholders if the fees are reduced too much or without suitable commercial justification, for example, the threat that the exporter will look for another instructing and issuing bank.

Overseas subsidiary

Subsidiaries of banks in overseas countries usually have their own balance sheets.

Bank guarantees issued by a subsidiary on the instructions of its parent bank will be shown as a contingent liability on the subsidiary's balance sheet. Being a separate corporate body subject to local laws, it will usually require a counter-indemnity from its parent company and this will show up on the parent's balance sheet.

So, in theory, there are two notional balance sheet costs to be considered. However, it is unlikely to influence significantly the level of composite fees that can be negotiated as compared with those obtained for guarantees issued by a bank's overseas branch.

Overseas branch

When the exporter can deal with an instructing bank that has a branch in the buyer's country, and bank guarantees issued by that branch are acceptable to the beneficiary, then the opportunity presents itself to reach deals on the bank guarantee charges.

There are occasions when the size of the bonding is sufficiently attractive for the exporter to ask for a composite rate from the instructing bank, which includes the local issuing bank's fees, particularly if there are no local restrictions on bank guarantee fees, or on such deals.

The exporter's bank will take an overall view on the profitability of a composite rate, taking into account that, as the issuing bank is of branch status, only the head office balance sheet will carry any contingent liability, and that there is no credit risk between a branch and its head office.

Generally speaking, the more institutions and regulations involved, the greater can be the cost of issuing a bank guarantee.

Bond insurance

Bond unfair calling insurance is covered in Chapter 8. However, it should be borne in mind that if this facility is used, the cost must be added to the cost of issuing and maintaining a bank demand guarantee.

The provision must allow for any extensions to the guarantee's validity. If a guarantee has expired but has not been cancelled, there is still a risk of it being called.

Agreement to extend (or to change guarantors) should be given only with the express approval of the bond insurer, which is usually forthcoming unless the *"extend or pay"* claims persist after the exporter has completed his contract obligations. Then it is a question of the insurer and exporter deciding the best course of action to minimise the risk of a call if the guarantee is no longer extended.

The exporter should not assume the extension of cover will be provided automatically if he accedes to such a demand. The extension of the validity period can cause much concern and lead to increased costs.

Frequent short extensions are better than single long extensions as they are usually cheaper and force the beneficiary to keep making demands. This keeps the exporter's attention on the problem and the prospect of an early solution.

Banks also prefer shorter extensions as this makes assessment and control of their exposure to the exporter that much easier.[1]

Hidden Costs

Extend or pay

A major concern for exporters is that the buyer can *unilaterally* obtain an extension to the bank demand guarantee validity by submitting a demand with the request either *to extend the validity or pay the amount* of the guarantee.

However, not all *extend or pay* requests are unreasonable. A buyer may simply be protecting his position because the exporter is running behind on his contract and the bank guarantee validity is about to expire. In most such circumstances, the exporter will willingly agree to extend for a reasonable period. The bank can continue to charge the same fee or increase it if it thinks the risks are greater.

If the bank takes the view that the exporter's credit-worthiness is declining, it may not be willing to extend the guarantee because it is concerned that a claim at a future date may expose it to the risk of the exporter's insolvency. The exporter may then have to find another bank or pay the claim.

Where the guarantee is covered for bond unfair calling (see below), the exporter must confer with his broker or insurer to ensure that cover is not jeopardised.

Unreturned guarantees

The exporter may also have to face unanticipated costs if the beneficiary or foreign bank fails to return the bank guarantee by the expiry date. Many banks are not willing to release the exporter from the counter-indemnity until the guarantee it issued is physically returned, because of the risk of a belated demand.

Some banks, particularly overseas local banks, can keep charging fees until the guarantee is physically returned and cancelled. These charges could go on indefinitely if the buyer loses the actual guarantee document. (The 458 Rules address this particular issue: see Chapter 10.)

For guarantees not incorporating the 458 Rules, contingency insurance to cover the risk of a guarantee being called unfairly, long after it should

---

[1] In Germany, initially it was considered that the extension of the guarantee period was the subject of a special contract and, therefore, substantive law provided the beneficiary with no legal justification for a demand for "extend or pay". However, a decision of the German Federal Court ([1985] N.J.W. 1829 (B.G.H.)) considered the demand "extend or pay" as a *valid claim*, and this opinion has prevailed.

have been returned for cancellation, is sometimes available in the London insurance market. It also covers the risk of a purportedly lost guarantee being called.

The issuing bank may agree to waive additional charges incurred after the expiry date, if it can assign to the insurer its contingency risk against payment of a single fixed premium.

One possibility of avoiding unfair calls in these circumstances is for the exporter to require the buyer, when signing a taking-over certificate or final acceptance certificate, to sign in addition a document to the effect that he *abandons his claim under the guarantee*. (Such a declaration of renunciation is, of course, not possible in the case of a warranty or maintenance guarantee which covers the period following taking over or completion.)

The existence of such a declaration of renunciation will, in most cases, constitute a psychological barrier against the buyer's making an abusive call at a later date. A further advantage of such a declaration of renunciation is that it will prove valuable evidence for the exporter if the case is brought before a court.

Foreign currency guarantees

Many bank guarantees are required to be issued in foreign currency. As it is rarely known whether a bank demand guarantee is likely to be demanded, those issued payable in foreign currency introduce exchange risks. The cost of the hedge or the alternative exposure could be significant in these circumstances. Exporters must have regard to the additional risk and impact of exchange rate fluctuations during the life of such guarantees.

The fluctuations can serve to increase the exporter's ultimate liability under the guarantee, affect the extent of the utilisation of his banking facilities, and can result in an increase in commission charges in respect of the guarantee itself.

For example, some contracts require bank guarantees to remain valid for several years, *e.g.* construction and process engineering contracts. These are often taken in dollars or sterling, and sometimes in both currencies. The implications of this can be significant.

For example, in November 1988, the United States dollar/pound sterling exchange rate was $1.77 = £1.00; in November 1989 it had strengthened to $1.60 = £1.00. By November 1990 the United States dollar had weakened to $1.95 = £1.00 and strengthened again to $1.72 = £1.00 by March 1992. It fell again to $1.83 = £1.00 by June 1992, and rose to $1.55 = £1.00 in November 1992.

These fluctuations are not atypical. In fact, some periods have witnessed even greater exchange rate volatility.

Many banks regularly monitor the impact of exchange rates on their customer's level of bonding and adjust banking line utilisation accordingly. Those customers operating at the *limits of their banking lines* many find their bank imposing constraints on their bonding and other facilities, such as foreign exchange and letter of credit lines, which can severely impair their ability to trade effectively.

For this reason, if for no other, it is worthwhile setting up modest bonding lines with a number of banks to spread the exposure and avoid one bank becoming unduly nervous over its commitment to, and ability to take effective recourse on, the exporter.

Chapter 7

RECOURSE-WORTHINESS

Not all export tenders or contracts require bank demand guarantees to be provided by the exporter or his agent. When they do, he can decline to provide them, but this can risk rejection of his offer and could prejudice the award of a contract or, in the case of performance guarantees, put him in breach of contract.

When bank demand guarantees are required, the guarantor needs the exporter's indemnity for the amount of the guarantee. However, the exporter has to show that he is recourse-worthy. This depends on tangible considerations such as:

(a)   the extent to which the exporter's banking lines have already been, and are committed to be, utilised;
(b)   the amount of his balance sheet assets; and
(c)   the extent they are otherwise secured, mortgaged or charged,

and less tangible aspects such as:

(a)   the quality of management;
(b)   the experience, and
(c)   the commercial standing.

The exporter can demonstrate his recourse-worthiness and provide an indemnity in three ways:

(a)   by using his own balance sheet, personal guarantee, cash cover, or commercial reputation and credibility;
(b)   by securing the guarantee against the balance sheet or guarantee of a related or associated company or person to provide the guarantor with the necessary added security; or
(c)   by providing the guarantor with an acceptable alternative method of security from an unrelated third party.

Using Own Balance Sheet

Most exporters are normally able to arrange facilities with banks for the issue of bank guarantees up to agreed limits. However, some often find that placing such extra contingent liability on their balance sheets can absorb too much of their banking facilities and is a serious financial constraint. Balance sheets are far better used for more profitable aspects of an exporter's business.

This point is particularly apposite in times of recession when the balance sheet needs to be free from unnecessary encumbrances in order to maximise the amount of, or reduce the cost of, borrowing in order simply to survive as a going concern.

Using the Balance Sheet of a Related Company

Some exporters are under-capitalised and close to overtrading. By themselves they are not totally recourse-worthy in the eyes of their bank and unable to raise additional guarantees against their own security.

They find that, although they are technically and commercially competent, their banking lines are insufficient to take on more bank guarantees. These add contingent liability to the other exporter's balance sheet, and make it difficult for his bank to accept the risk of a cash outflow following a demand on a guarantee.

Such exporters may find a willing third party, such as their parent company, an associate or major shareholder to provide the necessary additional security to his bank.

Whether there is a charge for this support or whether the third party requires a counter-indemnity from the exporter depends on the circumstances and, where appropriate, the inter-company policy.

This support would only be forthcoming if the third party were confident that the risk of a fair call on the guarantee was negligible. They would, for example, provide additional funds to complete a contract if necessary, rather than risk a demand on the guarantee. The risk of an unfair demand can usually be insured against (see Chapter 8: "Controlling the Risk of an Unfair Demand").

Unrelated Third Party Security

It is not just exporters operating at their limits or with weak balance sheets that choose to look for support to improve, or maintain, their recourse-worthiness. Many contractors who are competent, commercially and financially strong may be able but unwilling, for sound commercial and financial reasons, to submit bids which require large bank demand guarantees.

This could be because the size and nature of the bank guarantee make

the balance sheet risks and costs unacceptable. What is considered acceptable and unacceptable depends on the views and policies of the management of the exporter. These are often coloured by:

(a)   their existing level of profitability;
(b)   their future use of the balance sheet;
(c)   their aversion to risk; and
(d)   their experience with the buyer and the market.

Prudent financial managers do not like to encumber their balance sheets
with abnormally large bank guarantees with single buyers or markets.
They prefer a well-diversified spread of risk. They also try to keep their
banking lines free and, by implication, their borrowing costs down. This
would not be possible if they were carrying too much contingent liability
on their balance sheet.

Such financial managers do not wish their borrowing facilities to be ab-
sorbed by bank guarantees, which are a risk and a cost without being an investment. They may therefore try to persuade the issuing bank to accept an
indemnity from an acceptable unrelated third party.

This requirement for a strategy of laying off some of the contingent liability associated with bank guarantees first manifested itself in the 1970s
when, as a result of the sudden enormous wealth of many Middle East
countries following the oil price hikes of the time, many so-called "Jumbo"
projects were signed requiring bank demand guarantees of many millions
in United States dollar and pound sterling terms to be provided against
each contract.

As a result, the finance functions of even the largest companies had to set
limits on the size and nature of individual bank guarantees and overall exposure (see Chapter 11: "Grading and Controlling Risks" for details on
monitoring and recording bond risk).

This limit varies greatly according to the experience, size and financial
strength of the exporter, his pattern of business (and therefore his spread of
risk), the type of bank guarantee, the guarantee wording, and the commercial and political risks associated with the buyer and the buyer's country.

Many European exporters sought support from their respective governments and insurance agencies.

In the United Kingdom, the Export Credit Guarantee Department
(ECGD) introduced their Bond Issue Support Scheme and an equivalent
scheme was also offered by the private market. ECGD's scheme became
uneconomic as world recession restricted the size of projects and the level
of bank guarantees requiring support. It attracted heavy losses that proved
difficult to recover. By 1990, following the decline in exports caused by
Third World debt problems, it was no longer being made available to exporters and was subsequently withdrawn.

The scheme is described in the Annex to this Chapter. However, this and
its equivalent private market scheme are now only of academic interest.

Effect of Inflation

The value of a bank guarantee is intended to relate to the additional cost of finishing a contract that has been defaulted on. Inflation increases this cost and reduces the real value of the guarantee.

Inflation can *reduce the recourse-worthiness* of exporters. In times of high inflation, the exporter's bank must take a more stringent view than otherwise of the recourse-worthiness of the exporter because;

(a) contract values can increase at a rate faster than the exporter's capital structure and asset base, on which recourse-worthiness is assessed. Inflation can also result in liquidity problems which can reduce the asset base available for securing bank guarantees; and

(b) buyers may set bank guarantee amounts at a higher percentage of the contract value. Whereas 10 per cent. is normal for performance guarantees, 25 per cent. is not uncommon, particularly with World Bank and similarly-styled contracts.

On the other hand, inflation can *reduce the effective value* of an existing guarantee and therefore the impact of a call on the balance sheet.

Effect of Currency Volatility

Where a bank guarantee is payable in local currency or in a currency which is not the exporter's domestic currency, there may be additional problems due to unexpected changes in exchange rates. This not only has recourse-worthiness implications if the guarantee currency strengthens against the exporter's domestic currency, but it also affects the level of contingent liability.

Banks monitor currency movements and recalculate their exposure to an exporter's recourse-worthiness on a regular basis.

Annex: Bond Issue Support Schemes

The following paragraphs covering the United Kingdom's bond issue support schemes are now of an academic nature as such facilities are no longer offered due to a fall-off in demand. However, it is important to understand the exporter's problems and how they were resolved at the time. Circumstances could still arise when the scheme may have to be revived and updated in line with competitive schemes in Europe, the United States and Japan.

The terminology at the time referred to contract bonds rather than bank demand guarantees. For the purposes of this Annex, the earlier terminology is used.

ECGD bond issue support schemes

To help exporters who were trading at their financial and risk limits, a number of national export credit agencies developed facilities which enabled a bank to issue a contract bond on the exporter's instructions, but without the need for a direct counter-indemnity from the exporter. Representations from United Kingdom exporters in the mid-1970s prompted the United Kingdom government of the day to authorise ECGD to introduce such a scheme to assist exporters in the national interest.

ECGD's bond issue support scheme enabled exporters to bid for the larger projects (which many had until then been reluctant or unable to do). It provided the issuing bank with the necessary security from a known and undoubted third party.

ECGD was not authorised to issue the actual bonds, but gave support by means of a 100 per cent. unconditional indemnity to a bank or surety company which was willing to issue the bond. Under the bond issue support scheme, the issuing bank was indemnified by ECGD in the event of a claim.

ECGD's bond issue support scheme was designed to support rather than supplant the commercial bond issuers. However, such support was only available when the beneficiary of the bond was directly or indirectly a public sector buyer.

Eligibility
Originally, to become eligible for bond issue support the exporter had to demonstrate that he had difficulty in obtaining bonds on grounds of insufficient bonding capacity. However, this constraint was subsequently dropped by ECGD, and any United Kingdom-based exporter selling goods wholly or partly produced in the United Kingdom could take advantage of the scheme in order to control his risks and conserve his overdraft and other banking facilities, provided basic credit insurance had been taken out.

This proved especially restrictive for construction companies taking contracts through overseas associates or in joint ventures where they could not always meet eligibility criteria, because the origin of a number of the goods and services was not in the United Kingdom.

Recourse

Because ECGD took on an enlarged risk against the often limited recourse-worthiness of the exporter, it adopted underwriting methods no less rigorous than a commercial bank or surety company.

ECGD needed to be satisfied that the risk of a failure to perform was acceptable before it was prepared to provide this facility. An assessment was made as to the likelihood of a failure and the prospects of ECGD being able to recoup any claims payments it may have had to make to the bank.

Viewed as a whole, all the support that ECGD gave an exporter in respect of his contract had to represent a viable commercial proposition.

First, ECGD assessed the ability, not only of the exporter, but also of his major sub-contractors, to perform the contract, having regard to their various responsibilities, their experience and proven technical ability, and their financial resources and organisation. This is information similar to that required by banks and private insurance company underwriters. In addition, ECGD required details of existing bank facilities, budgets, trading forecasts and corporate strategy. It is important to realise that the information required was more detailed and intimate than that normally required by ECGD for their other services.

Secondly, ECGD examined the equity and feasibility of the contract in all its terms, and attached any appropriate conditions for its support for the issue of a bond. For example, adequate provision for arbitration was often an essential requirement of ECGD.

This was a difficult clause to incorporate in a demand bond, unless the exporter was in a position to draft and negotiate with the buyer the wording of each bond supported by ECGD. ECGD would indirectly be part of those negotiations as they had to approve the final wording.

To a great extent, this requirement for an arbitration clause incorporated in the demand bond usually restricted ECGD's support to major projects, rather than contracts for supply and installation of capital equipment where there was usually less scope to table and negotiate arbitration clauses in bonds.

ECGD did not give open-ended commitments and objected to any conditions in the contract, such as those that allowed the buyer unilaterally either to extend the validity period of the bond or to increase its amount by, for example, ordering more work.

ECGD entered into a recourse agreement with the exporter. Recourse was taken by ECGD on the exporter if a claim on the bond was due to the failure by the exporter in the performance of the contract which was not attributable to one or more of the ECGD-insured political risks, *e.g.* he may have encountered financial or management difficulties, or have been let down by his sub-contractors.

Within 30 days of the bond having been called and the bank having paid the beneficiary, either directly or through a local bank, ECGD repaid the exporter's bank both the amount paid out, and interest due for the intervening period under an indemnity agreement.

Any payment by ECGD to the bank became the subject of an immediate claim by ECGD against the exporter under the *recourse agreement*.

ECGD did not exercise recourse against the exporter if the bond call was considered *unfair, i.e.* if the exporter warranted his innocence (provided the warranty proved to be correct). In this way, bond issue support effectively included protection against unfair calling, and the exporter did not have to pay additional premium for this cover.

ECGD also did not take recourse if the exporter was able to warrant in good faith that the call was *fair*, but was due to his having been prevented from performing the contract by one or more of the political risks covered by ECGD under its basic credit insurance policy which the exporter was obliged to take out.

If the exporter warranted, and the warranty was subsequently shown to be false, or, unless ECGD agreed otherwise, if he failed to terminate the contract within six months of the bond call, recourse was exercised. If it was apparent that the exporter had failed in his performance under the contract, ECGD's recourse was unlikely to be deferred. In the event of a dispute between the exporter and the buyer about the former's performance, ECGD would normally maintain its support until the dispute was resolved by arbitration or otherwise in accordance with the contract provisions.

ECGD could not wait indefinitely for disputes to be resolved, and in practice they waited up to six months, although they were not legally obliged to do so.

Indemnity agreement

ECGD's support for the issue of a bond was given in the form of an unconditional guarantee, known as an *indemnity agreement*, directly to the issuing bank on behalf of the exporter. In this way, ECGD stood between the exporter and the issuing bank and took over the issuing bank's recourse to the exporter.

Incorporated in the indemnity agreement was an undertaking to reimburse the issuing bank following a bond call for whatever reason. This cover enabled an exporter to obtain bonds from his bank without reducing or breaking his credit limit with the bank.

Figure 4

Structure of bond issue support scheme

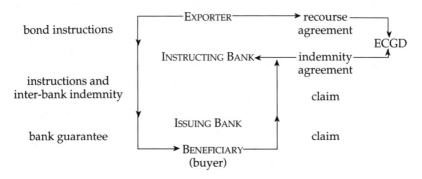

Sub-contractors

Where the exporter required bonds from his major sub-contractors, they were normally barred from obtaining bond issue support because they were not directly involved in exporting. It was therefore necessary to structure the sub-contract to expose the sub-contractor contractually to the overseas buyer and political risks so that he qualified for support and unfair calling cover.

Joint liability

Major projects are frequently undertaken by joint ventures or consortia, who give joint and several undertakings to the buyer. As the bonds invariably follow such commitments, contractors may be exposed to liabilities which considerably exceed their own contract value.

Where a number of exporters were involved as partners in a major contract, and where the acceptance of joint and several responsibility under the bond raised difficulties, ECGD helped by taking recourse to each partner only up to the extent of his participation in the contract.

Private market bond support

In 1982, a London-based company, Bond Support Advisers Ltd., introduced the bank guarantee indemnity scheme (BGI scheme) to assist small and medium-sized companies to raise bonds without affecting their working capital. Capacity was limited and inadequate to cover the major projects of the size seen during the mid-1970s.

The scheme worked by producing an indemnity in the form of an insurance policy to the exporter's bank.

In recent years, this scheme has also been dropped because of the economic downturn in the United Kingdom, and because the abnormal number of insolvencies has made the recourse risk too great for insurers.

CHAPTER 8

CONTROLLING THE RISK OF AN UNFAIR DEMAND

When an exporter agrees to provide a bank demand guarantee, he needs to weigh up the risks he could incur against the potential benefits.

The benefits are few and often short-term, *e.g.* initial cashflow benefits with an advance payment guarantee or retention release guarantee. Such benefits erode very quickly as the contract is performed and the guarantees remain unreduced.

The exposure increases when the value of the guarantee exceeds the exporter's residual contractual obligation; even more so when the contract has been completed, because then the exporter is in his weakest negotiating position. He can no longer threaten to delay or stop shipment or work to get the guarantees reduced or cancelled.

From the exporter's point of view, a bank demand guarantee is often a necessary evil that can leave him exposed to the risk of an unexpected demand and the abuse of it being called unfairly. However, failure to agree to provide a guarantee may result in the contract being awarded to a more compliant risk-taking competitor.

The purpose of this Chapter is to examine the risks and problems associated with bank demand guarantees. It will cover risk management techniques available to the exporter before the demand guarantee is issued and explain why legal action is rarely a viable alternative.

Reference is made in this Chapter to a number of European court cases and decisions. These show the extent to which courts of different nationalities and jurisdictions have attempted, and in most cases failed, to protect the exporter against the *unfair* claims by beneficiaries of guarantees payable on demand.

Nature of Risks

The most serious risks to the exporter are those of a demand guarantee being called *unexpectedly*, and possibly *unfairly*.

The nature of the risks falls into four main categories:

  (i) commercial;
 (ii) technical;
(iii) financial; and
(iv) political.

Commercial Risks

Certain buyers are considered more likely to make unfair claims on demand guarantees than others. For example, some exporters may decide
that a Danish government buyer is considerably less likely than a government buyer in Iraq, Libya, Syria or Iran to call a bank demand guarantee
unfairly. This is not necessarily the case. Perceived risk is usually a function of insufficient knowledge and confidence.

The insurance market considers that *private buyers* are generally more
likely to make an unfair demand on a guarantee than a *public buyer*, and for
this reason do not normally offer cover, except for clearly-defined govern-
ment-related risks. The insurer's attitude is usually based on experience.

A prudent exporter should be aware of a buyer's reputation in respect of
claims on bank demand guarantees.

A buyer's ability to make an unfair claim depends on the guarantee
wording. Not all exporters are in a position to dictate or negotiate wording
due to the competitive situation or the need to comply with published
tenders.

For example, the bank demand guarantee could be expressly worded so
as to permit it to be used as a means of drawing down payments under the
penalty and liquidated damages clause of the contract. In this instance, the
exporter loses control of the amount and timing of such payments, even if
some such payment is justified under the terms of the contract.

In other instances, a guarantee payable on *simple demand* can be called at
any time by an unscrupulous or capricious buyer, whether due or not.

Even the *threat* of a call on a guarantee payable on first demand can exert
unreasonable *coercive* pressure on an exporter to make concessions he
would otherwise be in a strong enough commercial position to resist. Unless such guarantees contain restrictive wording, they are as good as cash
in the hand.

In certain Middle East countries such as Syria, Iraq and Iran, guarantees
payable on demand are expected, although in others such as Saudi Arabia
and Kuwait a more reasonable guarantee wording can be negotiated depending on the circumstances. In some cases, the buyer may be obliged to
insist on bank demand guarantees with specified wording because of local
banking or finance ministry regulations.

The exporter should seek advice from his bank, other friendly exporters
trading in the area and government trade departments to establish the normal bonding requirements of the market.

Banks can sometimes advise exporters on areas of general difficulty and, via their correspondent bank, may be able to advise on local regulations and practices. However, few have or even claim to have wide in-house expertise on foreign laws, regulations and codes of practice. Exporters should therefore make inquiries and take local legal advice where appropriate.

Not all markets require guarantees payable on first demand. For example, those strongly influenced by United States trading practices will accept either stand-by letters of credit or surety bonds (see Chapter 2).

Such markets would include those in Latin America, the Far East and Pacific Basin. A little research in the early stages of a bid can help avoid a lot of potential problems later.

There are many areas of *commercial* risk which need to be identified and controlled:

Assignment and setting-off

In some cases, especially in Northern Europe, bank demand guarantees can be *assignable* and *transferable*. The risk here is that although the exporter's buyer may be trustworthy, honourable and beyond reproach, he may transfer or assign the guarantee as valuable security to somebody not connected to the contract who is only concerned with the monetary value of the guarantee. To realise its collateral value, the assignee has to cash the guarantee, whether or not the exporter is in default. From the exporter's point of view, this is totally unreasonable since the assignee, who has nothing to do with the contract, can make a claim for payment of the guarantee amount for reasons quite unrelated to the contract, or the exporter's performance thereunder. (The International Chamber of Commerce under their 458 Rules are encouraging a practice whereby only the *benefits* of the guarantee can be assigned. They require the original beneficiary to make the actual demand for payment. See Chapter 10.)

If the exporter wants to prevent assignment, the guarantee should expressly state that it is not assignable so that there is no doubt as to the identity and status of the key interested parties.

On the other hand, there is no reason why the *benefits* from the guarantee should not be assigned.

It is not clear to what extent a bank providing a guarantee may set off its own claims against a beneficiary's claim under a guarantee. What seems to be certain, however, is that, under German law, in view of the independent character of bank demand guarantees, the bank is not entitled to have itself assigned the *exporter's claims against the beneficiary* which result from the contractual relationship underlying the guarantee, and then subsequently to set these claims off against those of the beneficiary (this has been stated expressly by the Bundesgerichtshof (German Federal Court of Justice) on April 28, 1985: see [1985] N.J.W. 1829).

Misuse and abuse

Exporters should be aware of the risk that buyers can abuse the trust not to make demands on guarantees unfairly.

Some buyers use demand guarantees as a convenient mechanism to recover sums due from the exporter under the contract, such as penalties and liquidated damages. Unless expressly stated, this is a *misuse* of the guarantee. Normally such payments would have to be agreed with the exporter and paid by him in accordance with the appropriate clause of the contract.

Such misuse is not necessarily illegal and in some cases with Gulf State government buyers it has become a recognised accepted norm to use this mechanism to collect contractually due payments.

There is also the risk of *abuse*, for example, where the exporter instructs his bank to issue an effective demand performance or advance payment guarantee before the buyer has opened a letter of credit in accordance with the contract, and this is then claimed against.

In the United Kingdom's *Harbottle* case (see Chapter 4), the Libyan buyer called the guarantee on grounds of non-performance, even though it was the buyer himself who had failed to fulfil his contractual obligations to open an irrevocable letter of credit. (Harbottle had refused to ship until the letter of credit had been opened in an acceptable form.)

The English court was obliged to admit the Libyan claim because the call was *fair* in terms of the *guarantee*, although *manifestly unfair* in terms of the *contract*.

Extend or pay claims

A frequent *abuse* of a guarantee payable on first demand manifests itself in so-called *extend or pay claims*. Under this inequitable procedure the beneficiary is unilaterally able to maintain the validity of the guarantee, and therefore the threat of a claim, for periods far in excess of the original agreed validity date, and beyond the actual contract completion date.

The beneficiary simply asks the bank to *extend* the validity of the guarantee or to *pay* the guarantee in the event an extension of its validity is not agreed.

Whilst many extend or pay demands are unjustified, some beneficiaries make such calls in order to give the exporter an opportunity to make good an existing breach of contract without requiring payment if the guarantee is extended.

In these circumstances, an extend or pay demand could sometimes be welcomed if the alternative is a fair and justified claim on the guarantee.

Most exporters will, in order to avoid or delay the claim, agree to a limited extension to preserve the cashflow. The *period of extension* is often within the control of the exporter and the guarantor even if stipulated by the beneficiary.

Extend or pay demands of this nature can be repeated several times, with the result that the exporter may find himself at risk under the guarantee many months after its original expiry date. This is a problem which can arise with all demand guarantees, but particularly with those written in a *simple demand* form. This leads to a potential open-ended guarantee validity with increased, unforeseen risks and costs and, unless handled correctly, could prejudice any unfair calling insurance the exporter may have taken out.

This does not necessarily mean that the guarantee has to be extended on its original terms, but pressure is inevitably felt by the exporter not to do anything that could risk a demand to pay the guarantee.

Coercion

Demand guarantees can be used as a means of *coercion*. The risk is that an unreasonable beneficiary may simply use the *threat* of a demand for payment under the guarantee to force exporters to exceed their contractual obligations and concede extra-contractual concessions. For larger contracts, the buyer's government can impose its will via the buyer to exert political pressure.

This is the risk many exporters face in respect of outstanding demand guarantees in Iraq. Once sanctions are lifted, the Iraqi régime is in a powerful position to exert pressure on the governments of exporting countries because many extant demand guarantees remain unrecovered. Iraq could retaliate against their assets being frozen by Western banks as a result of sanctions.

The very threat of a demand usually precipitates quick action by the exporter to minimise exposure.

Many exporters have sought the protection of their government, asking that banks be prohibited from paying against demand guarantees relating to contracts that were frustrated by hostilities and economic sanctions.

The coercive power of a guarantee payable on *simple demand* can extend beyond its related contract to:

(a) apply pressure on unrelated contract performance;
(b) extend validity dates of tenders;
(c) get concessional terms on new contracts; or
(d) achieve additional discounts after the contract has been signed. (Some former Eastern Bloc state trading organisations had such a reputation.)

To the beneficiary, the exporter's perceived risk of a demand is an effective bargaining factor in any dispute concerning the bid or the contract.

The simple demand wording of guarantees *issued through local banks* puts the beneficiary in the strongest negotiating position when there is a dispute on the contract.

Maintenance and *warranty* obligations are also areas of particular vulnerability. Sometimes service engineers cannot be recalled from a job for fear of the buyer calling the warranty guarantee.

Top-up clauses

These clauses in the guarantee require the exporter to restore the original value of the performance guarantee every time a claim is paid. In this manner, the buyer is able to obtain payments from the guarantor and still retain 100 per cent. of the bank demand guarantee value even after the exporter has fulfilled all his contractual obligations.

Such clauses have been particularly popular with Iranian government buyers. The requirement creates an unacceptable open-ended exposure for the exporter, and often for the guarantor bank which is underwriting the risk on the exporter.

Bank charges are usually levied on the *full value* of the guarantee throughout its validity and not on its *reducing* value.

Failure to *top up* can in some circumstances be treated as breach of contract, permitting the buyer to cancel the contract, and call the bond.

Local laws and regulations

In some countries the local law, as well as local banking regulations, can cause difficulties for the exporter. These arise where the overseas correspondent/issuing bank imposes conditions on the exporter's instructing bank before they will issue a bank guarantee.

In the most extreme situation, an overseas issuing bank will insist on agreement from the instructing bank to cover and indemnify it fully until such time as the issuing bank is itself prepared to write and cancel the liability of the instructing bank.

In this situation, the inter-bank obligation effectively becomes open-ended and is no longer under the control of the exporter or his bank.

Technical Risks

Even the most experienced exporter can have contracts which suffer from technical delays, either in his own production or that of his suppliers or sub-contractors.

Some guarantees are issued to ensure the technical performance of a process, such as quality or volume of output. If the process underperforms, the guarantee can be cashed. The amount that can be claimed may be geared *pro rata* to the extent the process underperforms or, potentially more dangerously, to *stepped increases* in penalty payments that can be claimed from the guarantee.

Some buyers are prepared to be tolerant, particularly if the technical delay does not hold up the contract or project as a whole. Others may see this as an opportunity to call the guarantee. Very few contracts make provision for the repayment of the encashed guarantee if the problem is put right or the contract is actually completed on time.

Negotiation of guarantee wording (if any) is often left to the end of the contract when the exporter is in his weakest negotiating position, and this point is rarely covered. The best he could possibly hope for is to recover part of the claimed guarantee through an *ex gratia* payment. Payments against an unfair claim are probably lost forever. Local laws and regulations can, through exchange control regulations, make it difficult to reclaim payment made against an unfair demand.

Financial Risks

The actual issue of a guarantee creates a contingent liability on the exporter's and his bank's balance sheet. This ties up the exporter's banking lines. There can also be open-ended costs to keep the guarantee valid until it is returned to the issuing bank for cancellation or the issuing bank agrees to stop charging fees. In drafting a bank demand guarantee, the exporter should *avoid expressly stipulating* in the text that the beneficiary must return the guarantee document to the exporter, as banks may treat the non-return as a reason not to release the exporter from liabilty under his counter-indemnity. If the exporter is operating at the limits of his bank facilities he would, in addition, have opportunity costs.

With a limited balance sheet capacity the exporter must decide how to allocate these finite financial resources to maximise his profit performance. Loading up his balance sheet with the contingent liability created by bank demand guarantees is not a formula for success unless the risk of a call is minimal and far outweighed by the financial benefits of, say, advance payments.

On the other hand, the exporter's bank commits its own balance sheet to issue the guarantee and has an opportunity cost of not being able to use its balance sheet for other, more profitable, banking activities.

When a guarantee is called, the *contingent liability* becomes an *actual liability*. When the bank takes recourse, the exporter's cashflow suffers. Banks that issue guarantees take the risk that the exporter may not be able to meet the claim for cash payment, or meet it only by obtaining additional overdraft facilities. This raises the bank's financial exposure to the exporter, perhaps at a time when it is trying to reduce it.

In times of recession or boom, when cash is usually very tight as a result of undertrading or overtrading, a demand for payment under a guarantee can have a very serious impact on the financial viability of an exporter. Even in "normal" times, a guarantee call can upset profit/performance figures and have a very demoralising effect on those responsible for meeting targets.

Decisions to issue demand guarantees and to take risks are often taken at operating management level, based on corporate policy and advice from senior commercial and financial managers. Their advice should be based on analysis of existing exposure (see Chapter 11), projections of the strength of the balance sheet, and potential exposure on other contracts, present and future, during the life of the guarantee.

In many cases, however, exporters have no consolidated record of their contingent liabilities outstanding at any one time and often instruct the issue of new bank demand guarantees without a clear idea of the amount or nature of their existing or short- to long-term exposure.

Political Risks

Performance, technical and financial risks are to a large extent within the exporter's control. The decisions the exporter makes govern the risks and his exposure. However, whilst political risks, and the macro-economic risks that go hand-in-hand with them, are capable of being understood, they are usually outside the control of the exporter.

Some political changes can be of benefit, for example trade treaties, a greater relaxation of trading conditions or the local taxation system. However, others, particularly in those countries experiencing economic difficulties, changing political régimes, or subject to trade and political sanctions, as in the cases of South Africa, Libya, Iraq and the former Yugoslavian States, the exporter is justified in feeling that his guarantee is at risk.

Circumstances can change in the world as a whole as well as in individual countries. As a result of inappropriate economic policies, areas or industries within countries and regions can go into economic recession when the rest of the country or other industries are more buoyant. Wars can break out as in the case of Iraq/Kuwait in 1990, and civil war as in the case of the former Yugoslavia in 1992, which can totally affect the economic balance and viability of countries and regions. Uncertainty can abound, as in the States of the former Soviet Union.

Favourable forecasts about the financial strength of the exporter's company or industry can be reversed virtually overnight as a direct result of a change of policy by the government, *e.g.* the United Kingdom goverment's policy on British shipbuilding and coal mining. Suppliers can become nervous about their bonds; buyers can lose confidence and become anxious about the fulfilment of contracts and demand payment under guarantees even when the exporter is capable of fulfilling his responsibilities.

The economic situation in the buyer's country may also deteriorate so that the buyer cannot fulfil his own side of the contract, in turn making it impossible for the exporter to complete his contract.

Typical of this is the shortage of local currency in developing countries. This is often needed to cover the local costs incurred on projects. Such shortages have stalled and frustrated many export contracts. This can trigger a demand on the guarantee by the buyer even though the exporter is the innocent party, forced to slow down or suspend work on his contract for reasons totally beyond his control.

Some international companies are so large and powerful that they have sufficient influence on the local political scene to keep such risks under control. However, for most exporters they have to live with a constantly changing, and uncontrollable, political situation.

Exporters should be able to recognise the potential risks early in the contract negotiations and be able to monitor and control them effectively.

Guarantee-type Risks

There are also risks associated with the different *types* of bank demand guarantee.

Tender guarantees

The exporter is particularly at risk in respect of bid or tender guarantees.

A tender guarantee is a penalty bond. It should only be capable of being called if the exporter:

(i)   prematurely withdraws his tender, or

(ii) after being awarded the contract, fails or refuses to provide a performance guarantee or to proceed with the contract, forcing the buyer to select another, perhaps more expensive, tenderer.

As these are the only circumstances when a tender guarantee justifiably needs to be called, there is no apparent reason why the wording of the guarantee should not reflect this.

However, in many instances this is not the case. Tender security is often asked for in more onerous forms, for example:

(i)   cash deposits in local currency or United States dollars;
(ii)   banker's certified cheque;
(iii) payment on demand with statement of default or proof; or
(iv)   payment on simple demand.

Such requirements put off many would-be competitive tenderers from submitting offers.

Local businessmen trading regularly with the buyer would normally have no problem with the first two requirements. Because they operate in the same country as the buyer they are in a better position to control their risks.

However, an exporter would be more inclined to provide the demand guarantee or, if absolutely necessary, the *simple demand* guarantee. He would prefer to avoid any cash deposits blocked through exchange controls, currency fluctuation risks and restraints on working capital.

Often, the exporter may not have any option but to comply strictly with the letter of the tender, and submit an onerous tender guarantee, or risk having his offer rejected as *non-compliant*.

On other occasions, the tender documents may not be so specific, in which case the exporter can table his own wording to protect himself against an unfair call.

The problem is that the tender-inviting authority needs time to assess and evaluate the tenders received. For this reason, there is often a long adjudicating period of three and sometimes six months before awarding the contract.

Where the tender-inviting authority has not completed the evaluation of the various competitive tenders by the expiry date of the tender, there is a possibility that it will request an extension to the tender offer and also the tender guarantee. An extension to the guarantee validity takes away the pressure to make a decision to purchase within the offer validity.

Legally a tender guarantee cannot be used to enforce the extension of tenders which are limited in time. However, the beneficiary often achieves this objective where the tender guarantee is written in *simple demand* terms.

There is no justification in threatening to make a demand under a tender guarantee simply because the contract has not been awarded.

Unless the tender guarantee is worded otherwise, banks will usually be *unable* to refuse payment if the beneficiary, having made an *extend or pay* demand, then claims payment.

It goes without saying that an exporter can maintain his tender prices for only a limited period. Each extension of his offer or renewal of a tender guarantee will entail financial risks for him, for example through:

(a)   increases in labour and material costs;
(b)   increased overheads;
(c)   deterioration of currency; or
(d)   insolvency of suppliers, etc.

The costs resulting from validity extension are even greater in times of *rising inflation*. There is also the *opportunity cost* of holding open slots in the production schedule which have been provisionally allocated to meet the delivery requirements of the tender.

If the buyer is reasonable, he will permit a price revision to reflect the delay in awarding the contract. Possibly, subject to competitive pressures, a prudent exporter would even build a *price-adjustment formula* into his offer to be triggered at the first expiry date of the tender guarantee. This, however, does not help with any reprogramming of deliveries that may prove necessary if a production slot is lost, nor any associated "stepped" cost increase not picked up by a "progressive" price-adjustment formula.

The risk with tender guarantees is that there is no underlying contract to call on to protect the exporter in the event of an *unfair* demand, so there is nothing the exporter can do to stop the buyer *coercing* him to extend the offer. This threat may be *imagined* or *implied*.

Tender guarantee values can be high, so that the cost of issuing and maintaining such a guarantee usually is expensive and irrecoverable if, at the end of the day, the contract is awarded to a competitor. Many exporters tender for a number of contracts involving tender guarantees in the expectation of being awarded only a few of them. This can result in an accumulation of guarantees absorbing banking facilities. This problem is further aggravated if tender guarantees are not allowed to expire.

Follow-on guarantees

Exporters need to be very conscious at the time of tendering of the contract's total bonding requirements to ensure they do not exceed manageable limits. Each guarantee generates a contingent liability on the exporter's balance sheets and uses up valuable financing capacity.

Before instructing a bank to issue a tender guarantee, it is important to check that bank facilities are available for any subsequent performance and advance payment guarantees should the contract be awarded following a successful tender.

A prudent exporter would ensure that he is able to obtain any *follow-on guarantees*. This avoids the risk of having his tender guarantee called for failing to provide a subsequent *performance bond*, having been awarded the contract.

Banks should be asked, if they do not volunteer, to give the necessary written undertakings to provide additional future guarantees. This ensures that both the buyer and the exporter can be certain that specifically identified future bonding requirements will be satisfied.

This is in effect a *commitment* to provide guarantees, and a *commitment fee* may be charged. This is to compensate for the bank's risk of the exporter's financial standing weakening, and the opportunity cost to the bank of committing its balance sheet increasing.

Some banks may count all or just a percentage of such commitments against an exporter's facilities. Even where there is no formal obligation, banks will normally take into account their moral commitment to provide additional guarantees if a contract is won, before agreeing to issue a tender guarantee. Often banks insist on being given all the guarantee business, if they are to issue the tender bond.

They will take into account the existing level of exposure the bank has to the exporter, and that the exporter has to a particular market or buyer.

Most banks will also have a ceiling on the value of contract guarantees they themselves are prepared to issue to any one market as they like to see a spread of business and risk.

An excessive accumulation of contingent liability through the issue of bank guarantees can create problems when the exporter requires further bank loans or finance for which collateral may be required. Once an exporter has reached his credit ceiling a bank may well refuse to provide any further bank guarantees, or even loan, letter of credit or foreign currency facilities, etc.

Repayment guarantees

Advance payment and retention guarantees have in practice caused particular financial problems for exporters, as they are commonly issued for a value which can be very significant.

These guarantees are usually given to release payments to the exporter before he has contractually earned them. It is a concession granted by the buyer to improve the exporter's cashflow and to help fund his working capital.

Many exporters consider high advance payments, over and above what is required to achieve a neutral or marginally positive cashflow on a contract, good business. In many cases they can be right if the related guarantee wording is equitable. However, the dangers are self-evident for repayment guarantees payable on *simple demand* or against the beneficiary's *unsupported statement*.

During the production stage there exists an investment risk for the exporter (for example if the money had been placed on deposit with the Bank of Credit and Commerce International in 1990/91. This bank became insolvent, was accused of fraud, and subsequently lost its banking licence).

However, the main danger for the exporter is that, when much of the advance payment has been spent on raw material supplies or mobilisation costs, the buyer then demands payment under the guarantee in order to recover his down-payment. The sudden cash outflow can put a financial strain on the exporter, often causing serious financial difficulties.

Should the contract be terminated, cut back or curtailed for any reason, it is reasonable that any unearned part of such payment should be refunded to the buyer. Failure to do this entitles the buyer to cash the advance payment/retention guarantee.

However, the buyer should not be able to recover payments properly earned by the exporter. The wording should therefore permit the amount of the guarantee to reduce *pro rata* to delivery or performance milestones.

If the value of a repayment guarantee does not reduce as the contract progresses and the advance payments become earned, then the effect is for the guarantee effectively to become a performance/penalty guarantee.

The threat of a call on a repayment guarantee can be used to apply pressure, so as to obtain a post-contractual price reduction, a rebate or similar concessions from the exporter.

Whilst exporters should try to incorporate protective wording in the contract and guarantee, on most occasions this will at best show that the buyer's call was *unfair*. It will not necessarily prevent the issuing bank paying a demand.

The exporter could seek a favourable *arbitration award*; however, this is not a quick procedure, and even if the exporter wins the award he still has to enforce it in the buyer's country in order to recover the money. This may not be easy in some countries where the local law and exchange control regulations work in favour of the buyer.

Even if the financial authorities allowed the payment to be refunded, the exporter is still dependent on the buyer fulfilling all the necessary exchange control formalities. The risk is that he will not rush to do this. Meantime, the exporter is out of pocket until the money is transferred across the exchanges.

Performance guarantees

If a buyer is not certain that the exporter will be able to perform the contract, he will ask for a *performance guarantee*. The bank demand performance guarantee involves the exporter in serious risk, as was remarked by Kerr J. in *R. D. Harbottle (Mercantile) Ltd.* v. *National Westminster Bank Ltd.* [1977] 3 W.L.R. 752 at 756: "Performance guarantees in such unqualified terms seem astonishing, but I am told that they are by no means unusual, particularly with customers in the Middle East." Performance guarantees, like tender guarantees payable on demand, are *penalty guarantees*. They have the most serious cashflow implications because, unlike advance payment and retention guarantees, they do not repay any previous payment from the buyer.

The amount of the performance guarantee is usually set at a level high enough to make the contract unprofitable if called, typically 5 to 10 per cent. of the contract value.

Performance guarantees are sometimes called unfairly on the grounds of an alleged lack of conformity of the goods with the contract description, or, if defects have actually appeared, without giving the exporter the opportunity of remedying the defects.

They can be used to exert pressure on an exporter to force him to enlarge the scope of the contract, shorten delivery, or make other changes without additional cost. It is also possible that, having accepted the relevant goods, but before making payment, the buyer could still make an *unfair but legal* demand under the guarantee.

Performance demand guarantees can be called for reasons not at all related to performance, and in some instances for difficulties encountered on *totally unrelated* contracts. In other cases, calling the guarantee can be a means of obtaining a rebate or additional discount.

Maintenance/warranty guarantees

Performance guarantees can be so worded as to cover the maintenance period of a contract also. The reasons the buyer may have for making a claim during this period are different to those he may have for the delivery and installation period. These reasons and the appropriate claim documents should be spelt out in the contract and guarantee.

To avoid confusion, many exporters prefer to substitute a new guarantee with appropriate wording (sometimes called a maintenance or warranty guarantee).

The responsibility of the exporter during the maintenance or warranty period is to fulfil the obligations of his maintenance/warranty agreement. The cost to the buyer of the exporter failing in this duty is usually much less than failing to perform the contract *per se*. Therefore, this guarantee need only be for an amount sufficient to enable the buyer to bring in a third party to fulfil the exporter's contractual maintenance/warranty obligations.

The documents required to prove a claim would be no fewer than those required to make a demand on a guarantee for non-performance. A disputes settlement clause would be of value because of the subjective nature of a *fair* call during the maintenance/warranty period.

Nature of Demands

Generally speaking, once a bank demand guarantee has been issued, the exporter's negotiating position *vis-à-vis* his contract is weakened.

There are *fair* demands and *unfair* demands. *Simple demand* guarantees make it easy for the beneficiary to make an *unfair* demand. A distinction must be made between an unfair demand of the guarantee in terms of the *contract* and in terms of the *guarantee* itself.

Exporters agree to provide a bank demand guarantee to secure their performance under the contract. If it is called when the exporter does not consider himself to be in material default, for example if he is prevented from fulfilling his contract for reasons of *force majeure*, it would be considered *unfair* in terms of the contract by most reasonable people.

On the other hand, the bank issuing the demand guarantee assumes an irrevocable obligation to pay. Courts only look at the bank guarantee to see whether the claim is in accordance with the terms of this *separate and independent* legal document. If it is, then the bank must pay. Any protective clauses in the contract, unless also incorporated into the bank guarantee, cannot be enforced. As a result, the exporter exposes his balance sheet to the risk of a sudden outflow of capital following a *fair* demand under the guarantee.

Simple Demands

The most dangerous form of demand is under a bank guarantee payable on *simple demand*. With simple demand guarantees the beneficiary is not legally obliged to specify the reason for the demand.

Whilst it is quite unlikely that a prudent exporter would withdraw from his bank a large amount in cash to hand physically to his overseas buyer on contract signature as a security deposit for his own good performance, this is precisely the effect of issuing a bank guarantee payable on simple demand. Either way, the buyer has *immediate, unrestrained access* to the exporter's funds. Payment cannot be stopped.

With such one-sided guarantees the risk is real, and the effect on the exporter's liquidity/cashflow/balance sheet/gearing is usually significant, a point often appreciated more by the exporter's finance function than his sales department.

However, not all exporters recognise the serious dangers of *simple demand* guarantees, and readily agree to provide them if nothing else stands in the way of a valuable contract.

The impact of a demand will not be the same for all companies, but in all cases it will be:

- sudden;
- unwelcome;
- usually irrevocable; and
- possibly resulting in insolvency.

The popularity of simple demand guarantees is the result of buyers having been cheated by unscrupulous exporters. Buyers' former, more relaxed, approach to contracting based on trust was abused by the few and, as a result, many more trustworthy exporters are now having to accept much tighter, less comfortable contract and bank guarantee terms, biased in favour of the buyer and inequitable in respect of the exporter.

In Northern Europe particularly, simple demand guarantees have been frequently issued, and as a result many disputed claims have gone before courts in different jurisdictions. Originally, not all courts came to mutually consistent conclusions, although on appeal, and as experience was gained, there has been a convergence of views (see Chapter 4).

Fair Demands

Some buyers call guarantees *fairly* as a matter of corporate policy on the slightest default, often as a mechanism simply to collect liquidated damages or delay penalty payments.

What could be considered a *fair* demand would be one made in strict accordance with the agreed terms of the *contract*.

A fair demand can arise:

(i) when the exporter has defaulted on his contract for reasons that were expected to be within his control when he signed the contract, and for which he accepted responsibility, *e.g.* delivery, quality, quantity, specifications, etc.;

(ii) as a result of political actions of the exporter's government such as the imposition of export quotas or licences, trade embargoes, sanctions, or any form of government intervention or political cause of loss (and where any *force majeure* clause in the contract does not provide adequate relief) quite outside the control of the exporter or the buyer.

In these and equivalent circumstances it would be *fair* and *reasonable* for the buyer to try to recover any unearned *advance payments* made to the exporter.

It would be a *fair*, but *unreasonable*, demand if the buyer demanded payment under a *performance guarantee* for non-performance caused by events quite outside the exporter's control, or tried to claw back advance payments already contractually earned, or to which the exporter was irrevocably entitled. Such demands can arise:

(i) due to war in the buyer's country or in a country through which the goods must pass; or

(ii) by the imposition of exchange control regulations in the buyer's country which would prevent the exporter getting paid if he delivered the goods.

Where the contract is silent, or not obvious, about what would constitute a default by the exporter, there is a serious risk of dispute if the buyer makes a demand on the guarantee.

Buyers will react differently according to the circumstances. A prudent buyer, dependent on a sole supplier, is less likely to make a *fair* call, even if contractually entitled to do so, than a buyer that has reached the limits of his patience with a defaulting supplier that can be easily replaced.

A demand on a bank guarantee needs to be properly signalled in advance by the buyer, otherwise it could result in a serious *loss of goodwill*. Sudden, unexpected calls cause *shock* and *dismay*, and in many cases *panic*. For some exporters, the effect is like losing a wallet just after making a major cash withdrawal from the bank; for others, it is like losing someone else's wallet with which they have been entrusted in good faith.

For most reasonable buyers, the calling of the guarantee is an action of last resort after the exporter has shown that he is unwilling or unable to honour his contract. If the relationship between buyer and exporter is good, the buyer is more likely to give the exporter an opportunity to correct any contractual shortcomings before choosing to make a demand under the bank guarantee.

Some buyers use the possibility of a guarantee demand as a negotiating ploy to obtain their objective. The mere threat of a claim is like Damocles' sword hanging over the exporter's head. Only after all other reasonable measures had failed to give satisfactory contract performance would there be an actual demand. (*Once a demand has been made, the buyer's negotiating position is substantially reduced and the exporter's increased as a result of the new status quo.*)

Unfair Demands

The exporter is exposed to the risk that the beneficiary will make, or threaten to make, a demand which is *unfair*. It is the politically motivated or unjustified demand which causes exporters the most concern.

Statistically, considering the number of bank demand guarantees that are issued every year, very few demands are made on them *unfairly*. *Like an aeroplane crash, the probability of an unfair demand is very small, but the consequences can be very serious.* The adverse financial consequences can be high and include the risk of insolvency.

However low the risk of an unfair demand, it cannot be disregarded. It is always there and some effective measures of control are called for. These will depend on the nature and size of the demand guarantee.

Controlling risk of unfair demand

The ability to control the risk of an unfair demand depends on the relative experience and negotiating strength of the buyer and exporter, the statutory status of the buyer, his country's laws and regulations, the competitive situation, and precedents.

In most cases, the exporter is in the best position to manage his exposure by setting appropriate general guidelines and procedures.

As a general policy, he should set limits on the financial exposure that can be tolerated in a particular country or group of countries forming a political or economic bloc.

These limits should be supplemented by *tight monitoring* and *control* procedures to reduce outstanding exposure and recover bank guarantees at the earliest opportunity.

It is also important to have *export salesmen* understand the risks and exposures inherent in bank demand guarantees and encourage them to seek more explicit and tighter contracts and guarantee wording. They need to ensure that the cost of delays in getting bank guarantees returned is allowed for.

Any conflict of interest between the sales function and the finance function, *i.e.* the conflict between the responsibility to achieve turnover and the responsibility to control risk and exposure, should be eliminated or minimised through closer liaison.

There needs to be:

(i)   training of contract negotiators to incorporate risk minimisers into contracts and guarantees. (Insurance is not watertight and is no alternative to weak contract negotiation.);

(ii) assessment of sales success by different criteria, *e.g.* contract completion and guarantees returned intact;

(iii) a constant review of risk exposure (see Chapter 11). The outcome of this review should be taken into account in bid/no bid decisions for future business; and

(iv) contingency plans in the event of an unfair call on the bank guarantee.

Issuing Bank

Careful selection of the *instructing* or *issuing bank*, taking into account the political and commercial relationship of the bank with the beneficiary and the beneficiary's country, can often enable the exporter to reduce the risk of an unfair call. Some beneficiaries may be less inclined to make unfair claims on guarantees from certain banks/countries.

From the exporter's point of view, bank demand guarantees issued by a local bank in the buyer's country against the instructions of the exporter's bank offer the disadvantage of additional costs together with the risk that the local bank may be less impartial than, say, an international bank in the event of a demand. Annex I to this Chapter gives a list of countries in which beneficiaries normally require a local bank guarantee.

As an alternative to instructing his own bank to use a correspondent bank, an exporter himself could also try to give *direct instructions to a local bank* in the buyer's country to issue a guarantee. This could well result in reduced costs by avoiding commission charges of intermediate banks.

However, it has the disadvantage of the exporter not only having to deal at arm's length with the overseas bank when issuing and trying to recover bank guarantees, but also risks the local bank being less impartial than it would have to be when dealing with its valued correspondent bank in the exporter's country. In addition, the exporter's *counter-indemnity* may not be acceptable to the local bank.

For this reason the exporter would be in a stronger position to resist an unfair call if he were able to persuade his buyer to *accept direct guarantees from his bank*, provided this does not contravene local laws.

Consortia and Joint Ventures

Careful consideration needs to be given in respect of consortia and joint ventures to ensure that the bank guarantee risks are carried fairly by the members and partners.

The question of bank guarantees needs to be resolved at the time of deciding how best to set up a project requiring more than one discipline, particularly where one partner is located in another country. Typically risks can be reduced if:

(a)   a system of multiple bonding is used where a project is structured in discrete, independent sections that can be separately guaranteed by one or more partners;

(b)   effective cross-indemnities are obtained from each of the partners in the event that a guarantee of one partner is demanded as a result of the default of another; and

(c)   sub-contractors are asked to provide bank guarantees to the extent that is considered reasonable for their part of the project.

In this way, the risk of a demand on a guarantee can be limited to the area of default on the project to which each guarantee refers, and the amount of each guarantee that can be demanded is reduced accordingly.

Reducing Financial Exposure

The first place to start to reduce the exporter's financial exposure is in the contract and this should be reflected in the guarantee wording.

Contract and guarantee wording

The contract should state under what circumstances a particular bank demand guarantee can be called and the documents necessary to support the demand. This needs to be clearly reflected in the bank guarantee wording so that the guarantor bank will be in no doubt whether the claim is valid. *This may be all the security the exporter requires, coupled with tight contract performance.*

Such clauses may not be possible in all instances due to the strength of the buyer's negotiating position. However, the buyer does not hold the whip hand in all negotiating situations.

For example, in some defence contracts the exporter can dictate terms because the buyer has no choice but to deal with that particular exporter. In less obviously politically sensitive deals, the exporter may be the sole supplier of a particular piece of equipment, or the only exporter who can deliver in a reasonable time.

A further example of possible dilution of the buyer's negotiating position is with *government-aided* or *export-financed* contracts.

In all these circumstances the exporter may be able to negotiate equitably-worded contracts, irrespective of the status of the buyer, through the influence of the supporting government department and funding financial institution.

Wherever possible, bank demand guarantees should reflect the intentions of the parties as stated in the contract. For example, inappropriate use of performance guarantees to cover the warranty period obligations should be avoided. In these circumstances, performance guarantees should be cancelled and lower-valued warranty bonds issued, reflecting the reduced level of cost of bringing in another contractor to complete the contract, if the exporter defaulted on his warranty obligations.

Chapter 4 gives examples of more equitable guarantees whereby the bank only pays if there is *independently proven* or *documented default*.

If possible, a preferred guarantee text should be tabled with the buyer after clearance with the issuing bank. If a preferred text is offered by the buyer, the exporter may still find it possible to negotiate the wording.

The ideal is to *negotiate guarantee wording that limits the risk of an unfair call, the amount of the claim and when a claim can be made*. A key clause to incorporate in the guarantee should stipulate that when making a claim *the buyer must state that the exporter is in breach of his obligations, and the nature of such a breach*. This means stating in the contract and the guarantee the circumstances in which the guarantee can be called, and also the documents to be produced to the bank to enable them to pay a claim.

Whilst such a statement will not be verified by the bank, the exporter may be better placed to take legal action against the buyer under the contract if a false claim is made.

Banks are obliged to comply strictly with the letter of bank demand guarantees. If the wording is:

(a) one-sided in favour of the beneficiary;
(b) vague in respect of the amount that can be claimed;

or such that

(c) claim documents are not clearly stated;
(d) commencement date and expiry date are not clear; or
(e) no dispute settlement procedure is directly or indirectly incorporated,

then the exporter must expect complications in the event a demand is made.

For potential problems to be identified in good time it is important to avoid last-minute negotiations. The exporter should not wait until the contract is due to be signed and/or the guarantee is due to be issued before contacting the intended issuing bank. Legal advice, or simply help with difficult wording, needs time.

In theory, there are several methods of reducing the exporter's exposure to an unfair demand on a guarantee, some, if not all, of which may be appropriate for individual demand guarantees:

(i) Pre-empt an unfair demand by restricting the buyer's ability to make an unfair call through appropriate wording in the contract and the guarantee itself.

(ii) Control the amount of the guarantee.

(iii) Call for documentary evidence of default.

(iv) Reduce the period of risk.

(v) Make effective use of local agents.

(vi) Take the view that some small contingency should be built into the price.

(vii) Build the full value of the guarantee into the contract price.

(viii) Insure against the risk of an unfair call.

(ix) Perform the contract and have in-house procedures in place to monitor and control exposure and costs.

(x) Take legal action to stop a claim being paid or the bank taking recourse after payment.

(i) Pre-empting unfair demands

Controlling the risk of a demand on the different types of bank guarantee usually requires individual consideration. With the exception of tender guarantees and simple demand guarantees, which are usually the most vulnerable to *unfair* demand, a prudent exporter would first attempt to incorporate into his contract the precise circumstances under which each bank guarantee can be called and then try and have these reflected in the guarantee. Sometimes the contract is silent but the guarantee has protective wording. More often the contract and guarantee are silent on this subject.

(ii) Amount of guarantee

Few banks would issue a guarantee unless the maximum liability was clearly stated. However, guarantees that have the facility of being "*topped up*" create an *open-ended liability* for the exporter. Some banks have been known to issue these in respect of contracts with Iran.

Such *top-up* clauses and any clause which exposes the exporter to liability beyond the value of the bank guarantee should be avoided.

Reduction and *cancellation* of a guarantee should be made at the first opportunity. Suitable *pro rata*, or phased reduction or amortisation (self-liquidation) clauses (if the underlying commercial contract calls for part-shipments and part-payments), ensure that the guarantee value, and therefore the exporter's exposure, reduces in line with delivery or performance under a contract.

The stages of reduction and cancellation should be agreed in the contract and reflected in each type of bank guarantee as appropriate. For example:

(a) tender guarantee bonds should be cancelled when the related per-formance guarantee is issued, or the contract awarded to another party;

(b) advance payment guarantees should be reduced as contractual payments become due or are made;

(c) performance guarantees should be reduced at key stages in the pro-gress of the contract and cancelled when the warranty bond is issued.

Exporters need to pay attention to the precise wording of any reduction or amortisation clause, and to discuss and agree it with their insurance broker and guarantor bank prior to issue.

An example of a reduction clause is as follows:

"The maximum amount of this guarantee will reduce by...per cent of the total value of invoices and bills of lading (or other stipulated docu-ments) produced to us by the exporter which evidence the loading on board a vessel at port of shipment of...[description] supplied under the terms of the above contract.

This guarantee will expire for written demands on us when we have received the exporter's invoices and relevant bills of lading (and/or other stipulated documents), the total value of which produced as set out above equals or exceeds the maximum amount of this guarantee, or on...[date] whichever is the earlier. Our liability to you under this guarantee will then cease and the guarantee will be of no further ef-fect." (Source: Barclays Bank plc.)

Ideally, the bank should be given the *unilateral right* to reduce liability against appropriate evidence of contract performance without the prior consent of the beneficiary.

It is important to bear in mind that satisfactory reduction terms, if they are to operate to the exporter's benefit, will often require *continual mon-itoring and management* during the life of the guarantee. The occurrence of the events causing the reduction will not necessarily be known by the issu-ing bank and some notice or action by the exporter may be required. The exporter should ensure that his internal systems are adequate to allow these actions to be taken (see Chapter 11).

(iii) Claims documents

Very often the exporter's default under a contract of sale does not have serious financial consequences for the buyer. Therefore, if possible, the bank demand guarantee should only be called for those reasons of significance to the buyer, and then only in cases where the buyer has actually suffered as a result of the exporter's default.

For example, on grounds of goodwill and mutual understanding, it is arguably unreasonable for a buyer to demand the performance guarantee for late delivery of, say, heavy machinery, when it is commonly known that the necessary foundations and building to house the machinery have not been built and are behind schedule.

Equally, the performance guarantee should not be used as a means of drawing down a late delivery penalty. Such a penalty is the contractual responsibility of the exporter to pay. Only in default of this payment should the guarantee be called, and then only up to the amount of penalty due. However, the risk the exporter runs is that the entire guarantee can be *legally*, although *unfairly*, called.

If a bank guarantee requires documents supplied by an *independent party*, such as the engineer on a construction site, then the risk of an unfair claim is minimised.

However, the documents required to support a demand under many guarantees can often be supplied by the beneficiary. These may consist only of the beneficiary's statement of the exporter's default or, in the worst case, a *simple demand* for payment.

Such guarantees should be avoided if the risk of an *unfair* call is high.

(iv) Period of risk

Proper management of the issue and recovery of a bank guarantee limits the time during which an *unfair* call can be made. This means controlling the *operative* and *expiry* dates as best as possible, for example:

It can sometimes be difficult to determine the exact date when the guarantor's liability will commence. Normally the bank will consider itself liable under its guarantee from the date on which it is issued.

However, bank demand guarantees should not become enforceable until the contract is *fully effective*. So, for example, if contract payment is to be secured by a letter of credit, the performance guarantee should contain a clause stating that it only becomes operative upon receipt by the exporter of a letter of credit in a form acceptable to the exporter.

Similarly, advance payment guarantees should only become effective as and when the advance payment is received.

An example of an operative clause is as follows:

"This guarantee shall become operative upon issue of our amendment making it effective which will be issued upon receipt by us of written confirmation from the exporter that the latter has received an acceptable letter of credit." (Source: Barclays Bank plc.)

Effective expiry date

One of the biggest uncertainties and risks is knowing when the guarantee *effectively expires* and the exporter is no longer exposed to the risk of a demand. This seriously impacts on the cost of maintaining the guarantee and any additional insurance premiums. It also has an indirect cost as it ties up valuable balance sheet capacity.

The date that a guarantee expires depends on its *wording* and the *laws* to which it is subject. The guarantee may not necessarily expire on the date stated in the guarantee. Problems over expiry dates can often be overcome (and cancellation expedited) if the guarantee is governed by the exporter's country's law. (Guarantees issued direct by banks in the exporter's country may be more likely to be governed by the law and jurisdiction of the exporter's country than those issued by correspondent banks, whose guarantees would normally be expected to be subject to its local laws and jurisdiction.)

Any period of validity, which is usually fixed in the guarantee document, must be observed. This means that as a matter of principle a claim should normally be invalid if made after the expiry of this period. This principle is accepted by all legal systems in European countries, although in other countries different principles can apply. This point always needs checking if issuing a guarantee to a buyer in a new market for the first time.

"Extend or pay" claims can keep a demand guarantee in existence indefinitely, although responsible banks should question such repeated extensions if they are too frequent or too long relative to the original contract programme.

The risk of a late claim lies with the beneficiary. In England, if the guarantor has received the claim after the expiry of the period of validity, the beneficiary cannot maintain that the basis for the claim has arisen within the validity period. This is expressly confirmed by the English Court of Appeal in its judgment of June 6, 1984: *Offshore Enterprises Inc* v. *Nordic Bank plc* [1984] *International Banking Law* 86 (C.A.) (quoted from (1986) 17 *Recueil Dalloz-Sirey* 163).

A judgment of the Chambre Commerciale of the Cour de Cassation in France (dated March 18, 1986) confirmed that the risk of a claim after the expiry date of a guarantee lies with the beneficiary (*Banque Egyptienne M.I.S.R.* c. *Banque de l'Indochine et de Suez et Banque de l'Union des Mines* (1986) 17 *Recueil Dalloz-Sirey* 166).

A Swiss company had to give a performance guarantee under a delivery contract with the Egyptian Railways. The railway company, as the beneficiary under the guarantee, received the guarantee from an Egyptian bank. Upon instruction of the Swiss company, a French bank gave a counter-guarantee. Both the guarantee and the counter-guarantee provided that the expiry date should be the date of the provisional acceptance of the material to be delivered by the Swiss company.

Subsequent to the expiry date, the beneficiary demanded an extension to the guarantee using the *extend or pay* formula. The Swiss principal agreed to the extension without, however, consulting the French bank.

Some time afterwards, the Egyptian beneficiary claimed payment under the guarantee which was, however, rejected by the guarantors, *i.e.* the Egyptian bank. The case was referred to arbitration in Egypt, and the arbitral tribunal *ordered the Egyptian bank to pay the amount of the guarantee* on the grounds that the Swiss principal had agreed to an extension of the validity period of this guarantee.

The Egyptian bank then turned against the French bank which issued the counter-guarantee. But its action for payment of the amount of the guarantee was dismissed in the last instance by the Cour de Cassation on the grounds that there was *no doubt that the counter-guarantee had lapsed.*

The Cour de Cassation held that the Egyptian arbitral award cannot prejudice the position of the French bank as it did not participate in the arbitral proceedings. Similarly, the Swiss principal's consent to an extension of the guarantee could not have any consequences for the French bank which issued the counter-guarantee even if the Egyptian arbitral award considered the extension of the guarantee as lawful. *The counter-guarantee given by the French bank had not been claimed during the validity period, and thus the bank was discharged from its payment obligations by the lapse of time.*

This example shows the importance of two things:

- expiry dates in guarantee documents have to be strictly observed. However, expiry dates can be extended by agreement. The principle established by the French judgment is also to be found in other European countries;
- a counter-guarantee is absolutely independent of the guarantee. This French legal view seems also to be shared by the other European countries.

It is strongly recommended that the supplier requests, *in a letter separate to the guarantee*, the return of the guarantee document as soon as the guarantee has expired.

Difficulties can arise where buyers insist on demand guarantees which are open-ended, *i.e.* have no definite expiry date, for example one public buyer in the Middle East insisted on a bond "valid for ten months, automatically extendable and cashable on demand".

These problems are less likely to arise where the guarantee has a *final expiry date or, failing that, a clear validity period.* At the very least it should expire after a clearly defined event within the exporter's control, otherwise the exporter loses control of his costs. If the termination of the validity period is conditional on such an event, then the definition of this event and evidence thereof which the bank is authorised to accept must be specified in the bank guarantee to avoid any ambiguity.

Impact of local laws on expiry

A particular problem can arise when, on the insistence of the buyer, a guarantee has to be issued by an overseas correspondent bank on the instructions and responsibility of the exporter's own bank. In some cases the national law actually provides that bank guarantees issued in favour of residents of that country must be issued by a local bank. The bond commitment becomes subject to the laws or regulations of the domicile of the issuing bank which can over-ride the expiry terms of a guarantee, entitling the beneficiary to claim long after the expiry date stated in the guarantee.

Many instructing banks do not know how the local law treats expiry dates. It is important to *check the situation through local agents or banks* before committing to provide demand guarantees. They are usually able to advise the exporter on what risk he is exposed to under local law.

For example, local law affecting demand guarantees exist in several countries including Abu Dhabi, India, Pakistan, Saudi Arabia, Syria, Thailand and Turkey. In some countries, if the reason for a call on a guarantee occurred during its validity, then local law permits the guarantee to be called until such time as it has been *cancelled*. In Turkey, and India, local law requires the issuing bank to maintain its commitment under the bond irrespective of any stated expiry date. In Thailand claims are allowed up to 10 years after the expiry date.

This usually means that release from liability occurs only when the original guarantee document is *returned to the issuing bank for cancellation*, or when the instructing bank receives formal advice of release from its liability.

Consequently the exporter remains liable after the ostensible expiry date. For example, in India and Pakistan, claims can be made against guarantees even after 30 or even 60 years unless they are returned: see Williams, "On demand and conditional performance bonds" [1981] *Journal of Business Law* 13. (For further examples, see Pietsch, "Die Einheitlichen Richtlinien für Vertragsgarantien der Internationalen Handelskammer aus der Sicht der Kreditinstitute" in *Schriften zum deutschen and ausländischen Geld-, Bank- und Börsenrecht* (Frankfurt, 1983) Band 4, p. 42, n. 16 and p. 68.)

Where the exporter's bank is instructed to arrange the issue of a guarantee on behalf of the exporter, it gives appropriate instructions to its overseas correspondent bank and, in addition, gives a *counter-indemnity* to that bank. In some countries, local banking regulations or practice may require the provision of a particular form of counter-indemnity. Local banks are thus fully protected against post-expiry date claims.

The following is an example of an onerous clause imposed by one overseas correspondent bank as a condition of accepting instructions for the issue of a bank demand guarantee:

"We hold you indemnified against any claim that may be lodged against you by the beneficiary at a time even after the lapse of the expiry date specified in your bond, it being understood that our responsibility towards you shall continue to hold good until such time as the beneficiary agrees and releases you from your liabilities hereunder."

Exporters need to be aware of the way expiry is interpreted by buyers and banks, particularly local banks subjected to their own national laws, regulations or practices.

Sometimes "laws" are only central banking regulations, *e.g.* Syria's Central Bank Resolution 4407, and exceptions can be occasionally negotiated, particularly for large bonds relating to contracts with political or security/military associations.

The prudent exporter should deal only with those banks that know and understand the specific local law on bonds. The United Kingdom's Confederation of British Industry (C.B.I.) advice to exporters is that *it is up to exporters to find out about local law*. They do not consider it the direct concern of banks. From the exporter's point of view, it is important that the buyer does not lose the bond and that he gets him to return it to the issuing bank as soon as contractually possible for cancellation.

The 458 Rules (see Chapter 10) aim to establish a uniform practice which will make the stated expiry date more meaningful and equally understandable to all parties concerned. However, there is no attempt to circumvent local laws and regulations in the buyer's country which will continue to apply unless formally excluded.

Even with the ICC guidelines, the exporter is still best advised to have the bond sent back to the instructing bank through the banking chain. Alternatively, he can physically recover the bond himself from the beneficiary, together with a written request, signed by an authorised signatory, to the issuing bank from the beneficiary asking for the bond to be cancelled.

The practice of the United Kingdom in relation to problems of expiry is to treat each case on its merits and to take whatever practical steps are available to secure the termination of a bond commitment. Generally speaking, in the absence of a specific problem of local law or regulations, a United Kingdom bank will cease to charge bond commission once a clearly expressed expiry date has passed. Where, however, the bond has been issued by an overseas bank, commission may continue to be charged.

It will be appreciated, however, that the problems of expiry can be complicated and exporters can therefore find themselves in a situation where their bank facilities continue to be employed for a bond for quite long periods after an expiry date.

The inclusion of *"self-liquidation"* provisions in the bond wording, and preferably also in the contract (see p.177), would help ensure reductions in the bond in line with delivery or performance under the contract.

Not only does this reduce the risk of the bond being called long after the exporter has finished the contract, but it avoids the exporter's banking lines remaining tied up. It also reduces the exporter's liability to continuing bank charges which would otherwise continue to be applied on the full value of the bond until the bank agrees to waive charges.

Exporters may find a visit to the buyer's country is necessary to obtain release of the bond. Where it is not possible to obtain release of the bond, the issuing bank may agree to free the exporter's bonding facilities for the amount of the bond. This is not a straightforward decision for the bank. It has to take a long-term view of the credit-worthiness of the exporter, its customer. If a claim on the bond is then many years hence and the exporter is no longer in business, then the bank must pay. It may not regard itself as being "off-risk", and difficulties can arise particularly if there is an accumulation of such bonds.

(v) Use of local agents

In many instances the local agent is more keen to win the business than the exporter. It is then often possible to arrange for him to instruct his local bank to issue the demand guarantees.

This has several benefits for both parties:

(a)   the buyer has direct access to local funds;
(b)   the buyer's problem of trying to enforce claims through an overseas bank against guarantees often subject to foreign law and jurisdiction is eliminated;
(c)   the exporter is not using up his own banking lines and balance sheet;
(d)   it is unlikely that a beneficiary will make an unfair claim on a countryman who is able to deal with him face to face; and
(e)   the local agent has a vested interest after the sale in ensuring that the buyer is satisfied. This eliminates the risk of a call on the guarantee.

(vi) Contingency in price

For some low-risk buyers and markets, it is possible to reduce the impact of an unfair demand by including a small contingency in the price of all contracts, or selected contracts, and build up a *contingency fund* against the event of an unfair call on a guarantee. (The reality is that this pool of money is more than likely to be distributed as extra profit and will not be available to meet a demand when made on a guarantee.)

(vii) Build in full value

For some high-risk buyers and markets it may be necessary to expect the guarantee to be called and to build the full value of the guarantee into the contract price. This technique does not work for price-sensitive goods (unless all the competitors adopt the same policy), nor does it work with tender guarantee risks as there is no payment from the buyer until there is a contract.

(viii) Insure the risk of unfair demand

Whilst recognising that in the long term there is a remote prospect of recovering sums paid out against an unfair demand, an exporter can protect his short-term cashflow and profit position through insurance. This can be provided by the national credit insurer of the exporter's country (most OECD countries have such insurers), or the private market equivalent.

Most of the official unfair demand insurance schemes are modelled on, or developed from, those offered by the United Kingdom's Export Credits Guarantee Department (ECGD). Originally this cover was in respect of all eligible United Kingdom exports but, following privatisation of its short-term insurance services division, ECGD now only provides cover for eligible projects (see Chapter 7).

The private market has developed its own form of policy wordings for similar risks. Each has advantages and disadvantages which an exporter should discuss in detail with his specialist insurance broker. (See Annex II to this Chapter.)

Expiry of unfair call insurance
Insurance is probably the most expensive way of reducing the risk of an unfair call, as the premium is an actual cost paid to a third party and not a contingency or provision in the price which may or may not be used.

Insurance usually expires with the bank guarantee validity (subject to the three-year time limit usually imposed by insurers in the private market) and can cost additional premium to extend (tender guarantees' premium usually covers the period up to contract award).

Recovery of unfair payments
The more the intentions of the parties are expressed in the contract and the guarantee, the more likely it is for courts to identify an *invalid* claim. For even if the guarantee wording is issued in *simple demand* form, if the intention of the parties to the contract was to limit the circumstances in which a guarantee could be called, then it becomes easier to show *capricious or unfair* calling in any subsequent action under the contract.

If the exporter disputes the payment of a claim under the demand guarantee, it is his own responsibility to seek to recover any moneys due to him direct from the buyer through his contract, as he has no contractual relationship with the buyer under the guarantee.

However, it can take years, if in fact it is ever possible, to obtain this redress under the contract and in the meantime the exporter may have suffered a major setback to his cashflow, or even become insolvent.

(ix) Perform the contract

The exporter should make every effort to see that the contract is performed properly by himself and his sub-contractors or joint venture partners.

However, if the exporter fails to perform his contract properly, he can try to persuade the buyer, *before he makes a demand under the guarantee*, to give him an opportunity to rectify any default, or pay any liquidated damages to prevent a demand on the guarantee.

Having pre-empted the risk of a demand in this manner, the exporter should then, at the first permissible opportunity, recover the demand guarantee from the buyer to avoid the subsequent risk of an *unfair* demand.

If a demand is purely for commercial reasons, then there is the possibility that some honourable buyers will agree to a refund if the reason for the demand is rectified. This depends on the country, the buyer and the terms and nature of the underlying contract.

With speed being of the essence in the event of an unfair call, it is important for the exporter to have *in-house procedures* in existence to prevent the bank responding to a demand before there has been an opportunity to discuss it with the buyer.

These procedures should be aimed at preventing the bank:

(a)   paying; and/or
(b)   debiting his account under the terms of the counter-indemnity he signed with the bank.

The measures should include:

(i)   Requesting the bank to delay responding to the beneficiary.
      Some exporters rely on being able to pre-empt a payment of a demand by expecting the bank to give them prior notice of a claim and to withhold payment until the exporter has had an opportunity to persuade his customer, the beneficiary, to withdraw his demand for payment.
      However, many issuing banks have not been able to accept such an obligation to give notice and to withhold payment. Irrevocable obligations assumed by the bank have been considered the lifeblood of international commerce, and were such obligations not promptly fulfilled the bank's reputation would have suffered and trust in international commerce would have been irreparably damaged.
      The issuing bank is not expected to judge whether a demand is *fair* or *unfair*. All it is required to do is decide whether the demand is *in accordance with the guarantee*. If it is, and the guarantee has not expired, the bank will quite correctly pay the demand and take recourse on the exporter, or the instructing bank as the case may be,

unless the bank believes the demand to be *fraudulent*. Either way, the exporter's cashflow suffers.

On the other hand, no bank would want to prejudice its relationship with its customer by being accused of debiting its customer's account without first giving some prior warning of its intent. This dilemma has been partially solved under the 458 Rules (see Chapter 10).

If the beneficiary makes a demand, the bank is allowed a reasonable time to decide whether it complies with the guarantee, and to give notice of the demand to the exporter. If the demand does comply, then the bank must pay.

  (ii) Contacting the credit insurer or broker to seek their advice and assistance, where the guarantee is covered against unfair call.
 (iii) Immediately contacting the buyer to see why the demand was made on the guarantee.
 (iv) Instigation of injunction procedures where appropriate.

However, with many bank demand guarantees the exporter also concedes the right of objection, conciliation or arbitration in the event of an unfair call.

(x) Legal action to prevent unfair claim payment

When an exporter has exhausted all commercial means of protecting himself, he may be forced to resort to the courts for protection, should the bank insist on paying.

In the event of a disputed claim, some banks are likely to fulfil their obligations under the guarantee. Some have the reputation of preferring to pay claims rather than reject them because they are concerned to avoid harming their international reputation. This creates a conflict of interest between the bank and its customer, the exporter.

It is the exporter's bank account that will be debited, often directly. Therefore, the exporter has considerable interest in ensuring that an unjustified call under a guarantee is not honoured, and will look for whatever means are available, including the courts, to prevent payment following an unfair call. It is important to be able to react quickly and take immediate preventative measures. He therefore needs to have contingency plans to prevent payment by legal means, should such a need arise.

The European courts have developed legal instruments to assist the exporter in resisting unfair claims. However, many claims that are *unfair under the contract* have been considered by the courts as *fair under the guarantee*.

There have been more examples of action in continental European courts than in the United Kingdom to attempt to prevent banks paying unfair claims or, if not from paying the claim, then from debiting the exporter with the amount of the claim payment.

Where the exporter does have time, money and opportunity to dispute the demand, injunctions preventing the bank making payment or debiting his account may also be possible. In such cases, legal advice should always be sought as a matter of urgency.

As legal action against the bank would normally take too long, the exporter may have to resort to summary procedures available in his country for cases of great urgency. These will depend on the location of the bank instructed by the exporter to issue the guarantee, and on the legal jurisdiction to which it is subject.

Simple demand bonds cannot be called illegally by the beneficiary. Banks are able to pay the beneficiary without risk of being accused of negligence or manifest error.

Without any form of collaboration, all the European courts that have been approached by aggrieved exporters have eventually ruled, often after appeal, that in most circumstances a claim against a guarantee payable on demand is enforceable if the claim is in accordance with the guarantee wording. The only exception is in the case of *manifest fraud*. This legal exception permitted by the courts has so far proved of little value to the innocent exporter.

The reality is that the fraud has to be so obvious that the bank official handling the claim has to recognise it before paying the claim.

From the exporter's point of view, this is less than encouraging because it is difficult, if not impossible, for the bank to recognise a *fraudulent claim*, or for an exporter to provide the required evidence to support such allegations.

The legal remedies available to exporters in the various countries of Europe, whilst different in several respects, ultimately have the same outcome.

United Kingdom
In the United Kingdom, the exporter is able to apply for an interlocutory injunction which expires after 48 hours. So, at the very least, the exporter must persuade the bank not to settle the claim pending issue of the injunction, and then to take effective action to try to get the beneficiary to withdraw his claim within the 48-hour deadline.

This presupposes that the bank knows, or ought to know, the facts underlying an *abusive* or *fraudulent* call. The bank may, but should not, pretend to be ignorant of the facts, so, in order to protect his own interests, the prudent exporter should keep the bank informed of any risk of a possible claim, *fair or unfair*.

English courts hold the view that in principle no injunction should be granted if the bank guarantee is valid and the specified conditions are met.

Only in an exceptional case, where it can be proved that the bank knew that a demand for payment was *fraudulent*, may an injunction be granted. But in such circumstances the evidence must be clear, both as to the fact of fraud and as to the bank's knowledge (see *Boliventer Oil S.A.* v. *Chase Manhattan Bank N.A.* [1984] 1 W.L.R. 392; [1984] *Journal of Business Law* 59 (C.A.)).

In a decision of the High Court in England (*Edward Owen* v. *Barclays Bank plc* [1979] 1 All E.R. 978; [1978] 1 Q.B. 159 (C.A.)[1]) Lord Denning stated that "a bank must pay according to the terms of its guarantee. The only exception is when there is a clear fraud of which the bank has notice".

Germany

German procedural law knows two types of summary court procedure:

(a)   the *Einstweilige Verfügung* (section 935, ZPO—Code of Civil Procedure) *i.e.* a temporary interlocutory injunction requiring the issuing bank to refrain from paying the amount of the guarantee; and

(b)   the so-called *Arrest* (section 916, ZPO). The term *Arrest* means attachment for the exporter's benefit of the claim for payment that the beneficiary or the local guarantor has against the guarantor in the principal's country under the guarantee.

Lower courts sometimes prefer an interlocutory injunction accompanied by an application to prohibit the bank from debiting the exporter's account with the amount of the guarantee. In consequence, it lies within the bank's discretion whether it will pay at all.

These two procedures are designed to settle urgent cases provisionally where a normal, time-consuming procedure would entail serious and partly irrecoverable loss for the party concerned.

Consequently, it is the purpose of these procedures to *prevent a deterioration of the factual situation* until a final settlement is reached, for instance through a normal, ordinary litigious procedure.

The German Federal Court has held that a claim for payment under a guarantee will in equity fail only if it can be proved that, even though the formal requirements have been met, the event upon which the obligation to pay has arisen has not taken place ([1984] *Der Betrieb* 1389 (B.G.H.)). This in effect constitutes a fraudulent exercise of a right. The guarantor may put in a plea of unlawful exercise of rights (section 242, German Civil Code).[2]

By virtue of the *Geschäftsbesorgungsvertrag* (agency agreement) entered into between the guarantor and the exporter, the guarantor is, in such a case, actually under an obligation to raise the afore-mentioned plea, and will be liable to damages if he fails to do so (Pleyer, *op. cit.*, pp. 18, 19; Finger, "Formen und Rechtsnatur der Bankgarantie" [1969] B.B. 206–208).

The German Federal Court applies this ruling also in respect of abusive calls under a bank guarantee. In its judgment of March 12, 1984 ([1984] D.B.

---

[1]   See also *Pottom Homes Ltd.* v. *Coleman Contractors (Overseas) Ltd.* (unreported, Ct. of Appeal, February 28, 1984) and *United Trading Corporation* v. *Allied Arab Bank Ltd.; Murray Clayton Ltd.* v. *Rafidain Bank* [1985] *International Banking Law* 142; [1986] 17 *Recueil Dalloz-Sirey* 162, 163.)

[2]   This is undisputed in legal writings: see Liesecke, "Rechtsfragen der Bankgarantie". See Horn,"Bürgschaften und Garantien zur Zahlung auf erstes Anfordern" [1980] N.J.W. 2153–2156; "Einstweilige Verfügungen und Arreste im internationalen Rechtsverkehr, insbesondere im Zusammenhang mit der Inanspruchnahme von Bankgarantien" [1980] W.M. 1438; see also Mülbert, *op. cit.* pp.50 *et. seq.*

1389 *et seq.*), in a procedure where the plaintiff had to prove his claim by documents only—*Urkundenprozess*—the Federal Court held that the exporter could use the defence of abuse of rights to defeat the claim for payment if it was obvious or provable that the purported event giving rise to the obligation to pay had not happened, although the formal requirements were met (Canaris, *Grosskommentar HGBm* (3rd ed., 1981), Nos. 1139, 1140; Stumpf/Ullrich, "Die Missbruchliche Inanspruchnahme von Bankgarantien im internationalen Geschäftsverkehr" [1984] R.I.W. 843 *et seq.*).

The Federal Court affirmed this principle in a further decision (see [1986] Z.I.P. 1450; [1986] D.B. 2594). But, at the same time, the court made it clear that a call was not manifestly abusive if defences had to be examined by way of interpretation of the underlying main contract between the principal and the beneficiary. This would defeat the purpose of a demand guarantee.

Switzerland

In Switzerland, each Canton has its own code of civil procedure. But all these codes provide for summary procedures under which payments can be stopped (*e.g.* section 222(2) of the Zurich Code of Civil Procedure).

The *Zürcher Obergericht* ((1985) 85 *Blätter für Zürcherische Rechtsprechung* 44) and the Cour de Justice Civile de Génève ([1984] *Dalloz* 94) have both addressed the question of unjustified calls on bank guarantees. For example:

(a)   *U.B.S. et General Establishment for Cereal Processing and Trade* c. *Miranus International Trading Corporation, Inc. S.A.* (unreported, Cour de Justice Civile de Génève, September 12, 1985);

(b)   *Iranian Government Trading Corporation et Banque Melli Iran* c. *Segogest S.A.* (unreported, quoted from (1986) 17 *Recueil Dalloz-Sirey* 162–165).

In the view of the Zurich court, a bank does not have an obligation to pay if it can be adequately proved that the claim is *unjustified*. If a beneficiary claims a bank guarantee knowing the claim is unjust, he is unlawfully exercising a right. There are strict rules regarding proof of this unlawful exercise of a right.

France

In France the process is called an *interdiction de payer par voie de référé*—prohibition to pay by way of preliminary injunction.

Under this summary procedure, the court prohibits the bank from paying if the fraudulent nature of the beneficiary's claim stares you in the face (*crève les yeux*).

Some courts also admit *la mise sous sequestre* whereby a sum of money equal to the amount of the guarantee is deposited with a third person, pending litigation. By this means, a provisional prohibition to pay, which the exporter (the beneficiary of the *sequestre*) had obtained earlier, may be extended or reinforced.

There is yet another legal remedy called *saisie-arrête, i.e.* attachment of a debt (claim) in the hands of a third party. This remedy is only available if the principal (exporter) under the guarantee has a secure claim against the beneficiary, and if the issuing bank, where the claim is to be attached, is the beneficiary's debtor.

The latter is not the case when the guarantee is a counter-guarantee, because the bank which issued the counter-guarantee is then only the debtor of the bank which issued the guarantee. For this reason, *saisie-arrêt* is only of minor importance.

The French Cour de Cassation has held that the exporter can raise objections against the buyer's actions under the main contract where there is *fraude manifeste* or *abus manifeste*.

Belgium

This view is also share by courts in Belgium. In Belgium the process is called *procedure en référé, i.e.* interlocutory injunction. In the event of *abus ou fraude manifeste* the exporter may obtain a court order prohibiting the bank to pay.

There are two types of summary procedures:

(a)   a unilateral procedure called *requête*; and
(b)   a bilateral procedure called *citation*.

The latter process is rarely used.

The question as to whether a *saisie-arrête* would be useful is controversial, but a *saisie-arrête* must not affect the guarantee's total independence of the underlying contract.

The relevant cases are:

  (i)   [1982] J.T. 358 (Cour d'Appel de Bruxelles);
 (ii)   [1982] J.L.B. 349 (Cour d'Appel de Bruxelles);
(iii)   [1984] *Jurisprudence de Liège* 512 (Tribunal de Commerce de Liège);
(iv)   [1985] R.R.D. 73 (Tribunal de Commerce de Charleroi) (*référés*);
  (v)   (1986) 17 *Recueil Dalloz-Sirey* 162 (Tribunal de Commerce de Bruxelles) (*référés*).

Luxembourg

In order to justify non-payment by the bank, a fraud or an unlawful exercise of a right must stare you in the face. Such was the decision of:

 (i)   [1981] *Dalloz* 504 (Tribunal de Commerce de Luxembourg); and
(ii)   [1983] *Dalloz* 299 (Cour d'Appel de Luxembourg).

The Netherlands

The Dutch courts think it justified to refuse payment in the case of calls which are *manifestly arbitrary, fraudulent* or otherwise *deceitful*.

Here the summary procedure is called *Kort geding*. The courts may order a bank to refrain from paying the amount of the guarantee, provided the beneficiary's claim is manifestly arbitrary or fraudulent. The relevant cases are:

   (i) *Trengrouse* v. *Bank of America* [1982] N.J. 32 (District Court of Amsterdam); [1973] N.J. 188 (Court of Appeal of Leeuwarden); and
   (ii) *Tasmac* v. *Stevin Bahareth* [1981] K.B. 74 (District Court of Amsterdam); *Globogal* v. *Bax* [1983] N.J. 750.

Italy

Here the process is called *provvedimento d'urgenza* (Article 700, Code of Civil Procedure), *i.e.* summary procedure.

Under this procedure the bank may be ordered not to pay the amount of the guarantee. This procedure will not bring about the desired result unless two requirements are met:

   (a) There must be imminent, serious and irrevocable loss or damage if the amount of the guarantee were paid.
        Two examples are cited:
      (i) the principal might become insolvent or bankrupt as a consequence of the bank's payment; or
      (ii) the principal would have extreme difficulties in recovering the amount of the guarantee in the case where he obtained a judgment in his favour in subsequent proceedings.
   (b) The beneficiary's claim must be prima facie unjustified.

The relevant judgments of the Italian courts are:

   (i) *Gondwana Spa* c. *Istituto Bancario San Paolo di Torino* [1985] B.B.T.C. 84 (Pretura di Milano);
   (ii) *Safimi Babcock* c. *Banca Commerciale Italiana* [1985] II B.B.T.C. 87.

These refer to *"la prova pronta e liquida della frode del beneficiario"*. Evidence must be provided that the beneficiary claims in bad faith something which is not due to him.

As can be seen from the above, the principle is widely accepted in Europe that there must be an element of *"obviousness"* of unjustified claims or fraud.

It is, however, a major problem to prove this *"obviousness"*, with the result that, in the majority of cases in international practice, applications for interlocutory injunctions to restrain payments have been dismissed.

In all Western European countries, the courts base their decisions in this field on the principle of *"pay first and litigate afterwards"*.
Other approaches, mainly in France, are:

— *Banque Tejarat c. Pipe Line Service et Paribas* (unreported, Cour de Cassation, Chambre Commerciale, December 11, 1985);
— *BNCP c. S.A. Granit* (1986) 17 *Recueil Dalloz-Sirey* 159 (Tribunal de Commerce de Melun).

and bring out the following points:

• the unlawful exercise of a right must be beyond all doubt;
• a mere presumption will not be acceptable;
• obviousness does not exist if it is necessary to take further evidence or make further investigations.

The exporter's dilemma is that, as a rule, clear documentary evidence must be produced showing that the guarantee is the subject of a *fraudulent* or *unjustified claim*.

A court may take into consideration statements made by witnesses during a hearing, provided there is an oral hearing and that the witnesses are credible. However, courts do not allow the applicant (exporter) to establish a prima facie case of fraud through *statutory declaration*. The latter is possible, however, in the case of an *interlocutory injunction*.

In a number of cases, European courts have accepted evidence put forward of an obvious fraud. In these cases the fraud was so clear that courts in all countries would have probably reached the same opinion. The prerequisite of *"obviousness"* has to be present.

Typical examples are as follows:

(a) The beneficiary confirmed in the taking-over certificate that the goods supplied to him were in accordance with the contract (*Banque Tejarat c. Pipe Line Service et Paribas* (unreported, Cour de Cassation, Chambre Commerciale, December 11, 1985); *BNCP c. S.A. Granit* (1986) 17 *Recueil Dalloz-Sirey* 159 (Tribunal de Commerce de Melun)).

(b) The beneficiary claimed payment under a down-payment guarantee although he had not made the down-payment ([1984] *Dalloz* 93 (Cour de Justice Civile de Génève)).

(c) The beneficiary maintained that the ordered goods had not been supplied although relevant documents showed that the goods had been taken over.

(d) A call on an inter-bank indemnity was made by the bank which issued the guarantee against the bank which issued the indemnity, although payment of the bond had already been blocked through a court order (*U.B.S. et General Establishment for Cereal Processing and*

Trade c. *Miranus International Trading Corporation Inc S.A.* (Cour de Justice Civile de Génève); *Iranian Government Trading Corporation et Banque Melli Iran* c. *Segogest S.A.* (1986) 17 *Recueil Dalloz-Sirey* 162–165).

Relationships After a Demand

Disputed payment recovery

Once a bank demand guarantee is called and the payment made, recovering the payment, and any related costs, is often extremely difficult, unless it can be proved that the buyer is not contractually entitled to make a demand. In such situations, there is a chance of obtaining a favourable judgment under the contract.

Without any form of disputes settlement clause incorporated in the bank guarantee, the exporter can, at best, usually only proceed against the buyer for breach of contract. For this action to be successful he needs, at the very least, the buyer to state in writing the reasons for making a claim. On the strength of this, the exporter may be able to make a case to prove that the claim was unfair and that legally the money should be *refunded* to him.

Whether such an award could be enforced depends upon the circumstances, where the buyer has his assets and, if he has no assets in the exporter's country, the law of the country where his assets are held. Often complex exchange control regulations and bureaucratic procedures in the buyer's country can make the enforcement of any court order or arbitral award very costly and time-consuming.

Getting the contract and guarantee worded to anticipate such difficulties, and lay the grounds for recovery of payment, will help the exporter's case in arbitration or through the courts.

Avoiding disputes in the performance of any contract is of course highly desirable, if not always possible. With well-drafted contracts, the disputes clause should also cover the settlement of disputes under the bank demand guarantee and the guarantee wording should reflect this procedure.

However, few bank guarantees, except those especially negotiated for major projects, contain a disputes settlement clause. Many exporters assume that as the guarantee is issued under the contract then the disputes settlement clause in the contract (if any) covers the bank demand guarantee. This is not usually the case where the guarantee is totally *independent* of the contract.

In many cases the guarantee wording is often that customarily required by local laws and regulations to be issued by banks in the buyer's country and the exporter has no say in the matter. As a result, the exporter has no obvious neutral or independent mechanism for recourse against the beneficiary under the bank guarantee in the event that it is unfairly called.

If the contract and guarantee say nothing about the settlement of disputes, the remedies available to the exporter to prevent the bank paying an unfair claim, or to recover such payments, are greatly reduced. At the very least, a guarantee should state the *law and jurisdiction* which govern it so that there is some agreed legal framework within which disputes can be settled.

Better still, the exporter should incorporate an internationally-recognised code of practice (such as the 458 Rules—see Chapter 10) which contains a disputes settlement procedure.

A key consideration from the exporter's point of view is how he wishes to continue to value his future ongoing relationship with the buyer. Clearly, *demands on bank guarantees are not intended to create goodwill and cement long-term friendly relations.* In some instances, an unfair call on the bank guarantee can end the relationship.

Once a call has been made on a bank guarantee, the risk and threat of an unfair call that was once of concern to the exporter has been fulfilled and he has little else to lose from fighting to stop the bank paying the claim, or from trying to retaliate under the contract.

Not all buyers fully appreciate that calling a bank guarantee is like pulling the trigger of a gun. The results are usually irrevocable. Once called, the time for amicable solutions and remedial action is usually over. The damage has been done. The special relationship which may have once existed between the exporter and his buyer is often destroyed. The opportunity to work out problems amicably may have passed.

The exporter will, from this point on, do everything possible to cut his costs, to try to restore his negotiating position, to recover the guarantee payment, or possibly to suspend or even terminate the contract if the call was considered unfair. In many circumstances, the *insurer* will insist on a contract being terminated after a demand guarantee has been called unfairly and has become the subject of a claim.

In other instances, the exporter may decide that there is little alternative but to continue to deal with a buyer who abuses his power.

Role of the Insurance Broker

There is every argument for an exporter taking advantage of the skills and experience of *specialist brokers*. Brokers deal with other exporters as well as insurers, and are a *repository of collective experience* and a valuable source of, often free, advice. They can assist the exporter in several ways:

(i)   in negotiating bond unfair calling cover;
(ii) in helping select the appropriate insurer;
(iii) in giving advice on guarantee and contract wordings to ensure that they do not prejudice cover; and
(iv) in drafting contract terms and guarantee texts and indemnities that

do not conflict with, or contradict, each other, that are watertight and do not prejudice insurance cover.

On a continuing basis, they can monitor the progress of a contract and help ensure that cover is maintained whilst the guarantee remains valid; and ensure that any action taken to resist a demand on a guarantee would not prejudice the cover by ensuring that such action is only taken with the approval of the insurer providing bond risk cover.

Annex I—Fraud and Abuse

The exporter's only legal defence against an unfair claim is the bank's noticing the buyer's *manifest fraud*. However, the bank is not usually in a position to detect such fraud, nor is the exporter able to prove it. The result is that the bank has to honour the claim and to debit the exporter's account.

The only exception would be the case where the exporter is in the rare position of being able to present to the bank strong corroborative evidence of fraud, *i.e.* immediately available "hard" evidence that fraud actually has taken place. In this case the bank must not pay. However, such evidence normally is very hard to come by.

To avoid payment, some exporters have made use of other direct means.

Direct means of substance

These are based on the fact that the claim against the guarantee, according to the exporter, is *abusive* or *fraudulent*. The courts are more sympathetic to the exporter when this is shown.

The Commercial Chamber, in the first judgment establishing this attitude, rendered on December 11, 1985 in the Iranian case of the *Société Auxiliaire d'Entreprise* ([1986] D. 215, note Vasseur) said that: "Abuse and fraud keep in check the principle of autonomy in the matter of a guarantee or counter-indemnity." But the abuse or fraud, if any, must be an "obvious fraud" ([1987] D. 17, note Vasseur (Com.)) or an "obvious abuse" ([1987] D. Somm. 177, obs. Vasseur (Com.)).

A fraud or an abuse is obvious when it "hits you in the eye", and need not be evidenced by any measure of detection or verification ([1983] D. I.R. 299, obs. Vasseur (Luxembourg Court of Appeal)).

It should be apparent prima facie. According to the above-quoted judgment of December 11, 1985, in the case of the *Société Auxiliaire d'Entreprise*, it must exist "beyond doubt". "The fact, even apparently established, that the (exporter) fulfilled all his obligations" is not sufficient, as was decided by the Commercial Chamber in the *Fechoz* judgment of May 21, 1985 ([1986] D. 213, note Vasseur). Therefore, appearance is not enough, but is certainly required.

However, some first instance judges were led to show less stringency by favouring the principal (*e.g.* [1989] D. Somm. 155, obs. Vasseur (Versailles)). An example of a bad decision was the summary injunction of the commercial judge, dated September 29, 1988, which ordered a French bank, the counter-guarantor, to postpone payment. It stated that: "the circumstances of the case show that there may have been a fraud".

This injunction was reversed by a judgment of the Paris First Court of Appeal on February 15, 1989 ([1989] D. Somm. 158, obs. Vasseur), since, the court said: "only the existence of an obvious fraud or abuse can delay the performance of first demand commitments."

There are few judgments which have established an obvious abuse or fraud (nevertheless see [1986] D. 215 (Com.), quoted above).

What is an abuse and what is a fraud? The courts, in their decisions, usually use both words together or call "obvious fraud" something more rightly termed "obvious abuse" ([1987] D. 17, note Vasseur (Com.)).

Nevertheless, the judgment of the Commercial Chamber of January 20, 1987 rules that fraud and abuse must be kept apart, but without providing any standards for such a distinction.

Can fraud and abuse be distinguished? Considering the already-quoted judgment of December 11, 1985, in the case of the *Société Auxiliaire d'Entreprise (SAE)*, fraud requires a genuine plot aimed at making the principal pay sums he does not owe.

In this case, the SAE had concluded with Iran, in 1975–1976, contracts for the construction of thousands of houses.

The new Iranian régime had broken off relations with the French company, set up a bogus SAE-Iran company, entirely created by the government and entrusted with the task of pursuing the work, and confiscated and handed over to the Iranian company all the assets of the French company located in Iran. Neither paid what was owed to the French company, nor compensated it for the expropriation it had suffered.

Nevertheless, the Iranian authorities claimed the guarantee. *It was ruled that the fraud was obvious.*

Can there also be obvious abuse, as opposed to obvious fraud, when there can be absolutely no doubt that the principal effectively fulfilled all his obligations?

The *Fechoz* judgment of December 11, 1985 could be interpreted in this sense.

Obvious abuse would also exist (but this is no more than a reasonable, doctrinal suggestion):

(a)   if the guarantee is claimed after a final court decision cancelling the basic contract;
(b)   after a court declared the basic contract null and void because of the beneficiaries' actions; or
(c)   because the beneficiary acknowledged that he would not carry out the contract ([1989] D. Somm. 151, obs. Vasseur (Paris)).

In short, an obviously abusive claim against a guarantee would occur when the beneficiary has "beyond any doubt" no right to claim it.

In this respect it will be noted that no abuse was found in the fact that the beneficiary had put the guarantor in the difficult position of having to *"extend or pay"* (e.g. [1987] D. Somm. 171, obs. Vasseur (Paris)) since the beneficiary did not do so without any right.

On the other hand, no reference should be made to an obvious abuse, as was done wrongly by the Paris Tribunal de Commerce in its judgments of July 8, 1983 ([1984] D. I.R. 92, obs. Vasseur), when the guarantee is claimed outside its terms of implementation, *e.g.* because the time limit has expired. It is then sufficient to say that the guarantee is being claimed outside its terms of reference ([1979] *Dalloz* 259, note Vasseur (Paris)).

When an obvious fraud or abuse has to be considered, the situation becomes complicated when, as occurs most frequently, the operation is covered by a local bank's guarantee and a counter-guarantee by the exporter's bank.

If the beneficiary's claim is abusive or fraudulent, the claim against the counter-guarantee by the primary guaranteeing bank, considering the independence of the counter-guarantee *vis-à-vis* the primary guarantee, will only be fraudulent in case of *fraudulent collusion* between the primary guaranteeing bank and the beneficiary.

This was ruled by France's Commercial Chamber, in its judgment of December 11, 1985, in the repeatedly-quoted case of the *Société Auxiliaire d'Enterprise*. The judgment stated that under the circumstances, fraudulent collusion resulted from the fact that the primary guaranteeing bank, claiming the counter-guarantee, could "have no doubt whatsoever about the fraudulent nature of the claim against the guarantee" by the Iranian beneficiary.

This "no doubt whatsoever" must exist at the time when the primary bank claims the counter-guarantee.

In France, *obvious fraud* and *obvious abuse* are the means related to the merits of the case that may be quoted to counter a claim against the guarantee. It is the responsibility of the bank requested to pay to use spontaneously these means of opposition if it notes the existence of such a fraud or abuse. In practice, however, those means would rather be put forward by the exporter. The exporter therefore has an interest in being advised of a claim.

This leads to a review of the *procedural means available* and their acceptance by the courts.

Direct procedural means

When a guarantee or counter-guarantee is claimed, it is important for the principal claiming that he is a victim of an obvious abuse or fraud to act quickly.

Payment by the bank is normally due at short notice, since it is usually on demand. The principal will therefore rush to a judge in chambers or submit a petition for an interlocutory injunction.

It may be noted in this connection that the judge who, on the spot in France, acts as a pilot-judge in the matter of guarantees is the *"juge des référés"*.

The exporter will ask him to order the ban not to pay, or alternatively, to delay payment, at least until a decision on the merits of the case.

The exporter would succeed, more often without than with a real case, by making a judge pity him.

The Courts of Appeal, as well as the Cour de Cassation, have put this right several times. By its judgment of May 5, 1988 ([1988] D. 430, note Vas-seur), the Commercial Chamber denied the *juge des référés* any power to de-lay performance of first demand guarantees *in the absence of obvious fraud or abuse.*

It definitely ruled out that this judge could claim jurisdiction, on the ba-sis of Article 873, Nouveau Code de Procédure Civile (NCPC), in view of an impending damage threatening the exporter and liable, in the circum-stances, to deprive him of important, practically irrecoverable, assets if the payment were ill-founded.

Such a reason was considered unacceptable. Kind feelings do not mean good decisions. To recover some day the capital paid by the bank, the ex-porter must file a suit against the beneficiary if he feels that the latter wrongly claimed the guarantee.

The means used, however, did allow the exporter to win some time.

In one case that led to the judgment already quoted of May 5, 1988, the guarantee was claimed in 1986. The *juge des référés* stopped payment, a de-cision confirmed by the Court of Appeal, but there was a repeal of judg-ment by the Cour de Cassation on May 5, 1988. The guarantee, therefore, remained unpaid for two years.

This is a dangerous move since the exporter who succeeds in stopping payment against a guarantee, in this case the counter-guarantee, even if covered by the interlocutory judge, should be aware that if the Court of Appeal reverses the injunction, he can be sentenced to pay damages to the primary guaranteeing bank ([1986] D. I.R. 157, obs. Vasseur (Paris)). The time saved in the end will cost money.

Misguided by kind feelings not leading to the right decisions, some *juges des référés*, who were not sure of being entitled to issue an order to stop pay-ment or to delay performance, deemed it expedient, in the early 1980s, to compromise by stating the obligation to pay, but ordering the sequestra-tion or deposit of the funds with the counter-guaranteeing bank.

This measure failed when the First Chamber of the Paris Court of Appeal ruled, on December 3, 1984, that:

> "when a prohibition to pay, addressed to a counter-guaranteeing French bank, is not well founded, a sequestration order cannot be either since the result of such a provision is identical as regards the be-neficiary of the counter-guarantee, the purpose of the sequestration being to stop the on-demand payment."

The ban on sequestration seems final. In spite of this, the kindness of a *juge des référés* surfaced again in the *Zengor* case, leading to a judgment by the Paris Court of Appeal on September 23, 1988 ([1989] D. Somm. 156, obs. Vasseur).

This judge, whose injunction, open to criticism, was confirmed by the Court of Appeal, not daring to state fraud as a reason, but only the benefi-ciary's lack of fairness, did not delay the payment of the guarantee, but *made its collection by the beneficiary subject to the deposit by the beneficiary of a*

bank guarantee for the same amount, on the basis of Article 489, NCPC, providing that the provisional implementation of a right under an injunction
order can be made subject to a guarantee.

Arguably, all means are fair to avoid unfair payment. The exporter may resort
to *attachment*, *garnishment* or *arrestation* of the amount of the guarantee due
to the beneficiary.

Apart from technical difficulties in the way of seizing the guarantee, and
more particularly the counter-guarantee (as the counter-guarantor has no
debtor other than the guarantor, while the principal, in the best of circumstances, has only a claim on the beneficiary), this approach is doomed to
fail since the French Commercial Chamber, in the neighbouring field of
documentary credits, has through repeated judgments ([1986] D. 374, note
Vasseur; [1988] D. 195, note Vasseur) ruled that by instructing the bank to
give its guarantee, the principal forfeits his right to stop execution by
means of an attachment; he has made the commitment finally irrevocable.

There was one device attempted by an ingenious principal and revealed
by a judgment of the Paris Court of Appeal of December 14, 1987 ([1989]
Revue de l'Arbitrage 240, note Vasseur) worthy of note:

> "An ICC Arbitration clause was included in the basic contract, but not
> in the guarantee or counter-guarantee. The principal did not care. The
> guarantees were claimed. The principal went to the ICC Court of Ar-
> bitration, requesting that the claim against the guarantee be cancelled.
> He knew that his request was not admissible but he made use of it to
> ask the ordinary court to stop the French bank, the counter-guarantor,
> from paying the bank who is the primary guarantor until the issue had
> been settled. He speculated on the application of the principle that
> arbitral jurisdiction had priority over judicial jurisdiction."

However, the device was too obvious, and the principal failed. The French
courts, and especially the Supreme Court, are necessarily the watchful
guardians of orthodoxy in the matter of guarantees, as also is the banker.

In the banker's eyes, the principal is his client; he wishes to keep his customer and himself satisfied, but the principal should remember that he has
himself urged the banker to underwrite the guarantee and that this commitment, once accepted, is the banker's own commitment. The principal
(the exporter) no longer has any real control over it.

On the other hand, the banker is rightly eager to make his own name internationally trustworthy. As the Tribunal of Commerce in Grenoble
stated:

> "it would be serious if French banks could be accused of not com-
> plying with their undertakings; this would simply lead buyers to im-
> pose as counter-guarantors the banking establishments of countries
> where application is much stricter or to turn back to cash deposits."

French courts, therefore, allow the banker himself to go to the courts in opposition to an order not to pay or to postpone payment, or an attachment requested by the principal, and to request its withdrawal if the claim against the guarantee is obviously neither *abusive* nor *fraudulent*.

The banker who feels that he should pay must be empowered to do so. The means to reconcile his interest and that of the principal would perhaps be, as suggested by French authors (Mattout, [1987] 243 *Droit Bancaire International*) and by the Tribunal de Commerce in Brussels on December 7, 1988 ([1989] D. Somm. 148, obs. Vasseur) that the judge in doubt about the fairness of the claim against the guarantee would not stop the banker from paying, but would not allow him to debit the principal's account until a decision on the merits of the claim against the guarantee intervenes.

(The above is an extract from Professeur M. Vasseur, "Rapport de synthesis: le droit des garanties bancaires dans les contrats internationaux en France et dans les pays de l'Europe de l'Ouest", Colloque de Tours.)

Annex II—Bond Unfair Calling Cover

Where a bank demand guarantee has been called unfairly and is insured against such a risk, it is important to consult the insurer so that such cover remains valid and effective and that any action taken to minimise loss and exposure is taken only with the agreement of the insurer.

In many cases (except, perhaps, relatively low-value routine contracts printed in a standard format), insurers require to approve the wording of bank guarantees, counter-indemnities and related contract conditions before agreeing cover. This is to minimise the risk of an unfair call and to avoid prejudicing their own interests.

There are a number of grey areas in the *quality* and *duration* of cover, which can be very technical and complex. Few contracts are totally problem-free and it is therefore *difficult to establish if a call is unfair* under the terms of the contract.

ECGD bond risk cover

ECGD offers unfair calling insurance only to United Kingdom exporters in respect of bank demand guarantees relating to eligible contracts for the supply of goods wholly or partly produced or manufactured in the United Kingdom. There is similar cover for eligible contracts for the supply of services and constructional works.

Contracts must be taken by United Kingdom registered companies (or in some circumstances the United Kingdom branch of an overseas company) and must meet ECGD's other usual eligibility criteria, regarding, for example:

(a)   the availability of basic cover for the buyer's country;
(b)   the United Kingdom content in the contract value; and
(c)   the terms of payment and admissibility of goods.

ECGD provides unfair calling cover subject, *inter alia*, to the relevant contract being insured in respect of the pre-credit (*i.e.* pre-shipment) and credit (*i.e.* post-shipment) risks, or where contractual payments are accepted for financing under an ECGD buyer credit facility. The exporter can select the eligible contract for which bond risk cover is required.

There is a requirement that the buyer or end-buyer should be in the public sector. ECGD normally has to agree that the public buyer cause of loss under the credit insurance policy is applicable (*i.e.* failure or refusal on the part of the buyer to fulfil the terms of the contract).

There are, however, some cases (*e.g.* for utility companies and quasi-public bodies) where ECGD will consider giving bond cover when the public buyer cause of loss is not applicable under the basic credit insurance.

ECGD only underwrites risks prior to the risks attaching. They must therefore be approached for bond cover before the exporter is contractually committed to the buyer, although exceptions to this rule may be considered in special circumstances.

What bonds can be covered?

ECGD no longer provides cover against the unfair calling of tender bonds. Such cover is usually obtainable in the private market. However, it can cover any type of bank demand guarantee under a contract. It is important to note, however, that if the exporter wants unfair calling cover in respect of a particular guarantee, ECGD may insist that all the bank demand guarantees under the contract be offered for cover.

Demand guarantees relating to contractual payments (*e.g.* progress or retention payments) are exposed to risks normally covered under ECGD's basic credit insurance policy. Once the payment of these advanced sums has been earned under the contract by the exporter's performance, ECGD's liability is specifically excluded for any bond calls relating to such sums. This means that the exporter must have an effective mechanism to reduce the value of the bond by the amount of the payment *pro rata* to it being earned.

Guarantee wording

Not all bank demand guarantee wordings are acceptable to ECGD. For example, a guarantee which is expressly worded to permit the *restoration of the full amount* of the guarantee after any call (a so-called *"topping-up"* clause) makes it an open-ended liability. Insurers are not in the business of giving open-ended cover.

Depending on the nature of the contract, ECGD may exceptionally give cover for such a bond, but the initial cover would normally extend only to the original stated value and validity of the guarantee. ECGD would prefer the bond to be so worded that its amount could be reduced by the amount paid under any demand without provision for restoration of the value. Additional cover would need to be applied for at the time of any *"topping-up"* and would not necessarily be confirmed.

ECGD tries to avoid creating an *unacceptable open-ended exposure* on the period of bond validity. They would not normally accept bonds which expressly allowed the buyer either to demand an extension to the validity period of the bond, or the right to call the bond if an extension is not agreed (a so-called *"extend or pay"* clause).

However, ECGD recognises that a bond payable on demand is by its very nature often extendable at the unilateral request of the buyer, but does not commit themselves in advance to cover any extension. Nevertheless, in practice it is generally prepared to extend cover at the time of an *extend or pay* demand to avoid a payment of an unreasonable demand. This allows the exporter time to resolve with the buyer any outstanding issues which led to the demand on the bond.

Risks covered by ECGD

ECGD usually agrees to indemnify the exporter in respect of any loss sustained by the exporter by reason of the occurrence of any of the following causes of loss:

(a) ECGD will cover the risk of a demand being made on the bond when there has been no failure by the exporter to comply with:

   (i) any provision of the supply contract; or

  (ii) the provisions of any law (including any order, decree, or regulation having the force of law) in so far as that law affects the performance of the exporter's obligations under the supply contract, and there was no indication by the exporter that there would be such failure.

(b) ECGD's cover can include *fair* calling. Where any such failure by the exporter has occurred or has been indicated by the exporter, ECGD accepts claims for demands made on bonds when the failure is attributable solely to the occurrence of one or more of those causes of loss that ECGD normally insures against under their specific guarantee.

ECGD does not accept liability in respect of risks occurring outside the United Kingdom which are normally insured with commercial insurers in the private market. Typically these include wars, civil wars, hostilities, rebellions, insurrection, earthquakes, volcanic eruption and tidal waves, which in whole or part prevent performance of the supply or construction contract.

(c) After a demand has been made against a bond, ECGD would also normally pay a claim should the buyer fail to pay to the exporter the amount of a final and binding award by a competent court or arbitrator within 30 days of the duly authenticated award.

This is considered a remote cause of loss as the arbitration provisions under a contract do not normally include arbitration on bond-calling. The cause of loss could, however, apply, for example, when the whole amount of a bond had been called for a minor breach of contract, and arbitrators subsequently deemed that part of the bond amount should be returned, yet the buyer failed to do so.

However, ECGD *will not pay a claim* if there has been a failure to obtain any import licence or other authorisation necessary for the performance of the contract under any law, order, decree or regulation in force at the date on which ECGD's liability in respect of the contract commences under the specific guarantee, or if there is any indication by the exporter that there will be such a failure.

This means that the bond should not become effective and enforceable until these authorisations are in place.

It is necessary to advise ECGD of any material changes that could affect their underwriter's perception of risk, such as alterations to the contract or bonds, and to the time within which claims can be lodged.

Other conditions

The cover which ECGD offers is *not open-ended*, therefore the bank demand guarantee has to specify the maximum *amount*, the *currency* in which any payment under it has to be made, the *date it came into effect* and the date of its *expiry* (this could be a specified date or the occurrence of an event described in the contract).

ECGD also tries to restrict the maximum level of cover on bonding on any one contract to 50 per cent. of the total amount of the contract. If the exporter conceded a greater level of bonding to the buyer, then this could remain uninsured. For a prudent exporter, this is a reasonable restriction, as it would be very dangerous to tie up more than 50 per cent. of the contract value in bonds payable on first demand.

There are other conditions, such as those relating to the effect of a bond call on cover under the specific guarantee. For example:

(a)   Following a bond call, cover under the specific guarantee usually ceases, unless ECGD otherwise agrees in writing. There must therefore be a clear *termination provision* in the contract.

(b)   ECGD ceases to be liable for loss in connection with a bond if the exporter, without ECGD's prior consent in writing:

  (i)   departs from the terms of any agreement which relates to the bond and which is made between the exporter and ECGD, or between the exporter and the issuing bank;

  (ii) agrees to any variation in the terms of any such agreement, or the bond; or

  (iii) agrees to, or acquiesces in, any departure from such terms by any party to such agreement.

(c)   ECGD is not under any liability to make any payment in respect of any loss if, at the time the exporter gives a warranty, he is insolvent or bankrupt.

Liability only attaches after the exporter has provided ECGD with satisfactory recourse security.

Under the terms of the exporter's specific guarantee, he is required to prevent or minimise loss, and hold bond recoveries *in trust* for ECGD.

It is important to apply for ECGD bond risk cover at the earliest opportunity, since it cannot be considered if the bond is issued before ECGD have been able to indicate whether or not cover will be available and, if so, on what terms.

It is also advisable to apply as early as possible for credit insurance cover on the related contract, because such cover is a condition precedent to the availability of ECGD bond risk cover.

Private insurance market

The private insurance market issues policies specifically against the un-reasonable or unjustified calling of guarantees payable on demand.

Like ECGD, the private market covers the exporter not only against un-fair calling, but also where he defaults under his contract for specific rea-sons (usually political) beyond his control. The private market also covers him against the failure of the buyer to pay any arbitration award in respect of the bond-calling.

The leading players are:

(i) NCM Credit Insurance Ltd. (NCM), who took over ECGD's short-term insurance services division in 1992;
(ii) Lloyd's of London;
(iii) American International Group (AIG); and
(iv) PanFinancial Insurance Co. Ltd., who entered the political risk arena in 1987.

NCM   Subject to market limits, NCM offer substantially the same cover as ECGD; any differences reflect its private and international status. They specialise in short-term contracts on cash and credit terms. There is no cover for tender guarantees.

NCM are able to insure most non-United Kingdom goods and exporters, as long as they are approached before the exporter is contractually commit-ted to the buyer.

Lloyd's of London   Lloyd's has been market leader for a large part of this insurance, representing a number of independent competing syndic-ates. There are, however, only a few specialist underwriters who are ac-knowledged leaders in the political risk field, and for very large contracts or bonds it is sometimes necessary to obtain the support of all these lead-ers. In some larger deals, therefore, there can be little competition within the Lloyd's market for bond unfair calling cover.

AIG and PanFinancial   AIG and PanFinancial capacity is less than Lloyd's, but adequate for most requirements.

In addition to the above, there are other insurers who participate in this field, such as UIC in New York, PARIS in Paris, Citicorp International Trade Indemnity, Inc., New Jersey and Global Risks, Inc. in Dallas.

Eligibility criteria
Private market insurers do not normally require underlying credit insur-ance and are not restricted as to the origin of the goods or nationality of the exporter.

Any contract which is acceptable under normal underwriting criteria is eligible. The private market is, therefore, able to cover the bond risk in countries where the non-payment risk may be unacceptably high. It also enables the private market to cover bonds which have not been returned or cancelled, long after the underlying contract has been completed.

This ability of the private market to cover exporters of any nationality with no conditions as to the sourcing of goods and services is of considerable help to international traders and contractors who source their goods and services from the most competitive countries.

There are, however, some exceptions:

(a) United States insurers such as the American International Group (AIG) are subject to United States foreign policy considerations. They have therefore been restricted from covering contracts in countries such as Iraq, Iran, Cuba, Vietnam, North Korea, Kampuchea, Laos and Libya, when these markets were on cover with other insurers.

In addition they cannot, without special approval, support contracts for the sale of weapons capable of use for offensive purposes, as opposed to defensive applications.

They are also barred from covering contracts which breach United States boycott legislation. Such countries have included South Africa, Iraq, Cuba, etc.

(b) It is a general principle of the private sector market not to insure an exporter against the acts of his own government. This also applies if the exporter takes a contract through a local subsidiary or associated company. He cannot insure the bonds issued by that subsidiary to buyers in the same country.

His only insurable interest lies in the counter-indemnity (if any) he provides to the subsidiary's local bank issuing the bond.

Risks covered

The cover offered by all three leading insurers in the private sector is very similar, not only to each other but also to that offered by ECGD. In other words, cover is for a bond call when either:

(a) the exporter is not in breach of his obligations under the contract, nor of any law affecting that contract; or, if he is,

(b) when such breach is caused by a specified cause of loss (usually political, such as import/export embargo).

Cover is also offered against a buyer's failure to honour a judicial or arbitration award in respect of a bond calling.

Guarantees expressed in foreign currency

For bonds issued in foreign currencies, the private market issues a policy with amounts set in the same currency as the bond. Underwriters bear the risk, or reap the benefit, of currency fluctuations and there is no charge on the exporter.

Restrictions on cover

Lloyd's underwriters are not technically restricted to contracts with public buyers. However, they are concerned more with political risk than the commercial risk of non-payment, contractual default, insolvency, etc. (see "Exclusions from cover", below), and will therefore, in practice, usually only cover contracts with public or quasi-public buyers, or substantial private buyers.

Lloyd's underwriters are, however, reluctant to cover the increased risk of bonds being called in the maintenance or warranty period. They do not therefore normally cover pure retention bonds, and restrict cover on performance guarantees which continue into the maintenance period.

Exclusions from cover

The principal exclusions are:

(a) *War between any of the Great Powers and/or war between the buyer's country and the exporter's country*

By the former exclusion is meant The People's Republic of China, France, Great Britain and/or any of the British Commonwealth of Nations, the former Soviet Union and the United States; and

(b) *Insolvency and/or financial default*

This exclusion is a source of some difficulty. Lloyd's underwriters are not permitted to issue financial guarantees, and therefore exclude "any claim arising directly or in consequence of insolvency and/or financial default" of the exporter.

(Insolvency or financial default of the exporter which is incidental to, and not a cause of, the bond being called does not preclude a claim against unfair calling of the bond.)

It had always been assumed that it was not the underwriter's intention to exclude *wholesale calling* of bonds in any country which is in financial difficulties. However, this assumption was brought into question for bonds issued in favour of beneficiaries in Iraq.

As a result of the 1990–1991 Gulf War, commercial and financial sanctions were placed on Iraq and her trading partners. As a result, Iraq became technically insolvent, many contracts remained unperformed and many demand bonds remained suspended and uncancelled.

The fear that once sanctions are lifted Iraq, and any other countries in similar situations, would call the suspended bonds in order to generate cash is very real. Banks have been unanimous in their view that they will *not* release the exporter from his counter-indemnity obligations as long as a risk of a bond call remains.

If Iraq and any other such countries did make a general call of all outstanding bonds once controls on payment were removed from banks, it would greatly reduce the capacity of the private bond unfair calling cover market.

Special conditions

Lloyd's include in their policy a condition that the insured exporter should agree to do any additional work reasonably requested by the buyer, and also to grant any extension of the bond requested by the buyer.

Bond validity

Private market underwriters have a horizon on the period for which they grant cover. This is a matter of underwriting discretion rather than statutory authority. They do not normally like to commit themselves to provide cover for a period longer than three years at a time.

In some cases they prefer shorter periods and, in high-risk markets, may refuse to provide cover for periods longer than 12 months. This is because, in certain markets, political risks associated with bond unfair calling cover can change quickly and drastically (*e.g.* Iraq's overnight pre-emptive invasion of Kuwait and the West's economic and military retaliative stance in 1990; the abortive coup in the former USSR in 1991, etc.).

Lloyd's underwriters usually agree to extend the policy for up to 12 months, at a *pro rata* additional premium, in line with extensions to the validity period of the bond. This applies irrespective of whether extensions are formally authorised, or *de facto* as the result of the bond not being returned at expiry, or whether bonds were issued without a defined expiry date or event.

They prefer to see the contract provide specifically for the bond to be returned on expiry, and expect the insured exporter to make every effort to recover the bond as soon as possible. This includes sending his representatives out to the buyer's country, if necessary, to try to physically recover the bond.

Underwriters recognise some moral pressure to extend cover and there are few, if any, examples of insurers actually refusing to extend the validity of a policy, albeit for an additional premium greater than *pro rata* to the original premium rate in certain cases. (ECGD, however, has not been so willing.)

Extend or pay demands

In *extend or pay* demand situations, Lloyd's actually requires the insured exporter to extend for whatever period is required, or as long as Lloyd's is prepared to extend cover. Such demands may be repeated several times. Lloyd's may waive the requirement to extend in circumstances when it is apparent that further extensions are unreasonable.

The AIG policy is silent on the *"extend or pay"* issue, but AIG request consultation in the event of any change to the guarantee and emphasise the need for the insured exporter to take all action necessary to minimise loss. In practice, they take a similar view to Lloyd's.

PanFinancial gives the insured exporter the right "at or shortly before expiration of the original period of the guarantee, in the event of need arising, to procure the extension of the period not to exceed 25 per cent. of the original period of validity". PanFinancial usually will agree in such circumstances to extend cover at a *pro rata* additional premium.

It is important to appreciate that insurance cannot be used as a reason for defying an *extend or pay* demand or for refusing to negotiate under threat of a bond call.

Premium costs

There is no fixed scale of premium rates in the private sector. Rates vary not only between the countries of risk but also between exporters and individual contracts.

In the private sector, the premium rates are a function of many factors:

(a) Country analysis takes into account the political, economic and social/ethnic/religious factors in the buyer's territory.

(b) Underwriters also have regard to the:
   (i) technical and commercial competence of the exporter;
   (ii) complexity of the contract;
   (iii) length of the risk period;
   (iv) strategic importance or priority of the contract;
   (v) amount of competition; and
   (vi) exporter's experience of the country concerned and particularly of the buyer.

   The reason for this is that any demand, unfair or not, is likely to involve the underwriters in the expense of assessing a claim and they therefore wish to ensure that the chances of such demands are minimal. Hence the close attention paid to the exporter's competence and bargaining position.

(c) Other factors which are not readily apparent to exporters include:
   (i) the amount of capacity left for that country (underwriters will sell scarce capacity for whatever price they can get, on the basis of supply and demand);
   (ii) their allegiance to the client and vice versa (underwriters give preference to exporters who bring them a regular flow of good business); and
   (iii) claims experience.

Annex III—List of Countries in Which Beneficiaries Normally Require a Local Bank Guarantee

Abu Dhabi	Dubai	Libya	Saudi Arabia
Algeria	Egypt	Malaysia	Sri Lanka
Bahrain	Ethiopia	Malta	Sudan
Bangladesh	Greece	Mexico	Syria
Bolivia	Indonesia	Morocco	Taiwan
Brazil	Iran	Nepal	Thailand
Burma	Iraq	Oman	Tunisia
Chile	Jordan	Pakistan	Turkey
Colombia	Korea (South)	Peru	UAE
Cyprus (Greek)	Kuwait	Philippines	Yemen Republic
Cyprus (Turkey)	Lebanon	Qatar	

(Source: Midland Bank plc.)

CHAPTER 9

CORPORATE GUARANTEES

Many companies try to avoid the problems of bank demand guarantees by persuading their buyer to accept instead the exporter's *parent company's guarantee*, or the guarantee of a more substantial sister subsidiary or joint venture partner. These shall be referred to as corporate guarantees.

They consider that they have more control over their costs and the risk of an unfair claim if they can persuade their buyer to accept a *corporate guarantee*.

They also do this to save bank charges and to avoid using up finite banking resources. They believe that, in the event of a call on the corporate guarantee, they will be in a better position to resist payment of the demand, especially in a dispute situation.

Unlike the situation with a bank guarantee payable on demand, the exporter, at the risk of his reputation, will be able to hold up payment to the beneficiary, pending a court or arbitral ruling.

However, *the benefits are illusory*. Whereas by using a bank the exporter's exposure is finite to the extent of the maximum commitment of the bank, with a corporate guarantee there is no certainty that the limits of the financial obligation intended by the corporate cannot be breached. This could then possibly put his entire resources on the line, not just those of a lesser subsidiary, unless the guarantee contains effective limitation of liability clauses.

At best, there is considerable uncertainty as to the extent of the corporate's liability. It depends on the wording of the guarantee, *i.e.* whether it is written in the terms of a guarantee or an indemnity, and the extent to which it accurately reflects the protective clauses in the contract.

For example, there is the risk that, after the guarantee has been paid in full, or the underlying contract has been completely performed, the beneficiary may then seek compensation for additional costs or losses. In some circumstances, *the corporate's exposure could be open-ended*.

Minimising the Risks

The best protection is to ensure that the beneficiary physically releases and

213

returns the corporate guarantee as soon as possible. There are four possible scenarios when the guarantee is subject to English law:

(i)   Where there is an express provision for return and cancellation, there should be no argument that the corporate's liability is discharged.

A typical clause would be worded as follows:

"This guarantee shall be returned to [the corporate] immediately upon payment in full of the guarantee amount by [the subsidiary] or by [the corporate] under the terms of this guarantee, and [the corporate] shall thereupon be released from all its obligations hereunder.

If the document provides for return but nothing is said about cancellation, this should, nevertheless, be regarded as discharging the corporate's liability."

(ii)   Where there is an expiry date (or there is provision under which the corporate can give notice of termination), and no provisions about return and cancellation, nor provisions which provide for, or imply, a continuing liability, the corporate would normally be released from liability after such date has passed.

Whenever possible, the guarantee document should stipulate not only that its validity expires on a stated date, but also that all claims made thereunder must be submitted to the corporate by such date or within a specified period after such date.

(iii) As (ii), but with no expiry date, or notice provision. Where there are no clues at all in the document as to whether the corporate remains under a continuing liability, the position is as follows:

(a)   The corporate will be discharged from liability once the guaranteed payment has been made in full or the underlying contract performed (see *Perry* v. *National Provincial Bank* [1910] 1 Ch. 464 at 477 (C.A.)) if the document is a guarantee and not a contract of indemnity, but subject to (c) below.

(b)   If the wording of the guarantee can be construed as a *contract of indemnity*, the corporate will remain liable to make good any loss suffered by the other party to the guarantee document, *e.g.* where the subsidiary defaults on its contract and the beneficiary makes losses as a result (see *Goulston Discount Co. Ltd.* v. *Clark* [1967] 1 All E.R. 61 (C.A.)).

(c)   In either case, where the payment by the subsidiary is subsequently set aside or is, for some reason, ineffective, the corporate will remain liable, *e.g.* where payment is set aside for fraudulent preference (see *Petty* v. *Cooke* (1871) L.R. 6 Q.B. 790).

(iv)   The guarantee document may contain provisions which indicate a continuing liability or which could imply a continuing liability.

It is obvious that if the guarantee document indicates a continuing liability after payment of the guaranteed amount or performance of the underlying contract, the corporate will be at risk, although, as time passes, the risk diminishes.

Any such express provision should be qualified by imposing a long-stop date after which all liability ceases, *e.g.* six months after payment of the guaranteed amount or final completion of the underlying contract. This will allow for any claims of *fraudulent preference* to be presented in time (see scenario (iii)(c) above).

If there is no express provision, there may be some other provisions which imply a *continuing liability* if the guarantee document is not returned. For example:

(a)   a provision that the guarantee given is irrevocable;

(b)   a provision that the guarantee is the property of the beneficiary; or

(c)   a "sweep-up" provision under which it is provided that the corporate's liability shall not be affected by any act or omission on the part of the beneficiary which, but for such provision, would or might operate to discharge the corporate from its obligations under the guarantee document.

Wherever possible, the corporate guarantor should prefer to seek to achieve scenarios (i) and (ii) and strive to avoid situations in which there may be an indefinite liability such as (iii) and (iv). (Source: Peter L. Clarke, former legal adviser, BICC plc.)

Corporate Guidelines and Control of Risks

In view of the possible open-ended risk created by issuing loosely-worded corporate guarantees, corporates would be advised to introduce clear internal guidelines in relation to the offering or giving of corporate guarantees.

For example, these could typically be as follows[1]:

(i)   The provision of a corporate guarantee should be resisted wherever possible and only given where it is commercially important to do so. A corporate guarantee should never be offered or given as a matter of routine.

(ii) The subsidiary should seek consent from the corporate head office before the decision is taken to offer or give a corporate guarantee.

(iii) Subject to obtaining such consent, the decision to give a guarantee should be taken by the subsidiary's senior officer having delegated authority to approve tenders/contracts.

---

[1] Agents automatically commit the principal corporate to the obligations and liabilities assumed by them. A corporate guarantee should therefore not be necessary in respect of contracts taken by agents.

  (iv) Every effort should be made towards ensuring that the wording of
the guarantee does not undermine protections contained in the underlying contract for the benefit of the exporter.

  (v) Where a corporate guarantee in onerous form is requested in support of a contract with a company which trades as agent of the corporate, the policy should, wherever possible, be to resist the request
and instead to take the contract concerned in the name of the
corporate.

The decision to offer or give a corporate guarantee is a commercial one
and the following questions should be considered on each occasion in respect of the transaction:

  (i) Does the prospective contract involve the supply of highly complex
equipment or impose penalties for failure to achieve guaranteed
performance levels?

  (ii) Is the guarantee or delivery period unusual?

  (iii) Does the contract represent a particularly large obligation in relation to the subsidiary's balance sheet?

  (iv) Is the contract particularly onerous?

  (v) Does the contract cover the activities of more than one subsidiary in
the group?

  (vi) Is the subsidiary dependent upon technical assistance from the corporate parent and/or another subsidiary?

  (vii) To what extent is the subsidiary reliant on the efforts or skills of
unrelated third parties, *e.g.* suppliers, sub-contractors and joint
venturers, and is there sufficient contractual protection should they
default?

  (viii) What are the likely consequences of a default by the subsidiary?

  (ix) Is there adequate insurance cover?

  (x) What other safeguards will the buyer require, *e.g.* by way of retentions from the contract price, or performance bonds?

The above considerations should also apply to *omnibus or blanket guarantees*
covering an entire course of trading with a buyer, rather than an isolated
contract. In no event must an omnibus or blanket guarantee be expressed
to be *irrevocable*.

Letters of Comfort

The letter of comfort is a financial security of doubtful legal efficacy. It is often given by the parent company of a subsidiary to assure a buyer or a financial institution that the subsidiary will honour its contractual and
financial obligations.

Letters of comfort are generally simple to issue. Their terms are often vague, and any obligation is usually expressed in indirect terms.

Some letters of comfort are intended to contain no legal obligation, but only declare an *awareness* of the underlying transaction, be it a contract or credit facility. Such letters of comfort are normally intended to be *binding only in honour*.

Many contain a general statement of policy of always assuring the buyer/addressee that the corporate's subsidiary meets its obligations when required to. Others state that the parent will do what it considers best to keep its subsidiary in good financial health.

Yet others say that the parent will do whatever is necessary to ensure that the subsidiary performs its specific obligations. These give rise to a direct claim against the parent by the addressee, but only after exhaustion of the latter's remedies against the subsidiary and perhaps after years of litigation.

They were originally developed as a compromise where the prospective corporate guarantor preferred to keep its financial support off its balance sheet as a contingent liability.

They can be considered as providing direct recourse to the parent company only if it can be shown that the parent did not comply with its obligations and such non-compliance caused default by the subsidiary.

However, the French Banking Association, in a circular dated July 2, 1975, warned that *such devices were of questionable validity and effectiveness*.

In the United Kingdom case of *Kleinwort Benson* v. *Malaysia Mining Corporation Berhad* [1989] 1 W.L.R. 379 it was made clear that a comfort letter may be legally binding and give rise to a *liability, actual or contingent*, on the company which issues it. Brief details of this case are as follows:

Malaysia Mining Corporation Berhad (MMC) gave Kleinwort Benson Ltd. (KB) a comfort letter as part of the negotiations of a loan facility granted to MMC's subsidiary, MMC Metals Ltd. (Metals). The letter included a paragraph which stated: "It is our policy to ensure that the business of MMC Metals Ltd. is at all times in a position to meet its liabilities to you under the above arrangements."

Metals later ceased trading and went into liquidation owing KB £10m. KB wrote to MMC and requested them to ensure that KB received forthwith the payments due to them.

MMC renounced liability, claiming that the statement in the letter of comfort was not intended by either party to be legally binding. The case went to court, where it was held that the statement, even though it was not a guarantee, did give rise to contractual liability and MMC were in breach of contract. One of the points made in the judgment was that, in business matters, it is a prerequisite for defeating the presumption that such a stipulation has contractual force that it be expressed to the contrary "so precisely that outsiders may have no difficulty understanding what they mean" (see *Rose and Frank* v. *Crompton & Bros.* (1923) 2 K.B. 261).

KB were awarded £10m plus interest of £2.3m.

The case was decided by the High Court. It follows that any corporate which wishes to issue a letter of comfort that is not legally binding should ensure that it is adequately drafted to take this decision into account. This has sometimes been termed a *letter of discomfort*. (Source: *The Treasurer*, April 1988.)

Corporate Balance Sheet

Provisions for liabilities, actual or contingent, which may result from letters of comfort issued should be considered in the light of this case.

In the United Kingdom, the treatment of a contingency existing at the balance sheet date is determined by its *expected outcome*. In addition to accruals under the fundamental *concept of prudence*, contingent losses should also be accrued where it is probable that a future event will confirm a loss that can be estimated with reasonable accuracy when the accounts are prepared.

From the balance sheet point of view, bank and surety guarantees, corporate guarantees and letters of comfort often only get mentioned in the notes to the annual report saying that *the level of guarantees is not material, and have been issued in the normal course of business.* No amount is mentioned unless the auditors consider the level of such guarantees to be particularly high for the business, or where it is probable that a future event will confirm a loss that can be estimated with reasonable accuracy when the accounts are prepared.

The value of good record-keeping and good management and control of guarantees and letters of comfort is most appreciated at the time of *mergers and divestments*. These contingent liabilities can play a key part in negotiations. Often purchasers of guaranteed subsidiaries will refuse to take on the liabilities of the former parent company, which can find itself responsible for its ex-subsidiaries' performance, but *no longer having the authority to control it*.

This exposure can be controlled by being in a position to negotiate the transfer of each individual guarantee. The price of the corporate sale will reflect the obligations assumed by the purchaser and those remaining with the former parent company.

Chapter 11 covers the grading, recording, monitoring, reporting and controlling of bank demand guarantee risks.

CHAPTER 10

INTERNATIONAL CODE OF PRACTICE

"...What started off originally as a guarantee strictly so called, has over the years become something entirely different, usually called nowadays an 'on demand' bond or guarantee, simple or otherwise. The balance between the Principal (the contractor) and the Beneficiary (the client) has swung from one end of the spectrum to the other. The name of the document still has the words 'guarantee' and 'performance' in it...but the concern of the principal is the 'on demand' bit. The chrysalis has turned into a wasp with a fierce sting and not a honey bee carrying (beside a necessary sting) some sweetness for both parties."
(E. Lightburn, Solicitor, Trafalgar House plc.)

Chapter 8 explained where many of the risks, costs and other problems experienced by exporters arise in connection with bank demand guarantees. It also explained some of the contractual, administrative and legal solutions currently available to help minimise exposure to loss.

This Chapter will explain how banks are also exposed to uncertainties, risks and costs, and the efforts that have been made by the International Chamber of Commerce (ICC), the United Nations Commission on International Trade Law (UNCITRAL) and the Committee of London and Scottish Bankers (CLSB) (subsequently merged into the British Bankers' Association (BBA)) to bring the issue and use of bank demand guarantees within a recognisable uniform procedure and structure so that the risks, costs and problems can be identified, quantified and controlled.

The Annexes to this Chapter contain the uniform rules published by the ICC relating to *dependent, accessory guarantees* (the 325 Rules—published in 1978) and *independent, demand guarantees* (the 458 Rules—published in 1992).

Recognising and Controlling Risks

It is not only the exporter who is exposed to risks and related costs. Banks, which once considered guarantees as simply a useful source of fee income, generated at low cost, requiring little expertise on their part, came to realise that they were exposed to client- and balance-sheet-related risks.

As overseas buyers began insisting on bank guarantees payable on *first demand,* the true cost and risk of the growing level of outstanding demand guarantees on banks' balance sheets became apparent. This exposure was further highlighted by *reserve asset ratio* considerations of central banks which focused attention on the balance sheet cost of issuing bank guarantees and leaving them uncancelled after the related contract was completed.

Since December 1989, the United Kingdom clearing banks have been required by Bank of England regulations to operate within the Basle Agreement. This Agreement affects the way in which banks account for guarantees in their balance sheet. In practical terms it means that the banks are required to hold the necessary cash reserves to cover them, reserves which inevitably they cannot utilise to transact other business. (Source: Midland Bank Plc, "Export Today".)

The effect of this varies from bank to bank, reflecting the structure and utilisation of each particular balance sheet, the level of bonding and spread of business between markets, and the nature of the bank demand guarantee.

Other risks proved less easy to identify and quantify. For example, banks have problems at the best of times assessing the financial strength of the exporter and the value of his counter-indemnity. On most occasions they have only the historic information contained in the exporter's published balance sheets. From this, they have to forecast the exporter's *creditworthiness* during the life of the bank guarantee and the value of his *counter-indemnity.*

The security of a counter-indemnity signed by the exporter when the bank guarantee is issued is *acceptable at the time of issue*; thereafter it becomes uncertain, as it can diminish if the exporter is adversely affected by bad trading results as a result of competition or in times of economic recession.

Requests from beneficiaries to extend the validity of bank guarantees can greatly increase the period of exposure by the bank to the exporter beyond the original expiry date.

Once a bank has a reasonable understanding of its risks and costs, it can set its fee. It has to take a number of different considerations into account. Most fees are assessed on the basis that, if a bank demand guarantee were called, it would be a *valid and fair claim* and that the security put up by the exporter would be adequate to protect the bank. However, the probability and impact of an *unfair demand* on an exporter is difficult, if not impossible, to assess as it depends on when the unfair demand is made (*i.e.* during or after the period of the contract), how large the claim is, and the financial strength of the exporter at the time of a demand. An unfair demand can lead to the insolvency of the exporter.

There are other factors that banks have to consider before agreeing to issue a guarantee; for example, the fact that the larger companies are in a commercially competitive position to pressurise them to prevent or delay the payment of what these companies may consider an *unfair demand.*

The question whether a bank should pay an obviously unfair claim, even if the wording states that the guarantee is payable on first demand without objection, is difficult to resolve. Some banks are more prepared than others to *prevaricate* before paying a demand to allow time for the exporter to resolve his differences with the beneficiary. Others have felt more inclined to *honour* their obligation to the beneficiary immediately and to claim reimbursement under the exporter's counter-indemnity. All have their own policy and interpretation of the wording of the guarantee. The *international reputation* of a bank is always at stake, and it can incur legal costs defending it.

Following the Gulf War and the imposition of sanctions on Iraq, there was considerable uncertainty about outstanding bank demand guarantees. Following E.C. Regulation 3541/92: [1992] O.J. L361/1, passed on December 10, 1992, many banks decided to stop charging commission on outstanding guarantees in Iraqi hands, and to cease setting the value of those guarantees against the exporter's bank facilities. This was a one-off solution to a big problem. What banks and exporters needed was a blanket solution for lots of individual problems.

Until recently, there have been no workable international ground rules all banks could use. Many have had to take legal advice and action at considerable cost in order to clarify their legal obligations towards the exporter and the beneficiary in respect of guarantees payable on demand, issued independent of the underlying supply contract.

Need for International Uniform Rules

As early as 1964, the International Chamber of Commerce (ICC) Commission on Banking Technique and Practice began to concern itself with bank guarantees and related problems. From March-September 1968 onwards, a joint Working Party, set up by that Commission and the ICC Commission on International Commercial Practice, undertook a study.

Just prior to that, in January/February 1968, the United Nations Commission on International Trade Law (UNCITRAL), at its first session, decided to include in its agenda the subject of guarantees and sureties in international trade operations, at a more general level.

The following year the Secretariat, in preparation for the second UNCITRAL session, submitted a report (A/CN9/20, February 17, 1969) under the heading *Preliminary study of guarantees and sureties in international payments.* This report contained exhaustive developments on bank guarantees.

The Hungarian delegation proposed at this second session that the ICC should be requested to launch an inquiry into the issues raised by bank guarantees and to draft appropriate uniform rules governing them. UNCITRAL endorsed this proposal.

The ICC, thus entrusted with an UNCITRAL mandate, asked Professor

Lars Hjerner, a Swedish lawyer, to draft uniform rules to regulate such guarantees. Some rules did already exist in a few countries, notably Turkey, Egypt, Lebanon, Burma, the former Czechoslovakia and the former Yugoslavia, but none of an equitable or internationally acceptable nature. The Commercial Bank of Syria, for example, in its Resolution No. 4407 of May 1973, avails itself of the right to honour claims for payment under a guarantee *regardless of whether such claims are made within the validity period or after the expiration of the latter.* In one case, a claim was paid even though the actual guarantee itself had been returned to the issuer.

The aim of the ICC was to achieve a *fair balance* between the legitimate interests of the parties concerned—the beneficiary, principal and guarantor. This objective was to prove difficult, if not impossible, to achieve. The main contention was whether or not any rules should recognise *simple demand* guarantees. It had to moralise on their use and to outlaw their misuse on the part of beneficiaries.

The ICC's Commissions on Banking and on Commercial Practice worked for some 12 years to standardise the terms under which guarantees ought to be issued. Only after extensive consultation and drafting did they finally, in 1978, publish the ICC Uniform Rules for Contract Guarantees, Publication No. 325 (the 325 Rules—see Annex I).

The objective was to secure a uniformity of practice in international trade. The ICC also published a supporting brochure, ICC Publication No. 406, *Model Forms for Issuing Contract Guarantees*, containing specimens of guarantees together with model requests for payment under such guarantees.

The 325 Rules were heavily biased towards the control of guarantees payable only on *proven or admitted default.* They were intended to apply to different types of guarantees, bonds, indemnities, sureties or similar undertakings dependent on, and subordinate to, as well as independent of, the contract given on behalf of the exporter by banks, surety companies and other third parties.

They were aimed at regulating the legal relationship between the principal (exporter), guarantor and beneficiary with respect to the three major forms of guarantee: tender, performance and repayment guarantee.

Their intention was to constitute a reasonable compromise between the conflicting interests of the parties concerned (see Stumpf, "Einheitliche Richtlinien für Vertragsgarantien (Bankgarantien) der Internationalen Handelskammer" [1979] R.I.W. 1–4).

However, largely under the influence of the Nordic countries, notably Sweden, the 325 Rules were drafted in a form *hostile to first demand guarantees*, in spite of warnings from many who argued that it was pointless to ignore the reality of the increasing international use of such guarantees.

The 325 Rules linked the guarantee in several crucial points (for example, expiry) to the underlying contract. As a result, the *autonomy, or independence, of the guarantee was virtually abolished* and therefore of little interest to banks which had no wish to be drawn into the contractual conflicts of the buyer and exporter.

The 325 Rules tried to impose wholly new procedures for which there was neither enthusiasm nor broad acceptance in the international market, and which were anachronistic and not generally workable. By the time they were published, they no longer reflected normal international market practice which, by then, had made clear that such rules were inappropriate for *independent guarantees*. As drafted, they could only be effectively used for guarantees payable on simple or on first demand by specifically excluding Article 9, "Documentation to Support Claim" (see Annex I).

They placed on the bank duties and obligations of examination and verification which not only were outside the bank's scope of business but were also impossible to fulfil on the part of the bank.

Contrary to the stated principle of fair compromise, the 325 Rules were entirely one-sided, favouring the seller's/exporter's position, to the disadvantage of the buyer and banks.

In the event, the 325 Rules were not widely adopted, although some business circles, notably in Sweden, claim to have managed to have them accepted in some countries.

As far as the banks were concerned, there was a need to emphasise the *independence* of the guarantee from the underlying commercial contract; otherwise a surety bond would be the appropriate instrument, not a bank guarantee.

This concept of *independence* is similar to the relationship between commercial contracts and letters of credit and standby letters of credit, governed by the internationally-recognised ICC publication, the Uniform Customs and Practice for Documentary Credits 1983 Revision (ICC Publication No. 400 (No. 500 from January 1, 1994), "UCP").

The UCP is perhaps the ICC's biggest success. It is not only accepted universally by the world's banks, but also referred to frequently as the authoritative guidelines when disputes reach the courts. Ideally, the banks needed a similar set of rules for the *simple and first demand guarantees* which were featuring increasingly on their balance sheets, and which were causing great anxiety to their customers because of the risk of unfair calling and abuse.

Abuse by Beneficiaries

Exporters simply cannot trade if cash, which is paid to them through the contract, and which becomes an important part of the contract's and company's cashflow and working capital, is simply taken away again on first demand for no other reason than that the beneficiary is capricious or simply thinks the exporter is not properly performing the contract. That is the formula for cashflow problems and the path to insolvency.

The aim of the exporter is to avoid *undeserved financial loss* by preventing the bank paying a claim or debiting his account. The conflicting aim of the buyer is to *obtain payment on first demand* without contestation or delay. The ideal bank guarantee strikes a fair balance between this conflict of interests. What constitutes an ideal bank guarantee, however, depends on the individual circumstances. Ideal wording in one situation may not be suitable in another.

The advantage of *simple demand* wording for the bank is that the guarantee is *autonomous* from the supply contract between the exporter and his buyer. It is easy to handle, and the bank does not get directly involved in disputes between the parties to the supply contract. However, without legal precedent or uniform rules within which to operate, the bank can find itself in the middle of a *dispute* between its customer, the exporter, and the beneficiary for an *unfair or abusive demand* on the bank guarantee.

Abuse, or the risk of abuse, of guarantees by beneficiaries has been observed in those countries:

(a) relatively newly involved in international trade;
(b) which are short of foreign currency;
(c) where buyers try to improve their financial situation;
(d) where buyers try to improve their negotiating position; or
(e) where there is political motive.

In the main, unfair demands come from either private buyers whose business ethics are below internationally acceptable standards, or from government or quasi-government buyers adopting the ethics, attitude or policies of their political leaders.

In the event of an unfair call, the exporter is faced with the question of how to prevent the payment of an unfair claim. With *bank demand guarantees* the role of the bank is to comply with a demand for payment if it is in accordance with the wording of the bank guarantee. It is therefore important for the exporter to react quickly before the bank makes payment, because recovery of any money, once paid, is virtually impossible for reasons of legal jurisdiction and exchange control regulations in the beneficiary's country.

The prevention of unfair calls is extremely difficult, especially if the help of a court in the beneficiary's country is required, or if the beneficiary is a foreign state enterprise or authority (see Böckstiegel, "Besondere Probleme der Schiedsgerichtsbarkeit zwischen Privatunternehmen und auslandischen Staaten oder Staatsunternehmen" [1975] N.J.W. 1577 *et seq.*).

Exporters have increasingly resorted to summary legal proceedings to try to prevent banks from honouring their binding and irrevocable obligation to the beneficiary to pay. European courts have been asked to *interpret the responsibilities of the banks* in cases where exporters alleged claims were unfair. Initially the interpretations varied as European law at the time was lacking in precedent and void of case history.

The wording of most demand guarantees, and the circumstances surrounding each claim, are rarely the same or even consistent as regards their basic content. Uncertainties cause banks problems. In the absence of internationally-accepted guidelines on the minimum content and interpretation of the responsibilities of a bank under a demand guarantee, many banks have felt that, whatever the moral issues, they had to honour any prima facie proper claim.

The courts supported the banks on this. Chapter 4 gives a number of references to various cases, most of which conclude that the bank must pay a claim made in accordance with the guarantee wording unless there is a clear case of *fraud* or *manifest abuse*.

However, a call is not necessarily *abusive* if defences have to be examined by way of interpretation of the underlying contract between the exporter and buyer. This would defeat the purpose of a demand guarantee.

It is true that the exporter probably has a *counterclaim* against the buyer under the supply contract should the buyer claim on the guarantee when the contractual preconditions for such a claim have not been met, but he cannot be absolutely sure of this. Even in rare cases where it is possible to proceed under the exporter's or the contract's law, there is often the danger that a judgment cannot be enforced on the overseas buyer.

The question arises how best to prevent, or resist, an unfair claim, recognising that prevention is always better than any subsequent legal remedy to avoid a sudden cash outflow.

Many banks have found themselves in sympathy with the exporter, but bound by the wording of their guarantee to the beneficiary. Experience to date is that, with the courts unsympathetic to the exporter's plight, few have benefited by more than a just a few days' delay in the payment of the claim as a result of taking legal action.

In the light of this background, some of the leading banks in the United Kingdom under the auspices of the Committee of London and Scottish Banks (CLSB), having rejected the 325 Rules as offering only very limited application, realised they needed to bring some unified discipline to the issue of demand guarantees and the payment of claims. What was needed was a set of *uniform rules or a code of practice* covering independent demand guarantees that could be understood and accepted internationally by all parties to a demand guarantee.

They began work independently on a set of draft rules that would find acceptance with, and be adopted by, the United Kingdom banks. It was in their own interest, and also in the interests of their customer, the exporter, to avoid confusion, ambiguity and disputes.

The 458 Rules

On a totally separate initiative, early in 1980, an ICC Working Party was set up to look into the question of *stand-by letters of credit and demand guarantees* (see summary record of the meeting of April 24, 1980 of the ICC Commission on Banking Technique and Practice (Document No. 470/366, p. 10)).

Subsequently, at the beginning of 1981, the ICC Banking Commission, strongly supported by the Commission on International Commercial Practice, acknowledged that the 325 Rules were not universally acceptable. Having been intended for *dependent* guarantees, they were not capable of preventing abusive calls under *first demand guarantees* (summary record of the meeting of May 26, 1981 (Document No. 460/272, p. 2)).

In December 1981, the ICC decided to prepare (again jointly by the two Commissions) a separate code of practice for independent guarantees payable on *simple or first demand* issued to support commercial contracts.

Initially the drafting made slow progress, because there were serious conflicts in the respective interests and objectives of the various members of the ICC Working Party (mainly banks versus industry—initially beneficiaries were not directly represented). Under the chairmanship of Dr. Rudolf von Graffenried these were eventually overcome and broad consensus reached at a meeting in Frankfurt am Main in April 1983 which produced a joint draft paper entitled *Draft Code of Practice for demand guarantees and bonds which are issued to support commercial contracts* (Documents No. 470/407, 460/290).

On May 4, 1983 the ICC sent this joint draft to all its national committees for comment.

The uniform rules were to be based on a series of objectives. The initial joint draft contained, *inter alia*, the following important provisions which were capable of reducing the number of unfair calls:

(a) The liability of a guarantor should not exceed the maximum sum defined in the terms of the guarantee, and the bank guarantee would expire for claims on the date specified within its terms for expiry.

(b) A guarantee would expire, notwithstanding any expiry provision contained in it, on the day that a claim from the beneficiary for the maximum sum is paid to the beneficiary by the guarantor.

(c) The expiry of a guarantee may only be deferred or extended at the request of the beneficiary with the agreement of the guarantor (and instructing party if any) and the principal (exporter).

(d) Where notice of a claim is made by teletransmission, a signed written notice in confirmation must be received by the guarantor not later than 14 days following the receipt of such notice; otherwise, the beneficiary loses all right to receive the sum claimed. (*This requirement for confirmation was subsequently excluded from later drafts.*)

(e) On receipt of a claim from a beneficiary that satisfies the terms of a guarantee, a guarantor would be obliged to pay the beneficiary the amount of the claim without argument and, unless a guarantee contains a provision to defer payment, payment should be made on the seventh business day following the receipt of the claim by the guarantor. (*This time constraint was subsequently dropped from later drafts.*)

(f) The guarantor, or the instructing party when involved, should give notice of the receipt of a claim to a principal. In the event of an unfair call, the seven-day period, also called a "cooling-off period", would give the exporter an opportunity to clarify any misunderstandings with the beneficiary and endeavour to persuade him to withdraw his claim. (*The concept of a "cooling-off period" was dropped from later drafts.*)

(g) The written claim of the beneficiary should contain a statement specifying the nature of the default by a principal which gives rise to the claim and should be supported by any additional documents or certificates which may be stipulated in the guarantee.

Such additional documents or certificates must be received by the guarantor not later than 14 days following the receipt of the claim; otherwise, the beneficiary loses all right to receive the sum claimed. (*This requirement was subsequently excluded from later drafts.*)

It was accepted that:

(a) guarantors had to accept the *apparent authenticity* of documents, including any claim documents;

(b) there was always the possibility that forged documents might be presented to support a claim, but that a clever forgery would defeat even a careful bank officer/guarantor;

(c) the bank officer should not be made responsible for this. If an exporter wanted a proven document, notarised certificate, etc., then this needed to be defined and asked for in the guarantee itself;

(d) banks need a reasonable time to check the claim and any supporting documents against the guarantee; and

(e) it was in nobody's interest to have a quick, but wrong, decision. Rather it should be acceptable to everyone that the decision be slightly slower, but correct.

There were strong representations that the principal (the exporter) should have the right to have any statements, claims and other documents made available to him after the bank had paid a claim under a guarantee. Such documents and statements would not be sent for approval but only in the interests of fairness, so that if the principal felt aggrieved he could pursue a legal case against the beneficiary through the courts.

The aim of banks as guarantors was to try to avoid being involved in any dispute between the beneficiary and the exporter. The banks needed to know when they were liable to pay.

A second draft was produced in 1986. A fundamental point at issue was whether the ICC should formally recognise that a guarantee payable on first *simple* demand, without objection or contestation, was a morally acceptable document to be issued and put in the hands of a beneficiary.

Swedish bankers and their lawyers, who had played a leading role in the drafting and publication of the 325 Rules, strongly opposed the very concept of a separate set of rules covering first demand guarantees. They, and some United Kingdom exporters and contractors, wanted such guarantees *banned* by the ICC or, at worst, brought more closely within the scope of an amendment to the already published 325 Rules.

This opinion did not gain acceptance with other international bankers and their lawyers, particularly in Germany, Belgium, the United Kingdom and France, who were pragmatic in recognising that *independent, first demand guarantees* were already an established fact of international trade.

Many exporters and contractors recognised the futility of trying to turn the clock back to the days of a seller's market. Despite its worldwide recognition and standing, the ICC would not attempt to suggest a ban on *simple demand* guarantees (nor in fact does it pretend to exercise any such powers).

Also in 1986, the ICC National Committee—ICC United Kingdom— initiated a movement to have new rules written from scratch to reflect the reality of the market place. The British banks joined in the drafting, as did a number of international banks represented in London. They used as a working basis the draft code of practice for demand bonds mentioned above drawn up by the CLSB. The CLSB elaborated on their original draft, and presented a revised version in 1987, the *Code of Practice for Demand Guarantees and Bonds—1987 Edition* (May 14, 1987), for consideration via the ICC, having no formal presence of its own.

Selected articles from the ICC and CLSB drafts were extracted and a third *composite draft* discussed by a joint Working Party, including members of the ICC Commission on Banking Technique and Practice and the Commission on International Commercial Practice, meeting in Paris in September 1987.

After much effort and discussion, the ICC produced a single agreed draft which the CLSB subsequently agreed could form the basis of a new set of rules. ICC Paris took over the final drafting and international co-ordination.

On October 13, 1987 at a meeting of the Commission on Banking Technique and Practice (Document No. 470/510, p. 3), the Swedish Bankers' Association agreed that while Swedish banks were opposed to the use of first demand guarantees, they recognised that they could not avoid them, since they existed in practice, and the competitive pressures could put Swedish exporters at a disadvantage.

The reform trend was further characterised by the efforts of the banking representatives to make the rules for guarantees as similar as possible to the internationally-recognised ICC publication referred to previously, the Uniform Customs and Practice for Documentary Credits 1983 Revision (ICC Publication No. 400 (No. 500 from January 1, 1994), "UCP"). The underlying change acknowledged that a demand guarantee can only be properly invoked if the exporter is in default of his tender or contractual obligations—while at the same time the bank is not concerned with the fact of default, only with documents.

One of the major arguments to bring the new rules, as far as possible, into line with those covering documentary credits was that the so-called *stand-by letters of credit* are, almost without exception, obligatory for use in the United States in place of bank guarantees, as banks' operational mandates there prohibit them from issuing the latter type of instrument on behalf of customers. Stand-by letters of credit are also used extensively in Japan and, to a lesser (though growing) extent, in Europe. (See Brooke Wunnicke and Diane B. Wunnicke, *Stand-by Letters of Credit*, published in Denver, Colorado, United States.)

The two ICC Commissions completed their draft in September 1989, and, using the international network of the ICC National Committees and some affiliated organisations, it was submitted to a wide and extensive consultative process involving many national chambers of commerce, banks, exporters, contractors and beneficiaries. This was to ensure that their views and interests could be properly reflected in the rules when published in order to ensure widespread acceptance and adoption.

The draft of the rules was submitted to a meeting of UNCITRAL's Working Party in November 1988 for comment. In May 1989, at its 22nd session, UNCITRAL reviewed and approved its Working Party's report (A/CN9/316, December 12, 1988).

After considerable international input of views and opinions, some of which were conflicting, a smaller special Working Party was set up under the chairmanship of Professor Roy Goode to engineer a final draft which reconciled the various viewpoints of countries such as Japan, Germany and Sweden. This was circulated in April 1991 and approved for publication by the ICC Executive Board on December 3, 1991 and adopted and published in April 1992 as the ICC Uniform Rules for Demand Guarantees (ICC Publication No. 458) (the 458 Rules—see Annex II). It was subsequently supported by ICC Publication No. 510, *Guide to the Rules for Demand Guarantees*.

Application of the 458 Rules

The 458 Rules, while embracing *simple demand* bonds, discourage their use in principle. However, some exporters say that the 458 Rules will prove of little value to them because competition puts the buyer in a strong negotiating position. The buyer would ask for, and expect to get, a simple demand guarantee to his own requirements in almost every case.

In answer to this, the ICC hopes that, once beneficiaries get to understand the 458 Rules, they will come to accept simple demand guarantees as being inequitable in international business and also not needed to secure their genuine interests, and so will cease to ask for them.

The 458 Rules should prove acceptable because they:

(a)   are short and written in clear plain language;
(b)   are more in line with the trend of international commercial practice;
(c)   come closer to the declared, albeit unrealised, aim of the 325 Rules, namely "to achieve a fair balance between the legitimate interests of the parties concerned...";
(d)   state the minimum requirements for making a claim, but leave the parties to agree actual claim documents;
(e)   do not require an arbitration award or other independent documentary evidence of default;
(f)   determine exactly when the guarantor has to pay;
(g)   give the exporter an opportunity to resolve disputes with the beneficiary before a claim is paid;
(h)   ensure that claims, statements and documents are, after payment, forwarded to the exporter;
(i)   clarify the bank's responsibilities in the event of *extend or pay* claims; and
(j)   provide a method of ascertaining the applicable law in the particular circumstances and a clear method of resolving disputes.

In addition, they:

(k)   recognise the role of the instructing bank which forwards the exporter's instructions to the guarantor and counter-guarantees such instructions;
(l)   treat counter-guarantees as separate transactions from the guarantees to which they relate and from the underlying contract, or tender conditions;
(m) stipulate that the principles or rules of national law concerning the *fraudulent or manifest abuse or unfair calling* of guarantees are not affected.

Banks widely hold the view that the choice of guarantee should be left to the negotiations between the exporter and the beneficiary. The 458 Rules are more or less neutral in this respect. They do, however, require that all guarantees should stipulate:

• the principal (exporter);
• the beneficiary;
• the guarantor;

- the instructing party (where applicable);
- the underlying transaction requiring the issue of the guarantee;
- the maximum amount payable and the currency in which it is payable;
- the expiry date and/or expiry event of the guarantee;
- the terms for demanding payment; and
- the provision for reduction of the guarantee amount, if any.

The 458 Rules provide that the guarantee:

(a)   is non-assignable, although proceeds can be assigned;
(b)   comes into effect from date of issue unless its terms expressly provide otherwise, and that the conditions bringing it into effect are verifiable by the guarantor;
(c)   is subject to the rules and principles of national laws, where these conflict with the 458 Rules.

In addition, they:

(d)   provide a clear definition of the legal quality of the guarantee, stressing its *independence* of the underlying contract; and
(e)   clarify that all guarantees are *irrevocable* unless otherwise stated.

The guarantor can reject instructions for the issuance of a guarantee if the guarantor would be unable to fulfil the terms and conditions of the guarantee, if issued, by reason of a law or regulation in the country of issue.[1]

The 458 Rules favour the buyer, but less so than the 325 Rules favoured the exporter. This reflects the true market conditions and should make their incorporation into a guarantee text more acceptable to a buyer.

Under the 458 Rules, a demand guarantee is payable according to the conditions contained in it before its expiry date, or any expiry event, at its *place of issue*. The guarantor bank is not required to make payment of a demand immediately, but shall have *reasonable time* to examine a demand and to determine whether to pay or reject it. It is required to advise the exporter of a demand and transmit it to him with any related documents without delay.

If the bank rejects the demand it has to inform the beneficiary without delay and put the documents at his disposal. However, if the demand is not rejected, *the bank does not necessarily have to advise the exporter before paying the demand.*

---

[1] Situations involving local laws or regulations, as mentioned above, may sometimes occur such as, for example, where the instructions to the guarantor are to issue a guarantee for payment in, say, U.S. dollars, but local regulations require a bank to issue the guarantee for payment in local currency. Another situation may be that under local law the period of validity of a guarantee may not be freely reduced.

Guarantees are payable *on first demand*, but three sub-versions of demand are recognised, all of them regularly used in practice:

(a)   simple demand;
(b)   demand supported by a bona fide statement; and
(c)   demand supported by specific documents.

Simple demand

For bank guarantees payable on simple demand, where Article 20(a) has been expressly excluded (see Annex II to this Chapter), and unless there is *manifest fraud* or *abuse* of the bank demand guarantee, the bank pays on first written demand from the beneficiary without objection or contestation.

Demand supported by bona fide statement

Where Article 20(a) has not been expressly excluded, and unless there is *manifest fraud* or *abuse* of the bank demand guarantee, the bank pays on first written demand from the beneficiary, *including a statement* stating that the exporter is in breach of his obligations under the underlying contract or tender, *and the nature of the breach.*

As an equitable alternative to simple demand guarantees, the 458 Rules offer this automatic payment mechanism which requires only a bona fide statement of the exporter's default, in the absence of any other specific provision.

If the guarantee text itself only reads "Upon your first written demand" but in addition to that stipulates that the 458 Rules apply, then according to the 458 Rules, a bona fide statement of the exporter's default is *automatically required.*

Such a bona fide statement is the solution which in most cases best reflects an equitable balance of interests of the parties and should be encouraged as the *minimum requirement* in any demand for payment.

The obligation of the beneficiary to submit a document indicating that, and in what respect, the exporter has failed, does not prejudice the abstract and independent nature of the bank demand guarantee. The bank has only to examine whether or not there is a conclusive written document including such a statement. Though related to the underlying transaction, the bank does not have to examine and decide whether the claim is justified or the alleged fact is true or not.

Exporters should be able to expect fulfilment of these requirements by beneficiaries acting in good faith, and working on the basis of the real facts, to fulfil these requirements. The beneficiary does not have to invent anything.

However, the bank could risk being considered negligent if there were obvious inconsistencies between the bank guarantee wording and the bona fide statement. Banks are, after all, specialists in checking documents against letters of credit. The procedure for checking demands against bank guarantees is no different.

A fraudulent beneficiary would have to invent a fact which is not true. He would be forced to lie openly in writing. Blatant lies are a potential deterrent, because nobody likes to be proved a liar or an unreliable partner. With such a fraudulent document, the principal would have valuable evidence for any subsequent damage claim against the beneficiary.

In some cases the exporter could even be in the position to provide the kind of clear proof of *manifest misuse* which is necessary to prevent the guarantor bank from paying; for example, if the beneficiary claims payment stating that certain goods have not been delivered, whereas the exporter has a signed certificate of acceptance for those very goods which he could submit to the bank or the court.

To avoid this fair and equitable requirement to provide a statement describing the nature of the exporter's default, the parties must take the deliberate step of expressly excluding or modifying Article 20 by so drafting the text of the guarantee.

Demand supported by specific documents

Unlike the 325 Rules, the 458 Rules do not stipulate specific documents to be presented in the event of a claim.

Bank demand guarantees that are drafted requiring the submission of specific documents, such as, for example,

(a) the exporter's admission in writing;
(b) an engineer's certificate in respect of civil engineering contracts; or
(c) an arbitration award in favour of the beneficiary,

offer the exporter the greatest protection against *unfair* demands and sudden outflows of cash.

Such bank guarantees are usually related to the larger contracts and projects and are carefully drafted and negotiated. It would be up to the drafters to decide whether to include their own equitable safeguards, including the bona fide statement of default, or to incorporate the 458 Rules by reference.

Expiry Provisions

The 458 Rules provide that a guarantee terminates when any of the following events of expiry occurs:

(a) when its total amount has been paid;
(b) on a specified calendar date or upon presentation of the document

specified for the purpose of expiry (expiry event), whichever occurs
first;

(c)   if the guarantee is returned to the guarantor;

(d)   if the beneficiary releases the guarantor from liability in writing.

Possession of the guarantee or any amendments after termination does not
preserve any rights of the beneficiary under the guarantee.

In drafting a bank demand guarantee, the exporter should *avoid expressly
stipulating in the text that the beneficiary must return the guarantee document to
the exporter*. Banks should also be alert to such wording. The reason for this
is that the bank is likely to need to treat the guarantee as a *contingent liability*
against the assets of the exporter if the stipulation to return the guarantee is
not complied with, even though its expiry date has elapsed.

Extend or Pay Demands

In the case of a bank demand guarantee, the guarantor is not entitled to pay
the guarantee sum to the beneficiary if it is obvious that the beneficiary's
claim constitutes an *abuse of rights*; for instance, when the tender-inviting
authority tries to enforce an extension of the validity of the tender guarantee by the means of an *extend or pay* threat.

Under Article 26, the guarantor must, without delay, inform the exporter
of an *extend or pay* claim and delay payment for a time reasonable enough
for the exporter and beneficiary to agree a period of extension.

It is not enough that the exporter and beneficiary alone agree formally to
an extension. The instructing bank and guarantor bank must also agree to
such extension if it is to be operative.

There has to be *reasonable time* to permit the exporter and the beneficiary
to reach an agreement on an extension of the guarantee and also to arrange
for such extension through the exporter's bank. It is also expressly stated
that the guarantor bank shall incur no liability, in terms of interest or otherwise, for any delay in payment which may result from such procedure.

If there is no agreement between the exporter and the beneficiary within
a reasonable time, the bank can pay the demand without any further reference to the exporter.

If the instructing bank considers that the exporter's counter-indemnity
no longer offers adequate security to cover the period of the extension, he
can either ask the exporter to offer greater security to support the counter-
indemnity or, in the extreme, refuse to extend the bank guarantee. In these
circumstances, the only option is to pay the beneficiary the amount
claimed, adding to the exporter's solvency problems.

Settlement of Disputes and Governing Law

Unlike the 325 Rules, the 458 Rules contain no complicated *arbitration* procedure. Disputes are to be settled in the competent court of the country of the *place of business of the guarantor or instructing bank* as the case may be, unless otherwise specified in the guarantee or counter-guarantee.

Similarly, the *governing law* is to be that of the place of business of the guarantor or instructing bank as the case may be, unless otherwise specified in the guarantee or counter-guarantee.

Limited Objectives

The 325 Rules in Article 9b reflect the correct strict legal position in international law under a guarantee, namely proof being required of default by the exporter under the underlying contract before a demand is paid. Few beneficiaries, however, accepted the 325 Rules for this very reason.

The 458 Rules, banker-led, swing to the other extreme and reflect no requirement for such proof to support a demand.

Intentionally, the 458 Rules are not all-embracing, and thus avoid repeating that weakness of the earlier 325 Rules. With conflicting interests of the different parties to a bank guarantee, the 458 Rules are right to *concentrate on those areas where exporters, banks and beneficiaries could find common ground for agreement.* At best, it is a compromise established at the highest possible level of agreement achievable, at the minimum acceptable level of regulation.

The 458 Rules are a *framework* to help banks and other parties to the bank demand guarantee to understand their rights and responsibilities, particularly in the event of a demand on the guarantee. Both the exporter and the beneficiary are expected to be reasonable in their demands. Neither should abuse his power as an exclusive seller or as buyer in a highly competitive market.

The beneficiary should not be in a position to make an unfair demand unilaterally. The exporter should not be able to stop payment if the beneficiary complies with the terms of the guarantee and the 458 Rules.

Issues That Have Been Avoided

There are several aspects which the 458 Rules deliberately avoid attempting to address in detail, *e.g.* subjects such as the terms of the contract between the *issuing bank* (primary guarantor) and *instructing bank* (counter-guarantor). As was seen in Chapter 2, there is no contractual link through the bank guarantee between the exporter and the beneficiary. Each contractual link in the process is independent of the previous and next link, and of the whole guarantee and contractual transaction. Each can be in its own terms and subject to its own law and jurisdiction.

To have attempted to bring all these legal links in the bank guarantee transaction under a single law and jurisdiction would have proved extremely premature at this stage in any event, and probably even impossible to achieve in the longer term. It would have prejudiced the chances of getting the necessary international adoption of these Rules by exporters, banks and beneficiaries alike.

To have required the instructing bank to release to the exporter the text of its *counter-indemnity to the issuing bank* (primary guarantor) as a matter of course would have been likely to cause problems for some banks, and could have risked them rejecting the 458 Rules. There is nothing to stop the exporter asking to see a copy of this document, if he feels it introduces risks which exceed those in the guarantee which he has instructed to be issued.

Similarly, no attempt has been made to lay down rules governing the *counter-indemnity between the exporter and his bank*. The bank and the exporter's lawyer are perfectly capable of agreeing acceptable wording.

There has likewise been no attempt to initiate a procedure aimed at terminating the obligation to pay.

In the event of *suspension, frustration* or *termination* of the contract, a demand guarantee is not affected. It continues to be valid until its expiry date, unless returned or cancelled in writing. This became the predicament of those exporters with contracts with Iraq in 1990 which were frustrated or suspended as a result of the Gulf War. Banks have been prevented from paying any claims because of international sanctions against Iraq. However, once lifted, exporters may find themselves exposed to claims. It is unlikely that the UNCITRAL or any other body could draft acceptable rules which would help in this sort of situation. As mentioned earlier, it has taken E.C. Regulation 3541/92, and the action of the various E.C. governments to bring this Regulation into effect, to protect exporters against unfair Iraqi claims.

How to Benefit from the New Uniform Rules

The 458 Rules are *voluntary*. They apply only to those demand guarantees which state that they are "subject to the Uniform Rules for Demand Guarantees of the International Chamber of Commerce (Publication No. 458)".

The new 458 Rules are intended to encourage good practice. However, it has never been easy to change an established bad practice and all too easy to get into bad habits. Only time will tell whether the 458 Rules will find wider acceptance than the 325 Rules.

Having explained the nature of demand guarantees, highlighted the risks and techniques for their control, and detailed the attempts of the International Chamber of Commerce to bring some order into a complex subject, Chapter 11 explains how to *quantify, record, monitor and control risk and exposure* to unfair claims and, in principle, to control abuse of the basic application of demand guarantees to international trade.

To complete the ICC involvement in the area of bonds and guarantees in their widest application, the ICC Insurance Commission, with representation from the two Commissions above, is working to publish what initially has been called Uniform Rules for Contract Guarantees. However, to avoid confusion with the existing 325 Rules, the new Rules will eventually be entitled Uniform Rules for Contract Bonds.

These Rules will relate to contract bonds which are *dependent* on the contract and, where the liability of the guarantor arises from, and is conditional upon, *an established breach or default* by the contractor.

Given the negotiations over several years taken to reach an acceptable international compromise over the 458 Rules, no suggested target date has been set for the new publication; the 325 Rules remain in force for the time being.

Annex I

The following is the text of the 325 Rules reproduced by kind permission of the International Chamber of Commerce. These were adopted by the ICC on June 20, 1978.

UNIFORM RULES FOR CONTRACT GUARANTEES (PUBLICATION No. 325)—AUGUST 1978

INTRODUCTION

Guarantees given by banks, insurance companies and other guarantors in the form of tender bonds, performance guarantees and repayment guarantees in relation to projects in another country involving the supply of goods or services or the performance of work are currently an important tool of international trade.

* Broadly speaking the purpose of the tender bond (bid bond) is to provide an assurance of the intention of the party submitting the tender (principal) to sign the contract if his tender is accepted.

* Similarly, the performance guarantee is intended as a safeguard against the party to whom the contract is awarded (principal) failing to meet his obligations under such a contract, which, by its nature, normally requires a period of time for completion.

* Finally, the repayment guarantee protects the interest of the party awarding the contract (beneficiary) in respect of the repayment of payments or advances made by him, in the event of the principal not fulfilling the contract terms.

Thus in each type of guarantee three parties are involved—and their interests differ:

* The beneficiary, *i.e.* the party inviting the tender, or awarding the contract, wants either to receive a compensatory sum of money if the tenderer fails to meet his obligations arising from submission of the tender, or if the tenderer, having been awarded the contract, fails to perform the contract in accordance with its terms, or to secure repayment of any payments or advances made by him if the principal fails to perform the contract. He wants to be sure that he will receive such amounts as may be due to him, even if the principal fails to pay such amounts, whether by reason of unwillingness or inability to pay.

* The principal, *i.e.* the party tendering, or the party to whom the contract has been awarded, does not want to be compelled to pay by reason of the guarantee if he has met his obligations arising from submission of the tender, or if, having been awarded the contract, he has performed it in accordance with its terms.

* The guarantor, whether bank, insurance company or other party, wants to meet its commitment in the terms of the guarantee, without becoming involved in possible disputes between beneficiary and principal regarding correct performance by the principal of his

obligations arising from submission of the tender, or of the contract in accordance with its terms.

The "contract guarantee" has therefore the difficult tasks of creating a fair equilibrium among the legitimate interests of the three parties, and of defining the rights and obligations of the three parties with sufficient precision to avoid mistakes.

Unfortunately, these concepts have not always been appreciated, or applied, in practice. Lack of experience in certain cases, or abuse by a party of its dominant position in other cases, has tended to create inequitable situations, leading to dispute and distrust. This state of affairs is a hindrance to the development of international commerce.

Action by the International Chamber of Commerce

The International Chamber of Commerce, in close co-operation with interested inter-governmental and international commercial organisations, particularly the United Nations Commission on International Trade Law (UNCITRAL), has therefore drawn up a set of "Uniform Rules for Contract Guarantees", with a view to securing a uniformity of practice based upon an equitable balance between the interests of the parties concerned while observing the commercial purpose of the guarantee, *i.e.* to ensure the availability of funds with an independent third party in the event of the beneficiary having a justified claim against the principal.

In drafting these Rules care has been taken to maintain the maximum possible flexibility consistent with observing the concepts referred to above, and also, by establishing the principle of the need to justify a claim under a guarantee, to invest guarantee practice with a moral content. Thereby it is hoped that international trade conducted on the basis of contract guarantees may develop in an atmosphere of confidence. For the said reasons it has not been found advisable to make provision for so-called simple or first demand guarantees, under which claims are payable without independent evidence of their validity. Although the Rules do not encourage the use of such guarantees and are not drafted to apply thereto (and there is evidence of a decline of their use in certain areas as their economic disadvantages are more fully understood), parties who so wish may agree to apply certain of the Rules to such guarantees.

It has also not been found practicable to deal with the complex subject of the nature of the guarantee, *i.e.* whether it is a primary and independent obligation or whether it is a secondary and accessory one, because of the differing approaches to the matter under various national legislations. Instead, attention has been directed in a more concrete manner to the prerequisites for payment under the guarantee and the objections and defences available to the guarantor.

The relationship between the principal and the guarantor is, with a few exceptions (Articles 7.3, 8.2, 11.2), not dealt with in the Rules, it being felt that the question of recourse by the guarantor to the principal, and the provision of any collateral security deemed necessary, is a matter less in need of standarisation or guidance than the relationship between the beneficiary and the guarantor.

COMMENTS ON THE RULES

Article 1

Paragraph 1

The application of the Rules is voluntary. This means that it must be evidenced by a specific statement in the guarantee document itself, that the guarantee is "subject to the Uniform Rules for Tender, Performance and Repayment Guarantees ('Contract Guarantees') of the International Chamber of Commerce (Publication No. 325)".

The Rules are then binding upon all parties "unless otherwise expressly stated in the guarantee or any amendment thereto". This possibility of "partial application" enables parties to agree to apply the Rules to simple or first demand guarantees by specifically excluding Article 9.

N.B. To avoid difficulties when guarantees on behalf of the principal have to be submitted in respect of a particular project, it would be helpful for it to be specified in the invitation to tender that the International Chamber of Commerce Rules are to apply to any guarantees.

Paragraph 2

It may happen that in certain countries the whole of the International Chamber of Commerce Rules cannot be applied, *e.g.* where the text of certain guarantees for the public sector is prescribed by the authorities or by ministerial decree, or where claims under a guarantee may be made within a period of time laid down by the law or whilst the guarantee is still in the hands of the beneficiary—regardless of any expiry date stated in the guarantee—unless the beneficiary has specifically "released" the guarantor from his obligations.

N.B. Good faith and fair dealing require that a party, whether principal, instructing party, guarantor or beneficiary, who is aware of the effect of any such mandatory rules in his national law, shall advise the others thereof at the time of issue of the guarantee. This is of particular importance where the guarantee is given by a guarantor in the country of the beneficiary at the request of an "instructing party" in another country.

If such mandatory law is part of the proper law applicable to the guarantee (see also Article 10), the provision of the law prevails over the Rules, as over any other provisions of the guarantee contract, as is made clear in this paragraph.

Article 2

This Article makes no attempt to deal with the nature of the guarantee (see Introduction) and does not set out any legal consequences arising from such nature.

It merely defines and describes the different types of guarantees for which the Rules are made, by

(a) identifying the parties involved in the different types of "contract guarantee" transaction on the basis of the commercial part they play in such transaction;

(b) recognising that some guarantees are not legally acceptable in certain countries if issued by a guarantor outside the country of the beneficiary, so that they have to be issued by a "local guarantor", *i.e.* one in the beneficiary's country, acting on behalf of an "instructing party";

(c) recognising the possibility, in some countries, of the issue of a guarantee whereby the guarantor has to "arrange for performance of the contract" instead of to "make payment to the beneficiary within the limits of a stated sum of money".

(d) emphasising the link between the performance of the guarantor's undertaking and "default by the principal".

Article 3

Paragraph 1

Linking the liability of the guarantor towards the beneficiary to the wording of the guarantee is the nearest the Rules can come to defining the nature of the guarantee. Its own wording (as well as the content of the Rules) should provide the evidence as to whether the guarantor is assuming a primary or a secondary obligation as these concepts may be defined in the proper law applicable to the guarantee.

This calls for clear and precise drafting of the guarantee to give proper legal effect to what is commercially intended. It is obviously essential that the guarantee should show what the guarantor and the beneficiary need to know, *i.e.* precisely what the guarantor has to pay, and when.

In respect of the tender guarantee, for example, it would seem desirable that

(a) the amount or the percentage figure should be realistic, and avoid over-protection, since there might well be a less satisfactory response to the invitation to tender, or some reflection in the tender price, to the detriment of the party inviting the tenders, if the amount were fixed at too high a level;

(b) the expiry date should be related as closely as possible to the date fixed for acceptance of tenders, since it is not in the interests of either beneficiary or principal to insist on a tender guarantee being outstanding for an unnecessarily long period of time.

The levels of cost in tendering, and competition, are in themselves deterrents to the submission of frivolous or unsuitable tenders.

So far as the other types of guarantee are concerned, the fact that fulfilment of the guarantor's undertaking is linked with "default by the principal" would call for the inclusion in the guarantee of conditions relative to the submission of specified evidence of default giving the beneficiary a right of claim under the guarantee, and also the amount of such claim. These conditions should be of such a nature as to permit the guarantor himself to verify whether, or not, they have been met. (Attention is also drawn to the discussion of paragraph 2 below.)

Paragraph 2

This draws attention to an important fact which has a bearing on the wording of the guarantee, and hence, the possible liability of the guarantor.

Under the Rules there is no automatic presumption of a pro-rata reduction of the guarantee in keeping with partial performance of the contract in respect of which it is given.

Thus, where the intention of the parties is that the amount of the guarantee shall be reduced on a pro-rata basis (or any other basis) as performance of the contract progresses, a specific statement to this effect should be incorporated in the guarantee. It is obviously desirable that similar mention should be made in the contract.

Article 4

It is obviously desirable for the wording of the guarantee to specify a last date ("expiry date") by which claims must be received by the guarantor. The principal should, therefore, either directly to the guarantor, or through the "instructing party", state the "expiry date" to be inserted in the guarantee: and such expiry date should be linked realistically with the tender period or the period of performance of the contract as appropriate.

Sub-paragraphs (a), (b) and (c) of this Article only apply in cases where the principal has not stated an "expiry date".

It has to be borne in mind, however, that in certain countries legislation precludes the insertion of an expiry date in a "contract guarantee": and that such legislation, if mandatory, may result in the guarantor remaining liable under the guarantee for longer than may follow from the provisions in this Article or from what has been expressly stipulated in the guarantee.

The fact that the "expiry date" is the "last date by which a claim must have been received by the guarantor" means that the "non-business day" referred to in the final paragraph of this Article is a "non-business day" in the place or country of the guarantor, not the place or country of the beneficiary.

Article 5

The purpose of this Article is to explain precisely the time when a guarantee ceases to have effect.

This is of particular importance in respect of tender guarantees, as is shown in paragraph 2(b) of this Article, which clearly establishes the position *vis-à-vis* the beneficiary (who knows to whom he has awarded the contract) and the guarantor (who most probably lacks that knowledge), and in paragraph 2(c), which deals with the position created when the beneficiary declares his intention not to place a contract at all.

Article 6

The return to the guarantor of a guarantee which has ceased to be valid is desirable for reasons of certainty. The return of the original document confirms quite definitely that no claim under the guarantee will be made. This may be of particular significance in countries whose legislation provides that a guarantee remains in force until returned to the guarantor or unless the beneficiary specifically releases the guarantor from his obligations.

The return of the guarantee document is also desirable for balance sheet purposes, to remove any doubt that the figure of "Contingent Liabilities" may be adjusted.

The Rules, however, do not impose a sanction for failure to return such documents, while under the Rules possession or retention of the document embodying the guarantee does not, in itself, confer any right upon the beneficiary.

Article 7

Paragraph 1

This is intended to cover the situation which has arisen in the past in connection with tender guarantees where the beneficiary has demanded "either extension of the guarantee, or payment under it". The beneficiary may have valid reasons for extending the period for receipt and consideration of tenders: the principal, on the other hand, should not be forced to extend the validity of his tender or to renegotiate its terms by a threat that payment is demanded under the guarantee. The guarantor may, therefore, not make payment under the guarantee unless such claim is accompanied by the statement in the terms of Article 9(a), nor may the guarantor extend the period of validity of the guarantee without the consent of the principal or the instructing party as set out in Article 7(3).

Paragraph 2

Knowledge of the conditions of the basic contract may be essential for the guarantor to assess the ability of the principal to comply with his obligations, and therefore for deciding whether or not to give the guarantee.

Knowledge of these basic contract conditions becomes even more important when the guarantee is given in terms committing the guarantor to ensure performance of the contract in the event of default by the principal.

Knowledge of amendment to the terms of the contract may therefore be important to the guarantor. It is essential that the guarantor shall not be bound in excess of the amount, or beyond the expiry date, to which he originally agreed. This is expressly stated in the Rules. It may also be important for him to know of other amendments to the contract and its performance in order that he may assess his liability. If this is so, the guarantor should stipulate in the guarantee that he must be notified of such amendments for his approval.

Paragraph 3

It is desirable that the agreement of the principal or the instructing party should be expressed in writing or by cable or telegram or telex.

Article 8

Paragraph 1 links with Article 4 (see discussion above) to establish the "deadline" for receipt of a claim by the guarantor; and provides specifically for such claim to be made by such speedy methods of communication as "cable, or telegram, or telex".

It is therefore necessary for the guarantee to indicate precisely on whom the claim is to be made, *i.e.* the name and address of the guarantor, the address being particularly important where the guarantor has many offices—and possibly several offices in the same city.

The exceptional case of a claim being made by the beneficiary in good time, but not being received by the guarantor until after the "deadline" by reason of "force majeure" is not dealt with in these Rules. It is felt that this is a matter for decision under any "force majeure" rules of the applicable law.

Paragraph 3(c) establishes a subsequent time limit within which the supporting documentation required by the terms of the guarantee or by these Rules must be in the hands of the guarantor.

Article 9

It has been pointed out in the introduction that the concepts on which these Rules are based are

(a)   that a claim should only be made, and honoured, if the beneficiary has a legal right to make the claim based on a failure of the principal to perform, or correctly to perform, the underlying contract;

(b)   that the claim should be justified by the production of some form of "evidence" of such default by the principal. It is reasonable to expect the nature and form of such "evidence" to be stated in the guarantee. The parties to the contract can very well specify the necessary documentary evidence ("documentation") in the contract, and it can then be stated in the guarantee, for example, a certificate, possibly in a stated form, given by a named party such as an accountant, surveyor, arbitrator or other person. (As indicated in discussion of Article 3 above it should be of such a nature as to permit the guarantor himself to verify whether or not the documentation submitted is that called for.)

If, however, the guarantee is silent, as are guarantees payable on first or simple demand, Article 9 speaks and says that documentation as stated therein must be submitted.

For the purpose of the beneficiary's declaration "that the principal's tender has been accepted" (paragraph (a) of this Article) the acceptance must, of course, have been unconditional.

Also, the "court decision or an arbitral award" referred to in paragraph (b) of this Article means a decision or an award given in proceedings between the beneficiary and the principal.

Article 10

The ICC's Uniform Rules do not claim to solve all the problems that can arise in connection with guarantees. For this reason it was important to include in the Rules a provision making it possible to determine the applicable law without any ambiguity. In specifying that the solution which they formulate shall apply when the parties have not chosen the municipal law applicable to the guarantee, the Rules recall the parties' freedom in this respect and it is preferable that the parties avail themselves of it. Where the parties are silent, the guarantee is subject to the law of the guarantor's place of business. This may come as a surprise to those who look upon the guarantee as a contract accessory to the basic contract and therefore consider that the guarantee should be governed by the same law as is the contract. There are various reasons why this solution was not adopted. First of all, as has been repeatedly pointed out, the Rules refrained from taking any stand as to the nature of the guarantee. Furthermore, the application of the law of the place of business of the guarantor appeared to be preferable to that of the basic contract

(a)   because it is not always possible to determine the latter accurately;

(b)   because the obligation which characterises the guarantee operation is that of the guarantor;

(c) because it may happen that guarantors can issue guarantees only according to their own national law.

Article 11

The Rules make a point of drawing attention to the advisability of providing that any dispute which might arise in connection with the guarantee shall be settled by means of arbitration. But a special agreement must exist between the guarantor and the beneficiary so that they will be bound by an arbitration clause and, in this connection, they are left entirely free to choose the type of arbitration. The Article does however mention the two most important sets of rules of international arbitration, *i.e.* of the ICC Court of Arbitration with regard to arbitration under the auspices of a permanent institution, and of UNCITRAL (United Nations Commission on International Trade Law) with regard to an ad hoc arbitration, *i.e.* arbitration which is freely instituted by the parties.

Should a dispute arise between the beneficiary and the guarantor, it can be useful that the principal or the instructing party be able to intervene in the proceedings. Special provision is made for this (Art. 11.2). While this provision does not make it possible to compel the principal or the instructing party to intervene, it does however make it impossible for the guarantor or the beneficiary to invoke the confidential nature of the arbitration as a pretext for objecting to such intervention.

Without an arbitration clause, the parties to a dispute would have been exposed to the jurisdiction of courts in several countries. To avoid this, it has been stipulated in this Article that only the courts in the country of the guarantor's place of business are competent or the courts in the country where the branch issuing the guarantee is situated.

UNIFORM RULES FOR CONTRACT GUARANTEES

Article 1

Scope

(1) These Rules apply to any guarantee, bond, indemnity, surety or similar undertaking, however named or described ("guarantee"), which states that it is subject to the Uniform Rules for Tender, Performance and Repayment Guarantees ("Contract Guarantees") of the International Chamber of Commerce (Publication No. 325) and are binding upon all parties thereto unless otherwise expressly stated in the guarantee or any amendment thereto.

(2) Where any of these Rules is contrary to a provision of the law applicable to the guarantee from which the parties cannot derogate, that provision prevails.

Article 2

Definition

For the purposes of these Rules:

(a) "tender guarantee" means an undertaking given by a bank, insurance company or other party ("the guarantor") at the request of a tenderer ("the principal") or given on the instruction of a bank, insurance company, or other party so requested by the principal ("the instructing party") to a party inviting tenders ("the beneficiary") whereby the guarantor undertakes—in the event of default by the principal in the obligations resulting from the submission of the tender—to make payment to the beneficiary within the limits of a stated sum of money.

(b)   "performance guarantee" means an undertaking given by a bank, insurance company or other party ("the guarantor") at the request of a supplier of goods or services or other contractor ("the principal") or given on the instructions of a bank, insurance company or other party so requested by the principal ("the instructing party") to a buyer or to an employer ("the beneficiary") whereby the guarantor undertakes—in the event of default by the principal in due performance of the terms of the contract between the principal and the beneficiary ("the contract")—to make payment to the beneficiary within the limits of a stated sum of money or, if the guarantor so provides, at the guarantor's option, to arrange performance of the contract;

(c)   "repayment guarantee" means an undertaking given by a bank, insurance company or other third party ("the guarantor") at the request of a supplier of goods or services or other contractor ("the principal") or given on the instructions of a bank, insurance company or other party so requested by the principal ("the instructing party") to a buyer or to an employer ("the beneficiary") whereby the guarantor undertakes—in the event of default by the principal to repay in accordance with the terms of the contract between the principal and the beneficiary ("the contract") any sum or sums advanced or paid by the beneficiary to the principal and not otherwise repaid—to make payment to the beneficiary within the limits of a stated sum of money.

Article 3

Liability of the guarantor to the beneficiary

(1) The guarantor is liable to the beneficiary only in accordance with the terms and conditions specified in the guarantee and these Rules and up to an amount not exceeding that stated in the guarantee.

(2) The amount of liability stated in the guarantee shall not be reduced by reason of any partial performance of the contract, unless so specified in the guarantee.

(3) The guarantor may rely only on those defences which are based on the terms and conditions specified in the guarantee or are allowed under these Rules.

Article 4

Last date for claim

If a guarantee does not specify a last date by which a claim must have been received by the guarantor, such last date ("expiry date") is deemed to be:

(a)   in the case of a tender guarantee, six months from the date of the guarantee;

(b)   in the case of a performance guarantee, six months from the date specified in the contract for the delivery or completion or any extension thereof, or one month after the expiry of any maintenance period (guarantee period) provided for in the contract if such maintenance period is expressly covered by the performance guarantee;

(c) in the case of a repayment guarantee, six months from the date specified in the contract for delivery or completion or any extension thereof.

If the expiry date falls on a non-business day, the expiry date is extended until the first following business day.

Article 5

Expiry of guarantee

(1) If no claim has been received by the guarantor on or before the expiry date or if any claim arising under the guarantee has been settled in full satisfaction of all the rights of the beneficiary thereunder, the guarantee ceases to be valid.

(2) Notwithstanding the provisions of Article 4, in the case of tender guarantees:

(a) upon acceptance by the beneficiary of the tender by the award of the contract to the principal and, if so provided for in the written contract, or, if no contract has been signed and it is so provided for in the tender, the production by the principal of a performance guarantee, or, if no such guarantee is required, the signature by the principal of the contract, the tender guarantee issued on his behalf ceases to be valid;

(b) a tender guarantee also ceases to be valid if and when the contract to which it relates is awarded to another tenderer, whether or not that tenderer meets the requirements referred to in para. 2(a) of this Article;

(c) a tender guarantee also ceases to be valid in the event of the beneficiary expressly declaring that he does not intend to place a contract.

Article 6

Return of guarantee

When a guarantee has ceased to be valid in accordance with its own terms and conditions or with these Rules, retention of the document embodying the guarantee does not in itself confer any rights upon the beneficiary, and the document should be returned to the guarantor without delay.

Article 7

Amendments to contracts and guarantees

(1) A tender guarantee is valid only in respect of the original tender submitted by the principal and does not apply in the case of any amendment thereto, nor is it valid beyond the expiry date specified in the guarantee or provided for by these Rules, unless the guarantor has given

notice in writing or by cable or telegram or telex to the beneficiary that the guarantee so applies or that the expiry date has been extended.

(2) A performance guarantee or a repayment guarantee may stipulate that it shall not be valid in respect of any amendment to the contract, or that the guarantor be notified of any such amendment for his approval. Failing such a stipulation, the guarantee is valid in respect of the obligations of the principal as expressed in the contract and any amendment thereto. However, the guarantee shall not be valid in excess of the amount or beyond the expiry date specified in the guarantee or provided for by these Rules, unless the guarantor has given notice in writing or by cable or telegram or telex to the beneficiary that the amount has been increased to a stated figure or that the expiry date has been extended.

(3) Any amendment made by the guarantor in the terms and conditions of the guarantee shall be effective in respect of the beneficiary only if agreed to by the beneficiary and in respect of the principal or the instructing party, as the case may be, only if agreed to by the principal or the instructing party, as the case may be.

Article 8

Submission of claim

(1) A claim under a guarantee shall be made in writing or by cable or telegram or telex to be received by the guarantor not later than on the expiry date specified in the guarantee or provided for by these Rules.

(2) On receipt of a claim the guarantor shall notify the principal or the instructing party, as the case may be, without delay, of such claim and any documentation received.

(3) A claim shall not be honoured unless

(a) it has been made and received as required by para. 1 of this Article; and
(b) it is supported by such documentation as is specified in the guarantee or in these Rules; and
(c) such documentation is presented within the period of time after the receipt of a claim specified in the guarantee, or, failing such a specification, as soon as practicable, or, in the case of documentation of the beneficiary himself, at the latest six months from the receipt of a claim.

In any event, a claim shall not be honoured if the guarantee has ceased to be valid in accordance with its own terms or with these Rules.

Article 9

Documentation to support a claim

If a guarantee does not specify the documentation to be produced in support of a claim or merely specifies only a statement of claim by the beneficiary, the beneficiary must submit:

(a) in the case of a tender guarantee, his declaration that the principal's tender has been accepted and that the principal has then either failed to sign the contract or has failed to submit a performance guarantee as provided for in the tender, and his declaration of agreement, addressed to the principal, to have any dispute on any claim by the principal for payment to him by the beneficiary of all or part of the amount paid under the guarantee settled by a judicial or arbitral tribunal as specified in the tender documents or, if not so specified or otherwise agreed upon, by arbitration in accordance with the Rules of the ICC Court of Arbitration or with the UNCITRAL Arbitration Rules, at the option of the principal;

(b) in the case of a performance guarantee or of a repayment guarantee, either a court decision or an arbitral award justifying the claim, or the approval of the principal in writing to that claim and the amount to be paid.

Article 10

Applicable law

If a guarantee does not indicate the law by which it is to be governed, the applicable law is that of the guarantor's place of business. If the guarantor has more than one place of business, the applicable law is that of the branch which issued the guarantee.

Article 11

Settlement of disputes

(1) Any disputes arising in connection with the guarantee may be referred to arbitration by agreement between the guarantor and the beneficiary, either in accordance with the Rules of the ICC Court of Arbitration, the UNCITRAL Arbitration Rules or such other rules of arbitration as may be agreed between the guarantor and the beneficiary.

(2) If a dispute between the guarantor and the beneficiary which touches upon the rights and obligations of the principal or the instructing party is referred to arbitration, the principal or the instructing party shall have the right to intervene in such arbitral proceedings.

(3) If the guarantor and the beneficiary have not agreed to arbitration or to the jurisdiction of any specific court, any dispute between them relating to the guarantee shall be settled exclusively by the competent court of the country of the guarantor's place of business or, if the guarantor has more than one place of business, by the competent court of the country of main place of business, or at the option of the beneficiary, by the competent court of the country of the branch which issued the guarantee.

Annex II

The following is the text of the 458 Rules reproduced by kind permission of the International Chamber of Commerce. These were adopted by the ICC in April 1992.

UNIFORM RULES FOR DEMAND GUARANTEES (PUBLICATION NO. 458)—APRIL 1992

The ICC Commission on Banking Technique and Practice and the Commission on International Commercial Practice have published a set of rules for independent guarantees payable on demand which are intended to help establish a uniform code of practice for their issue and use.

Entitled the Uniform Rules for Demand Guarantees (ICC Publication No. 458), they will be used in parallel with the 1978 ICC Uniform Rules for Contract Guarantees (Publication No. 325), which relate only to dependent guarantees payable when certain contract conditions have been fulfilled. The frequency of use of such guarantees has been diminishing as independent guarantees payable on demand have gained greater popularity with buyers.

A third form of guarantee, the stand-by letter of credit, continues to be governed by the Uniform Customs and Practice for Documentary Credits (1983 Revision No. 400.)

Introduction

Section A: Scope and application of the Rules

Section B: Definitions and general provisions

Section C: Liabilities and responsibilities of guarantors

Section D: Demands

Section E: Expiry provisions

Section F: Governing law and jurisdiction

INTRODUCTION

These Uniform Rules for Demand Guarantees (ICC Publication No. 458) result from the work of the ICC Joint Working Party of members representing the Commission on International Commercial Practice and the Commission on Banking Technique and Practice and from the work of the Drafting Group set up to finalise the text.

The rules are intended to apply worldwide to the use of demand guarantees, that is, guarantees, bonds, and other payment undertakings under which the duty of the guarantor or issuer to make payment arises on the presentation of a written demand and any other documents specified in the guarantee and is not conditional on actual default by the principal in the underlying transaction.

Demand guarantees differ from documentary guarantees in that they are properly invoked only if the principal has made a default. However, the guarantor, like the issuer of a documentary credit, is not concerned with the fact of default, only with documents.

Standby credits are already governed by the Uniform Customs and

Practices for Documentary Credits (UCP) (1983 Revision No. 400). They have developed into all-purpose financial support instruments which are used in a much wider range of financial and commercial activity than demand guarantees, and regularly involve practices and procedures (*e.g.* confirmation, issue for a bank's own account, presentation of documents to a party other than the issuer) which are infrequently encountered in relation to demand guarantees and which ally standby credits more closely with documentary credits. Accordingly, while standby credits are technically within the definition of a demand guarantee, it is expected that issuers of standby credits will continue to use the UCP, which are both more detailed and more appropriate to the particular requirements of standby credits.

These Rules do not apply to suretyship or conditional bonds or guarantees or other accessory undertakings under which the guarantor's duty to pay arises only on default by the principal. Such instruments are widely used, but are different in character from demand guarantees and are outside the scope and purpose of these Rules.

These new Uniform Rules have been introduced because the 1978 ICC Uniform Rules for Contract Guarantees (Publication No. 325) did not gain general acceptance. The new Rules reflect more closely the different interests of the parties involved in a demand guarantee transaction. However, since Publication No. 325 continues to be used to some extent it will be retained in force for the time being so as to be available for those who may wish to use it in preference to the new Rules. The future of Publication No. 325 will be reviewed at a later date in the light of experience.

The Beneficiary

The beneficiary wishes to be secured against the risk of the principal not fulfilling his obligations towards the beneficiary in respect of the underlying transaction for which the demand guarantee is given. The guarantee accomplishes this by providing the beneficiary with quick access to a sum of money if these obligations are not fulfilled.

The Principal

Whilst recognising the needs of the beneficiary, the principal can expect on the grounds of equity and good faith to be informed in writing that, and in what respect, it is claimed he is in breach of his obligations. This should help to eliminate a certain level of abuse of guarantees through unfair claims by beneficiaries.

The Guarantor

For these Rules to apply, the guarantee should not stipulate any condition for payment other than the presentation of a written demand and other specified documents. In particular, the terms of the guarantee should not require the guarantor to decide whether the beneficiary and principal have or have not fulfilled their obligations under the underlying transaction, with which the guarantor is not concerned. The wording of the guarantee should be clear and unambiguous.

The Instructing Party

The new Rules recognise the existing widespread practice whereby an instructing party may forward to the guarantor instructions received from or on behalf of the principal and counter-guarantee such instructions.

General

The ICC wishes to encourage good demand guarantee practice which is equitable to all concerned, and believes that these Rules will result in a fair balance of interests, recognising the rights and obligations of all parties. Compared with the ICC Rules published in 1978, these Rules incorporate a major change in favour of beneficiaries in that they are no longer confined to guarantees which require the presentation of an arbitration award or other independent documentary evidence in support of any demand. However guarantees which do require such evidence are still within the scope of these Rules. These new Rules also incorporate provisions relating to counter-guarantees.

It is a characteristic of all guarantees within these Rules that they are payable on presentation of one or more documents. The documentary requirements specified in demand guarantees vary widely. At one end is the guarantee which is payable on simple written demand, without a statement of default or other documentary requirements. At the other end is the guarantee which requires presentation of a judgment or arbitral award.

Between these two extremes lie various intermediate forms of guarantee, such as guarantees requiring a statement of default by the beneficiary, with or without an indication of the nature of the default, or the presentation of a certificate by an engineer or surveyor. All these fall within the scope of the new Rules. However, the interests of the beneficiary must be balanced against the need to protect the principal against an unfair claim on the guarantee. The ICC considers it reasonable to provide that in accordance with principles of equity and fair dealing a demand should be in writing and should at least be accompanied by a statement by the beneficiary that and in what respect the principal is in default, and Article 20 so provides. A party who wishes to avoid or alter even this requirement is free to do so but must take the deliberate step of excluding or modifying Article 20 by the terms of the guarantee. However, Article 20, when read with Articles 2(b) and (c), 9 and 11, also makes it clear that guarantors are not concerned with the adequacy of any statement of breach. The documents must, of course, appear to conform to the guarantee, so that where a non-conformity is apparent on the face of the documents the beneficiary is not entitled to payment. Moreover, these Rules do not affect principles or rules of national law concerning the fraudulent or manifest abuse or unfair calling of guarantees.

Like the UCP, these new Uniform Rules for Demand Guarantees apply where expressly incorporated into the guarantee and depend for their success upon their use by the international business community. The ICC, through its National Committees and international fora, will strongly encourage industrial and financial circles to adhere to these Rules, which will help to secure uniformity of practice in the requirements for demand guarantees.

A. Scope and Application of the Rules

Article 1

These Rules apply to any demand guarantee and amendment thereto which a Guarantor (as hereinafter described) has been instructed to issue and which states that it is subject to the Uniform Rules for Demand Guarantees of the International Chamber of Commerce (Publication No.458) and are binding on all parties thereto except as otherwise expressly stated in the Guarantee or any amendment thereto.

B. DEFINITIONS AND GENERAL PROVISIONS

Article 2

(a) For the purpose of these Rules a demand guarantee (hereinafter referred to as "Guarantee") means any guarantee, bond or other payment undertaking, however named or described, by a bank, insurance company or other body or person (hereinafter called "the Guarantor") given in writing for the payment of money on presentation in conformity with the terms of the undertaking of a written demand for payment and such other document(s) (for example, a certificate by an architect or engineer, a judgment or an arbitral award) as may be specified in the Guarantee, such undertaking being given

(i)   at the request or on the instructions and under the liability of a party (hereinafter called "the Principal"); or

(ii) at the request or on the instructions and under the liability of a bank, insurance company or any other body or person (hereinafter "the Instructing Party") acting on the instructions of a Principal to another party (hereinafter "the Beneficiary").

(b) Guarantees by their nature are separate transactions from the contract(s) or tender conditions on which they may be based and Guarantors are in no way concerned with or bound by such contracts, despite the inclusion of a reference to them in the Guarantee. The duty of a Guarantor under a Guarantee is to pay the sum or sums therein stated on the presentation of a written demand for payment and other documents specified in the Guarantee which appear on their face to be in accordance with the terms of the Guarantee.

(c) For the purposes of these Rules "Counter-Guarantee" means any guarantee, bond or other payment undertaking of the Instructing Party, however named or described, given in writing for the payment of money to the Guarantor on presentation in conformity with the terms of the undertaking of a written demand for payment and other documents specified in the Counter-Guarantee which appear on their face to be in accordance with the terms of the Counter-Guarantee. Counter-Guarantees are by their nature separate transactions from the Guarantees to which they relate and from any underlying contracts or tender conditions and Instructing Parties are in no way concerned with or bound by such Guarantees, contracts or tender conditions, despite the inclusion of a reference to them in the Counter-Guarantee.

(d) The expressions "writing" and "written" shall include an authenticated teletransmission or tested electronic data interchange "EDI" message equivalent thereto.

Article 3

All instructions for the issue of Guarantees and amendments thereto and Guarantees and amendments themselves should be clear, precise, and avoid excessive detail. Accordingly all Guarantees should stipulate:

(a)   the Principal;
(b)   the Beneficiary;

(c)   the Guarantor;
(d)   the underlying transaction requiring the issue of the Guarantee;
(e)   the maximum amount payable and the currency in which it is payable;
(f)   the expiry date and/or expiry event of the Guarantee;
(g)   the terms for demanding payment;
(h)   any provision for reduction of the Guarantee amount.

Article 4

The Beneficiary's right to claim under a Guarantee is not assignable unless expressly stated in the Guarantee or in an amendment thereto.

This Article shall not, however, affect the Beneficiary's right to assign any proceeds to which he may be, or may become, entitled under the Guarantee.

Article 5

All Guarantees and Counter-Guarantees are irrevocable unless otherwise indicated.

Article 6

A Guarantee enters into effect as from the date of its issue unless its terms expressly provide that such entry into effect is to be at a later date or is to be subject to conditions specified in the Guarantee and determinable by the Guarantor on the basis of any documents therein specified.

Article 7

(a) Where a Guarantor has been given instructions for the issue of a Guarantee but the instructions are such that, if they were to be carried out, the Guarantor would by reason of law or regulation in the country of issue be unable to fulfil the terms of the Guarantee, the instructions shall not be executed and the Guarantor shall immediately inform the party which gave the Guarantor its instructions by telecommunication or if that is not possible by other expeditious means of the reasons for such inability and request appropriate instructions from that party.

(b) Nothing in this Article shall oblige the Guarantor to issue a Guarantee where the Guarantor has not agreed to do so.

Article 8

A Guarantee may contain express provision for reduction by a specified or determinable amount or amounts on a specified date or dates or upon presentation to the Guarantor of the document(s) specified for this purpose in the Guarantee.

C. LIABILITIES AND RESPONSIBILITIES OF GUARANTORS

Article 9

All document(s) specified and presented under a Guarantee, including the demand, shall be examined by the Guarantor with reasonable care to ascertain whether or not they appear on their face to conform with the terms of the Guarantee. Where such document(s) do not appear so to conform or appear on their face to be inconsistent with one another, they shall be refused.

Article 10

(a) A Guarantor shall have reasonable time in which to examine a demand under a Guarantee and to decide whether to pay or to refuse the demand.

(b) If the Guarantor decides to refuse a demand, he shall immediately give notice thereof to the Beneficiary by teletransmission or, if that is not possible, by other expeditious means. Any documents presented under the Guarantee shall be held at the disposal of the Beneficiary.

Article 11

Guarantors and Instructing Parties assume no liability or responsibility for the form, sufficiency, accuracy, genuineness, falsification, or legal effect of any document presented to them or for the general and/or particular statements made therein, or for the good faith or acts and/or omissions of any person whomsoever.

Article 12

Guarantors and Instructing Parties assume no liability or responsibility for the consequences arising out of delay, and/or loss in transit of any messages, letters, claims or documents, or for delay, mutilation or other errors arising in the transmission of any telecommunication. Guarantors and Instructing Parties assume no liability for errors in translation or interpretation of technical terms and reserve the right to transmit Guarantee texts or any parts thereof without translating them.

Article 13

Guarantors and Instructing Parties assume no liability or responsibility for consequences arising out of the interruption of their business by acts of God, riots, civil commotions, insurrections, wars or any other causes beyond their control or by strikes, lock-outs or industrial action of whatever nature.

Article 14

(a) Guarantors and Instructing Parties utilising the services of another party for the purpose of giving effect to the instructions of a Principal do so for the account and at the risk of the Principal.

(b) Guarantors and Instructing Parties assume no liability or responsibility should the instructions they transmit not be carried out even if they have themselves taken the initiative in the choice of such other party.

(c) The Principal shall be liable to indemnify the Guarantor or the Instructing Party, as the case may be, against all obligations and responsibilities imposed by foreign laws and usages.

Article 15

Guarantors and Instructing Parties shall not be excluded from liability or responsibility under the terms of Articles 11, 12 and 14 above for their failure to act in good faith and with reasonable care.

Article 16

A Guarantor is liable to the Beneficiary only in accordance with the terms specified in the Guarantee and any amendment(s) thereto and in these Rules and up to an amount not exceeding that stated in the Guarantee and any amendment(s) thereto.

D. DEMANDS

Article 17

Without prejudice to the terms of Article 10, in the event of a demand the Guarantor shall without delay so inform the Principal or where applicable its Instructing Party and in that case the Instructing Party shall so inform the Principal.

Article 18

The amount payable under a Guarantee shall be reduced by the amount of any payment made by the Guarantor in satisfaction of a claim in respect thereof and, where the maximum amount payable under a Guarantee has been satisfied by payment and/or reduction, the Guarantee shall thereupon terminate whether or not the Guarantee or any amendment(s) thereto are returned.

Article 19

A demand shall be made in accordance with the terms of the Guarantee before its expiry, that is, on or before its Expiry Date and before any Expiry Event as defined in Article 22. In particular, all documents specified in the Guarantee for the purpose of the demand, and any statement required by Article 20, shall be presented to the Guarantor before its expiry at its place of issue, otherwise the demand shall be refused by the Guarantor.

Article 20

(a) Any demand for payment under the Guarantee shall be in writing and shall (in addition to such other documents as may be specified in the Guarantee) be supported by a written statement (whether in the demand itself or in a separate document or documents accompanying the demand and referred to in it) stating:

  (i)   that the Principal is in breach of his obligation(s) under the underlying contract(s) or, in the case of a tender guarantee, the tender conditions; and
  (ii) the respect in which the Principal is in breach.

(b) Any demand under the Counter-Guarantee shall be supported by a written statement that the Guarantor has received a demand for payment under the Guarantee in accordance with its terms and with this Article.

(c) Paragraph (a) of this Article applies except to the extent that it is expressly excluded by the terms of the Guarantee. Paragraph (b) of this Article applies except to the extent that it is expressly excluded by the terms of the Counter-Guarantee.

(d) Nothing in this Article affects the application of Articles 2(b) and (c), 9 and 11.

Article 21

The Guarantor shall without any delay transmit the Beneficiary's demand and any related documents to the Principal or where applicable to the Instructing Party for transmission to the Principal.

E. EXPIRY PROVISIONS

Article 22

Expiry of the time specified in a Guarantee for the presentation of demands shall be upon a specified calendar date ("Expiry Date") or upon presentation to the Guarantor of the document(s) specified for the purpose of expiry ("Expiry Event"). If both an Expiry Date and an Expiry Event are specified in a Guarantee, the Guarantee shall expire on whichever of the Expiry Date or Expiry Event occurs first, whether or not the Guarantee and any amendment(s) thereto are returned.

Article 23

Irrespective of any expiry provision contained therein, a Guarantee shall be cancelled on presentation to the Guarantor of the Guarantee itself or the Beneficiary's written statement of release from liability under the Guarantee, whether or not, in the latter case, the Guarantee or any amendments thereto are returned.

Article 24

Where a Guarantee has terminated by payment, expiry, cancellation or otherwise, retention of the Guarantee or of any amendments thereto shall not preserve any rights of the Beneficiary under the Guarantee.

Article 25

Where to the knowledge of the Guarantor the Guarantee has terminated by payment, expiry, cancellation or otherwise or there has been a reduction in the total amount payable thereunder the Guarantor shall without delay so notify the Principal or where applicable the Instructing Party and, in that case, the Instructing Party shall so notify the Principal.

Article 26

If the Beneficiary requests an extension of the validity of the Guarantee as an alternative to a demand for payment submitted in accordance with the terms and conditions of the Guarantee and these Rules, the Guarantor shall without delay so inform the party which gave the Guarantor his instructions. The Guarantor shall then suspend payment of the claim for such time as is reasonable to permit the Principal and the Beneficiary to reach agreement on the granting of such extension and for the Principal to arrange for such extension to be issued.

Unless an extension is granted within the time provided in the preceding paragraph, the Guarantor is obliged to pay the Beneficiary's conforming demand without requiring any further action on the Beneficiary's part. The Guarantor shall incur no liability (for interest or otherwise) should any payment to the Beneficiary be delayed as a result of the above-mentioned procedure.

Even if the Principal agrees to or requests such extension, it shall not be granted unless the Guarantor and the Instructing Party(ies) also agree thereto.

F. GOVERNING LAW AND JURISDICTION

Article 27

Unless otherwise provided in the Guarantee or Counter-Guarantee, its governing law shall be that of the place of business of the Guarantor or Instructing Party (as the case may be) or, if the Guarantor or Instructing Party has more than one place of business, that of the branch which issued the Guarantee or Counter-Guarantee.

Article 28

Unless otherwise provided in the Guarantee or Counter-Guarantee, any dispute between the Guarantor and the Beneficiary relating to the Guarantee or between the Instructing Party and the Guarantor and relating to the Counter-Guarantee shall be settled exclusively by the competent court of the country of the place of business of the Guarantor or Instructing Party (as the case may be) or, if the Guarantor or Instructing Party has more than one place of business, by the competent court of the country of the branch which issued the Guarantee or Counter-Guarantee.

CHAPTER 11

GRADING AND CONTROLLING RISKS

It is the nature of bank demand guarantees that few appreciates the risk unless they have cause to think about it, are warned of it, or suffer actual loss.

In this final Chapter, we discuss the measures required to administer and control bank demand guarantee risk exposure effectively.

Education and training are usually the best ways to avoid the pitfalls of bank demand guarantees. It is the responsibility of senior management to ensure that all decision-makers, including those with delegated responsibility, understand the risks associated with bank demand guarantees.

Exporters need to establish corporate guidelines on the issue and control of bonds and guarantees of all types. These guidelines should state the company's policy on bond exposure, and delegate responsibility for their *issue, recording, monitoring, reporting, control and recovery* to a manager of sufficient calibre and authority to achieve these objectives.

The various Annexes to this Chapter suggest a typical corporate policy, advise on the minimum requirements to be incorporated into a bank guarantee from the exporter's point of view, and list a number of questions an exporter should address before agreeing to provide a bank demand guarantee.

Recording and Control Systems

Management requires good up-to-date information to ensure that their risks are regularly reviewed and controlled.

Without a clear policy and an effective monitoring and control system, keeping track of *outstanding bank guarantees* and *levels of contingent liability* can be haphazard, labour-intensive, and time-consuming.

Once a bank guarantee is issued, there needs to be an effective system for tracking it. Not only does each bank guarantee issued and cancelled need to be recorded, but also expiry dates need to be monitored, extensions to validity noted, changes in value made, and recovery action initiated.

Only a few bank guarantees are ever returned *voluntarily* once the exporter's obligations have been fulfilled. Those that are due to expire need to be highlighted and the appropriate action taken to ensure recovery.

Where all parties agree that a bank demand guarantee can incorporate the 458 Rules, *physical recovery* of the guarantee is no longer essential, as long as local law does not over-ride the 458 Rules.

Clear reports should analyse:

(a)   the volume and value of outstanding bank guarantees;
(b)   whether the guarantee is payable on demand or on proven default;
(c)   potential exposure to buyer and to country;
(d)   exposure trends; and
(e)   status of insured guarantees.

Controlling Risks

Risks need to be controlled in two ways:

(i)   quantitatively; and
(ii)   qualitatively.

Quantitatively, because the greater the value of bank guarantees outstanding, the higher the cost in the form of fees, taxes and insurance.

For senior management reporting purposes, only *summary information* is usually required. The simpler the presentation of the information, the easier it is for senior management to digest and understand. So an executive report could be in the form of Figure 5.

Figure 5

Regional analysis as at: 30 June 19...

	(m)	(m)*
AFRICA	12.57	12.93
EC	84.26	80.67
FAR EAST	52.17	13.69
MIDDLE EAST	39.50	52.80
PACIFIC	13.77	11.66
S&C AMERICA	4.88	5.40
SE EUROPE	3.18	3.33
USA & CARIBBEAN	8.67	6.78
WESTERN ASIA	30.55	25.77
TOTAL	249.55	213.03

(Figures in (m) column asterisked show comparative position at 31.12.19...)

This regional analysis informs senior management of the level of overall bonding, how exposure is distributed across the various regions of the world in which they are trading, and the trend since the previous report six months earlier.

Further down the management hierarchy, the information has to be more specific and detailed in order to identify the individual risks and exposures that make up the whole.

For operational management, the first information required is a *complete list* of outstanding bonds; that is to say, all those bank guarantees against which a bank is still holding a counter-indemnity. Until the counter-indemnity has been released, the exporter remains exposed to bank charges and even the risk of a demand on the guarantee, under some local laws, after the expiry date.

This list needs to be analysed into *type of bond* and its relevant details. Figure 6 shows typically how this information can be recorded on a computer database. Some professional treasury management systems include facilities for recording guarantees (see Appendix B for useful addresses).

Figure 6

Bond analysis—performance guarantees as at: 30 June 19...

Bond Number	Company Risk	Guarantor Beneficiary Country	Company Contact Date of Review/ Expiry
87023	100%	Barclays Min of Comm Pakistan	J Smith 1/94
		Currency: Sterling	Amount in Curr: Stg.Equiv: 25,165
		Reason: Gtee Contract Performance	Comment:
4032	100%	Citibank Bechtel USA	F Jones 3/93
		Currency: US Dollars	Amount in Curr: US$675,980 Stg.Equiv: 375,544
		Reason: Gtee Contract Performance	Comment:

	STERLING TOTAL:	124,820,076

There is also a need to record and assess the outstanding guarantees *qualitatively*. That is to say, the quality of the risk needs to be graded in order to understand the reality of the exposure to *unfair demand*. For example, surety bonds and bank guarantees that can only be called to the extent of *admitted* or *proven default*, or paid against a favourable award from a court or *arbitration*, carry an extremely *low risk* of unfair demand. The demand would need to be *fraudulent*, and the beneficiary is most unlikely to succeed in obtaining the exporter's or the court/arbitrator's approval for payment under these circumstances.

On the other hand, *simple demand* guarantees carry a high risk of *unfair* demand. This can often be mitigated by *unfair calling insurance*, and stays mitigated as long as the insurance remains effectively in place for the value and validity of the guarantee. Good records can ensure this.

The exporter is also less exposed if demand guarantees are issued against a payment of equivalent value. This applies particularly to *advance payments*, or the *release of retained money* which would not normally be paid until all contractual obligations had been fulfilled. This risk is mitigated as long as the payment guarantee is reduced *pro rata* to contractual perform- ance. If it is not, then the payment guarantee converts *de facto* into a per- formance guarantee in respect of the unreduced amount. Good records can show when the amount of a guarantee can be reduced.

Figure 7 provides an indication of how guarantees can be graded qualit- atively. Records of tender, advance payment, performance and retention guarantees need to be kept and regularly consolidated, analysed and com- pared with the previous period. This comparison is important, as it pro- vides a *"feel"* for the quality of potential new business in the pipeline, through analysis of new tender guarantees, and an indication of whether the quality of risk is improving or deteriorating.

Figure 7

Consolidated risk analysis as at: 30 June 19...

Type	Default		Demand Insured		Demand Uninsured		TOTAL	
	(m)	(m)*	(m)	(m)*	(m)	(m)*	(m)	(m)*
Advance	5.68	1.17	9.55	11.14	42.07	41.36	57.30	53.67
Perform	73.73	48.11	23.26	29.23	27.82	19.45	124.81	96.79
Retent	3.77	4.30	22.88	29.93	27.97	17.38	54.62	51.61
Tender	4.70	4.86	1.61	.82	6.51	5.28	12.82	10.96
TOTAL	87.88	58.44	57.30	71.12	104.37	83.47	249.55	213.03

(Figures in (m) columns asterisked show comparative position at 31.12.19...)

The consolidated risk analysis shows at a glance the *contingent liability* that the exporter is carrying in respect of bank demand guarantees on the company's balance sheet, and how this is divided between existing busi- ness and attempts to get new contracts (tender guarantee figure).

It shows the amount which cannot be called without the exporter's agreement or an arbitration award against him ("Default" column), the ex- tent he is vulnerable to the unfair call of demand guarantees, particularly performance guarantees, and the extent to which the insurer is mitigating the risk.

This qualitative analysis is important because of the need to *nurse* those contracts and guarantees given to buyers and/or countries which may be more inclined to call bank demand guarantees, or not reduce them when contractually required. To do this, it is important to know the exposure by *country*.

Figure 8 provides a typical example of the breakdown of unconsolidated data that was used to develop Figure 7.

Figure 8

Country/bond type risk analysis as at: 30 June 19. . .

Malaysia

	Default		Demand Insured		Demand Uninsured		Total	
	(k)	(k)*	(k)	(k)*	(k)	(k)*	(k)	(k)*
Advance	–	–	–	–	1006	538	1006	538
Perform	611	320	992	680	279	250	1882	1250
Retent	–	–	–	–	367	180	367	180
Tender	81	60	–	–	708	621	789	681
Total	692	380	992	680	2360	1589	4044	2649

(Figures in (k) columns asterisked show comparative position at 31.12.19. . .)

There is a higher risk of an *unfair* demand from some countries than from others and so these need to be analysed and controlled separately. Figure 9 provides an analysis of *high-risk territories*, exposure to which requires *intensive monitoring and control.*

Figure 9

Exposure in high-risk territories as at: 30 June 19. . .

	Default		Demand Insured		Demand Uninsured		Total	
	(k)	(k)*	(k)	(k)*	(k)	(k)*	(k)	(k)*
Iraq	–	–	–	–	1006	538	1006	538
Ex-USSR	611	320	992	680	279	250	1882	1250
Zaire	–	–	56	56	367	180	423	236
Yugoslavia	81	60	–	–	708	621	789	681
Total	692	380	1048	736	2360	1589	4100	2705

(Figures in (k) columns asterisked show comparative position at 31.12.19. . .)

Exporters need to know their *exposure to buyers and markets.* Limits are usually set on such territories, and new business should be declined or de-layed once those limits have been reached. This is to ensure that an imbal-ance of risk beyond corporate limits does not occur. Like banks, most exporters prefer to avoid having all their risks in one place.

To obtain a more balanced perspective of *uninsured* demand perform-ance guarantees, Figure 10 provides a country analysis containing valuable information of the current situation and trend compared with the previous period of analysis. This could be further analysed into public and private buyers if the information gained is useful.

Figure 10

Uninsured demand performance bonds as at: 30 June 19...

Total Qty	Country	TOTAL (k)	TOTAL (k)*
11	AUSTRALIA	8092	4697
2	BAHRAIN	6834	8877
2	BANGLADESH	125	135
1	BELGIUM	2	2
4	BULGARIA	34	29
2	CAMEROONS	439	–
9	PR CHINA	560	360
2	COLUMBIA	599	602
1	DENMARK	9	9
4	EGYPT	66	72
1	ETHIOPIA etc	91	91
2	ZAMBIA	21	57
	TOTAL	113,820	97,320

(Figures in (k) column asterisked show comparative position at 31.12.19...)

A key report is the ageing analysis of *time-expired bonds—uncancelled* to highlight guarantees that have *expired*, but have *not been cancelled*. Failure to recover and cancel guarantees not subject to the 458 Rules unnecessarily increases risk, as well as the cost of bank demand guarantees and unfair calling insurance. As a measure of the company's efficiency in reducing ex-posure, a report showing *bank guarantees expired but not cancelled* can be very revealing—see Figure 11.

Figure 11

Time-expired bonds, uncancelled as at: 30 June 19...

Summary—geographical analysis

Country	Cancelled this Period	Uncancelled (k)	of which expired more than nine months prior (k)	(k)*
ALGERIA	124	1133	213	213
AUSTRALIA		58	23	14
BAHRAIN	45	189	33	33
BANGLADESH		17	10	8
BELIZE		249	34	34
CAMEROONS	160	1969	54	–
PR CHINA		103	–	34
COLUMBIA		100	100	–
DENMARK	2	9	–	–
EGYPT		6	–	2
etc				
ZAMBIA		50	10	10
TOTAL	1204	23919	8584	9678

(Figures in (k) column asterisked show comparative position at 31.12.19...)

Finally, it is valuable for the company finance director or treasurer to know which *banks* are getting the company's bank guarantee business. This is good information on utilisation of banking lines.

It also helps with the negotiation of fees and the cost of other facilities. There is a risk that *too many* banks are being asked to issue bank guarantees and this can reduce the company's competitive buying power (see Figure 12—analysis by guarantor).

Figure 12

Analysis by guarantor as at: 30 June 19...

Total Qty	Guarantor	TOTAL (k)	(k)*
16	ANZ Banking Group Ltd.	480	480
12	Bank of America	305	305
1	Bank of New Zealand	51	51
106	Barclays Bank	23768	22975
3	Canadian Imperial Bank of Commerce	205	205
2	Citibank	163	163
15	Credit Lyonnais	8416	7590
(etc)			
7	Grindlays Bank	219	208
3	Hongkong Shanghai Bank	584	584
215	Midland Bank	85439	80359
4	Standard Chartered	856	856
3	Toronto Dominion	87	68
4	Westpac Banking Corp	43	43
TOTAL		249,550	213,030

(Figures in the (k) column asterisked show comparative position at 31.12.19...)

Guarantees expressed in *foreign currency* involve a potential foreign ex-change risk when called, unless suitably claused to eliminate it. Banks regularly adjust the value of bank guarantees outstanding to an up-to-date exchange rate, and increase or reduce the amount of banking facilities to an exporter accordingly. Exporters need to keep their own records in line with those of the banks, with regular reconciliations, say quarterly, with the guarantor bank.

Sub-contractor Guarantees

With some companies, a record also needs to be kept of guarantees that have been *received* from sub-contractors and major suppliers to ensure that the security in them is not lost before the related contract has been duly performed, and in some cases until the exporter is released from his liability under the main contract.

Computer Software

Fortunately, there are now computer packages on the market suitable for PCs to keep track of bond movements and to provide regular management reports to enable them to take action to reduce costs and exposure.

Annex I—Suggested Company Policy for the Issue and Control of Bank Demand Guarantees

It is Company policy to:

(i)   control the issue of bank demand guarantees;
(ii) control the Company's exposure to any one territory (especially those deemed from time to time to involve high risk) and to any one customer;
(iii) limit the exposure to the risk of an unfair call of demand guarantees;
(iv) ensure that where bank guarantees are given to customers either in the domestic market or overseas, they are drafted, approved, obtained, monitored, controlled and cancelled in the most efficient and cost-effective manner; and
(v)   establish a consistent and uniform approach throughout the Company in achieving (i)–(iv) above.

1. Scope

This policy applies worldwide.

2. Definitions

2.1   *Demand guarantee*
      A demand guarantee is a written guarantee given by one party, generally a bank, surety or insurance company (guarantor) to another (beneficiary/customer) for the fulfilment of contractual obligations undertaken by a third party (contractor). A surety company traditionally issues bonds under which they are liable only if the terms and conditions of the underlying contract have not been fulfilled.
      For the purposes of this policy, the term "demand guarantee" is used throughout to indicate both bonds and bank guarantees.
2.2   *Types of demand guarantee*
      The principal types of guarantee are:
      (a) *Bid or tender guarantee*
      A demand guarantee to support a bid or tender for a contract. Its purpose is to provide an assurance of the intention of the tenderer not to withdraw his tender and to sign the contract if his tender is accepted and to eliminate frivolous tenders.
      (b) *Performance guarantee*
      A guarantee intended as a safeguard against the contractor failing to fulfil his contract.
      (c) *Advance payment guarantee*

A guarantee which protects the customer's interest in respect of the repayment of advance payments made by him, in the event of the contractor failing to fulfil his contract.

(d) *Retention guarantee*

A demand guarantee which is substituted for money retained by the customer in accordance with the contract.

2.3   *Demand and default guarantees*

The most important distinction is between "demand" and "default" guarantees.

Unless specifically precluded by the terms of the guarantee requiring independent endorsement of default, a guarantor will pay the beneficiary on his written statement that the contractor has defaulted, without involving himself in the accuracy or otherwise of the claim.

(a) *Demand guarantee*

A demand guarantee becomes payable to the beneficiary immediately the beneficiary makes a formal request to the guarantor. If such a guarantee is called unfairly, the contractor's only recourse will be that allowed under the law of the beneficiary's country and/or of the relevant contract.

(b) *Default guarantee*

A default guarantee becomes payable to the beneficiary only when the contractor admits default or where the arbitration award or court judgment is made against the contractor. It cannot be cashed by means of a simple unilateral demand by the beneficiary (or his agent).

3. Interpretation

Any questions of interpretation of this policy should be referred to the Company Finance Director.

4. Selection of guarantor

The guarantor (bank, surety or insurance company) should be selected from a list published from time to time by the Company Finance Director, using the following criteria:

- strength of representation of the guarantor in the customer's country;
- guarantor's ability to provide guarantees directly to the customer without involving a chain of banks/surety companies, etc.;
- guarantor's ability to react speedily and flexibly in what may well be an ever-changing situation;
- the commission-charging structure;
- the extent to which the guarantor may possibly be involved in other Company financial activities;
- customer preference.

As a general rule, where the option exists, bonds issued by surety companies should be offered where it is considered this would provide additional security against an unfair call.

5. Issue of bank guarantees

5.1   Guarantees, particularly demand guarantees, should be resisted wherever there is an opportunity to do so. However, advance payment and retention guarantees may be considered desirable where this improves cashflow, and where risk of unfair call is low.

5.2   When drafting guarantees and choosing its guarantors, the Company's exposure to an unfair or capricious call should be kept to a minimum.

6. Text of guarantees

6.1   Guidelines for the drafting of guarantees are appended hereto. However, it is recognised that in certain countries the type of guarantee to be supplied is laid down by local law or custom. In addition, certain standard forms of contract include standard texts of guarantees.

6.2   The text of guarantees should be drafted in accordance with legal advice so as to minimise exposure to pre-emptive or capricious calling. It should not introduce risks additional to those accepted under the contract. For example, wherever possible:

(a)   the customer should not be given any express unilateral right to demand an extension to a guarantee and so effectively extend the period of exposure;

(b)   all guarantees should expire on a fixed date;

(c)   advance payment guarantees, especially when payable on demand, should automatically reduce in value *pro rata* to the earning of such payments during the performance of the contract, and a procedure should be agreed with the beneficiary and guarantor to achieve this;

(d)   any guarantee given against release of retention moneys should reduce in accordance with the date upon which retention under the contract should be released; and

(e)   performance guarantees should only be capable of being called for an amount equal to any actual loss suffered by the customer, up to the value of the guarantee. If the contract is divisible in stages then, if possible, there should be a guarantee for each stage that can be cancelled on completion of the relevant stage.

7. Limiting exposure

7.1   Guarantees may be either for fixed amounts or for the amount of losses suffered by the beneficiary up to a maximum amount. The latter approach is preferable provided that the maximum amount is reasonable. Whichever approach is applicable, the amount (or the maximum amount) should not be penal. In general, performance guarantees should not exceed 10 per cent. of the contract price. As regards tender bonds, these should not, in general, exceed 5 per cent. of the tendered price.

Advance payment and retention guarantees should be for the amounts advanced or released (as the case may be) and should reduce as mentioned in 6.2(c) and (d) above.

7.2 The total bonding requirement of any ultimate contract should be ascertained before bidding, as once a tender is submitted with a tender guarantee, this could entail an additional obligation to provide other demand guarantees if the tender is accepted.

8. Obtaining guarantees from major suppliers, sub-contractors, and joint tenderers

8.1 The Company must protect itself against contractual or financial failures by major suppliers, sub-contractors and joint tenderers. In appropriate cases this is achieved by obtaining "back-to-back" bonds or cross-indemnities.

8.2 The terms of the suppliers', sub-contractors' and joint tenderers' guarantees should be no less onerous than the terms of the guarantees under the main contract.

Wherever possible, such guarantees should be obtained prior to the issue of demand guarantees under the main contract.

8.3 The Company's contribution to guarantees in joint venture situations should be *pro rata* to the Company's participation in the joint venture and should be on a *several* basis unless specifically agreed otherwise by the Company Finance Director. Where, however, excessive exposure is necessary, it should be reflected in the margins.

9. Counter-indemnities

The terms of the counter-indemnity required by the guarantor may impose greater exposure on the Company than the guarantee it covers; wherever possible, such greater exposure should be avoided. Counter-indemnities must be approved by the Company lawyer and signed by the Company Finance Director.

10. Insurance of demand guarantees

10.1 *Availability of insurance*
Insurance is normally available from the national credit insurer

and the private market where policies are obtained against unfair calling of demand guarantees.

10.2 It is essential to comply in all respects with the terms and conditions of the policy to avoid prejudicing the ability to substantiate a claim.

10.3 *When to insure*

The decision whether to insure demand guarantees against unfair calling through the national credit insurer or private market depends on the particular circumstances, *viz*:

(a) Demand guarantees in high-risk situations or territories must be insured. A situation or territory falls into the high-risk category when any of the following apply:

   (i)   the tender or contract is with a country where there is significant risk of an unfair call;

   (ii) the level of Company bonding in the relevant territory (or the political bloc of which the territory is currently or is likely to form part) is particularly high;

   (iii) the type of guarantee is question is particularly vulnerable. In this regard, performance guarantees are considered to be the most vulnerable and should normally be insured.

(b) Tender guarantees usually fall into a separate category and insurance against a risk of an unfair call should be considered on an ad hoc basis. Insurance should be considered where it is practice to threaten calling a guarantee as pressure for improved commercial terms.

(c) Advance payment and retention guarantees established in high-risk territories should generally be insured (notwithstanding that the underlying contract may be covered by credit insurance) in cases where the applicable legal system is such that the credit insurance cover would not provide protection against unfair calling.

(d) The Company Finance Director may decide from time to time to insure, wherever possible, all demand guarantees for contracts directly with customers in those countries considered to expose the Company to particularly high risks or for sub-contractors where the ultimate customer is in such a country.

(e) Low-value guarantees—Where a demand guarantee would normally be required to be insured, there is a point at which costs could outweigh the benefits of cover. Advice on establishing such lower limits should be obtained from the Company Finance Director before the guarantee in question is issued.

11. Avoidance of claims

Before a claim is made under a demand guarantee, the Company will usually receive a prior hint or notification that such a claim is likely. In such an event:

(a) all necessary action must be taken to avoid a claim or to mitigate losses;

(b) advice of the Company Lawyer must be obtained at the earliest opportunity; and

(c) the Company Finance Director should be notified of all potential claims of significant value.

12. Charges and premiums

Both the instructing bank and the guarantor in the buyer's country make charges for giving guarantees; the latter's are often very heavy. These charges will vary from country to country and may include, but not be limited to, stamp duties, local taxes and levies. Some costs may be avoided by selecting a bank able to issue local guarantees without double charging, or by persuading a local guarantor to accept a Company counter-indemnity.

At the time of bidding/tendering, it is necessary to establish what guarantees are likely to be required, the cost of their issue and, if appropriate, the premium for their insurance.

13. Authority limits

13.1 The decision whether or not to insure against unfair calling, and/or to exempt a transaction from this Company policy, can only be taken by the Company Finance Director.

13.2 It is the responsibility of the Company Finance Director to:

(a) ensure that all commercial, sales and contract managers, are fully informed of Company policy on demand guarantees and comply therewith; and

(b) ensure that all guarantees are promptly reduced in value and cancelled when the appropriate performance milestones entitle the Company to any reduction or cancellation.

13.3 The Company Finance Director is responsible for:

(a) providing half-yearly information to the Executive Board of Directors on the total Company involvement and potential exposure for each territory, group of territories or political bloc;

(b) recommending from time to time to the Executive Board of Directors:

(i) financial limits for the Company's exposure in a particular territory or group of territories, etc.; and

(ii) the inclusion or deletion of particularly high-risk territories as referred to in 10.3(d) above.

(c) keeping closely under review the impact on Company profits, gearing and cashflow which might result from a pre-emptive or capricious calling of bank demand guarantees by a specific territory or group of territories, and make due allowance for such de-

mands when developing plans for financing acquisitions and
other requirements of the Company;

    (d)   approving the selection of banks, surety companies and other
guarantors; and

    (e)   reporting annually to the Main Board on the cumulative expos-
ure on demand guarantees.

The Executive Board of Directors shall:

    (a)   review half-yearly the Company's total bonding position and
give guidance regarding the types of guarantee or particular territories where insurance of demand guarantees is considered
necessary,

  (b)(i)   give guidelines on financial limits for the Company's exposure
in a particular territory or group of territories;

    (ii)   review the inclusion or deletion of particular high risk territo-
ries as referred to in 10.3(d).

Attachment to company policy on the issue and control of demand guarantees

Guidelines on text of guarantees

1. General

1.1 Where a contract requires guarantees to be issued, the circumstances giving the beneficiary the right to call such guarantees should,
wherever possible, be clearly stated in the contract.

1.2 Demand guarantees should reflect the agreed terms of the contract, preferably in the text, otherwise by specific reference to the relevant contract clauses.

2. Fundamental points to be covered:

  (a)   coming into force of guarantee;

  (b)   reason for claim;

  (c)   payment to be subject to seller's admission or official arbitration
award or court judgment against the Company;

  (d)   maximum liability;

  (e)   automatic reduction mechanism against clearly distinguishable
performance milestones, *e.g.* shipment;

  (f)   fixed or determinable validity date;

  (g)   cancellation procedure;

  (h)   law and neutral arbitration.

3. Risks to be avoided where possible:

  (a)   clauses permitting payment on simple demand;

  (b)   open-ended liabilities;

(c)   customer's right to "top-up" after a claim has been paid;
(d)   contract or guarantee subject to local law and arbitration;
(e)   open-ended validity dates or express right automatically to extend validity dates;
(f)   non-reducing advance or progress payment guarantees, valid for full amount until expiry date or cancellation;
(g)   guarantees which only reduce on some instruction or signature by the buyer;
(h)   guarantees expressed in a currency other than the currency of the contract;
(i)   undocumented claims.

Annex II—Possible Questions

(Extracted from: CBI booklet, *Contract Bonds and Guarantees* (3rd ed.).)

When asked to provide a bond, the seller should ask several important questions before committing himself. It should be stressed that sellers must allow as much time as possible for negotiation of the bond requirements with the buyer, bringing in the guarantors at an early stage of the bargaining.

   (1)   Does the buyer want a default bond or demand bond; what will be my liability?

   (2)   What type of bond does the buyer want—tender, performance, advance payment, retention, etc.?

   (3)   What is my legal position when I provide a bond?

   (4)   Who should provide the bond—a surety company or bank?

   (5)   What criteria should I choose for selecting the most suitable guarantor? Should I restrict myself to one bank or surety company?

   (6)   What indemnity must I give the bank or surety company?

   (7)   What considerations will a bank give attention to before assisting me?

   (8)   Should I resist a buyer's insistence that bonds be issued by a bank in the buyer's country?

   (9)   What considerations will a surety company give attention to before assisting me?

 (10)   What are the direct and indirect costs of providing bonds?

 (11)   What foreign costs may I incur?

 (12)   Will the bank/surety company continue to charge fees after the bond has expired?

 (13)   Can I get further bonding if my tender is accepted?

 (14)   Are the terms of the contract and the bond consistent? Does the bond give the buyer greater rights than agreed in the contract?

 (15)   Have I thoroughly examined the bond for any onerous conditions?

 (16)   What rights do I have in the contract in respect of the recovery of the bonds including the tender bond?

 (17)   Can I include wording so that payment is made only on certain conditions?

 (18)   Can I use a letter of credit instead of a bond?

 (19)   Is the date of expiry of the bond clearly stated and understood by all?

 (20)   How do I ensure the bond is cancelled on expiry?

 (21)   Are there any laws or practices in the buyer's country which might affect the expiry date or final date for claims under the bond?

 (22)   Is there any special bond wording for the buyer's country?

 (23)   In the event of an imminent bond calling, what defence is permitted under local law or relevant foreign jurisdiction?

(24) What if the buyer makes an "extend or pay" demand?

(25) What effect will the provision of several tender or bid bonds have on my credit facilities?

(26) Have I ensured that there is a suitable reduction or amortisation clause in any advance payment bond or other bonds?

(27) How can I cover the risks of exchange rate fluctuation of a foreign currency bond?

(28) Have I structured the bond package in the most competitive way?

(29) What can my competitors put together and at what cost?

(30) Can I draw comfort from the ICC Uniform Rules covering demand guarantees?

(31) Is my contractual relationship with the main contractor the most appropriate? What are the problems in providing bonds if I am a sub-contractor?

(32) How can I obtain cover against unfair calling?

(33) What cover does the private insurance market give against unfair calling?

(34) What additional bond support can I get from either ECGD or the insurance market?

(35) What other sources of advice are there?

(Published by kind permission of the Confederation of British Industries.)

These are just typical examples of the type of questions a prudent exporter should ask himself. Inevitably the list is not exhaustive as every contract and bonding situation can raise new questions.

BIBLIOGRAPHY

Interlocutory Injunctions and Attachments

Not only the courts but also legal writers have occupied themselves with the problems arising in connection with bank guarantees. This is shown by several books and articles which cite and explain cases of abusive calls and examine in detail the many problems involved.

Here too the main subject of controversial discussions is the question of whether an interlocutory injunction or attachment of the payment claim is the most effective instrument.

Horn (in "Bürgschaften und Garantien zur Zahlung auf erstes Anfordern" [1980] N.J.W. 2153 *et seq.*) and Mülbert (in "Missbrauch von Bankgarantien und einstweiliger Rechtsschütz" in *Tübinger Rechtswissenschaftliche Abhandlungen* (Tübingen, 1985, Band 60); "Neueste Entwicklung des materiellen Rechts de Garantie auf erstes Anfordern" [1981] Z.I.P. 1101 *et seq.*) hold the view that the principal under a guarantee may obtain legal protection against abusive calls by way of an interlocutory injunction.

Aden (in "Der Arrest in den Auszahlungsanspruch des Garantiebegünstigten durch den Garantieauftraggeber" [1985] R.I.W. 439 *et seq.*) finds that injunctions against the beneficiary are possible but that, in the long run, only the attachment is likely to be successful.

Schütze (in "Einstweilige Verfügungen und Arreste im internationalen Rechtsverkehr, insbesondere im Zusammenhang mit der Inanspruchnahme von Bankgarantien" [1980] W.M. 1488; "Zur Geltenmachung einer Bankgarantie 'auf erstes Anfordern' " [1981] R.I.W. 83; "Die Sicherung von Ansprchen aus missbruchlicher Inanspruchnahme von Bankgarantien auf ersten Anfordern durch Arrest" [1981] D.B. 779) affirms the legal admissibility of an interlocutory injunction against the beneficiary, and probably also against the issuing bank (in "Zur Geltenmachung einer Bankgarantie 'auf erstes Anfordern' " [1981] R.I.W. 83–85, n. 17).

Zahn (in "Zahlung und Zahlungsicherung im Aussenhandel" [1986] 6. Aufl., Berlin Rdnr, 9/130 *et seq.*), on the other hand, advocates the injunction procedure exclusively against the beneficiary.

Von Mettenheim (in "Die Missbruchliche Inanspruchnahme bedingungsloser Garantien" [1981] R.I.W. 581 *et seq.*) and Pilger (in "Einstweiliger Rechtsschütz des Käufers and Akkreditivstellers wegen Gewührleistung durch Arrest in den Auszahlungsanspruch des Akkreditivbegünstigten" [1979] R.I.W. 588 *et seq.*) consider the attachment as the only possible procedure.

Heinsius (in "Zur Frage des Nachweises der rechtsmissbräuchlichen Inanspruchnahme einer Bankgarantie auf erstes Anfordern mit liquiden Beweismitteln, Festschrift für Wilfrid Werner, 'Handelsrecht und Wirtschaftsrecht in der Bankpraxis' " [1984] *Berlin* 229 *et seq.*) rejects the applicability of interlocutory injunctions.

Graf von Westphalen (in "Die Bankgarantie im internationalen Handelsverkehr" [1982] *Heidelberg*), Coing (in "Probleme der internationalen Handelsverkehr" [1983] Z.H.R., ss. 125 *et seq.*) and Neilsen (in "Rechtsmissbräuch bei der Inanspruchnahme von Bankgarantien als typishes Problem der Liquiditölsfunktion abstrakter Zahlungsversprechen" [1982] Z.I.P. 253; "Ausgestaltung internationaler Bankgarantien unter dem Gesichtspunkt etwaigen Rechtsmissbräuchs" [1983] Z.H.R. 147, ss.145 *et seq.*) have also examined in great detail the question of bank guarantees.

Stein/Berrer (in "Praxis des Exportgeschäfts II" [1981] Landsberg Kap. F 11 *et seq.*) deal comprehensively with the risks inherent in unconditional bank guarantees.

Hein (in "Der Zahlungsanspruch des Begünstigten einer Bankgarantie 'auf erstes Anfordern' [1982] Diss. Giessen) gives a basic and dogmatic description of the legal nature of the contract of guarantee and also the problems involved when seeking legal protection against abusive calls.

Horn (in "Bürgschaften und Garantien zur Zahlung auf erstes Anfordern" [1980] N.J.W. 2153) also deals with these problems and suggests a "counter-guarantee" to be given by the beneficiary of the "first" guarantee. In the event of the "first" guarantee being abusively called in, the counter-guarantee seems quite suitable as a security and also as a deterrent. In practice, however, it will hardly be accepted by the beneficiary under the "first" guarantee. At any rate, this would cause a chain of counter-guarantees and thus considerably reduce the effectiveness in international trade of the original guarantee, which would lose its practical value.

The fear of abuses should not devalue an effective instrument of trade to the point of making it completely useless.

(Source: *Bankgarantien (Vertroygarantien* (5th ed., 1987), published by Machinebau Verlag GmbH, Frankfurt/Main, Germany, with kind permission.)

Other relevant reading includes:

- Confederation of British Industry, *Contract Bonds and Guarantees* (3rd ed., March 1987);

- Prof. Clive M. Schmitthoff, "Bank Guarantees and Other Guarantees", *Export*. (Journal of the Institute of Export, September 1985);
- Phillippe De Smedt, "First Demand Guarantees in Belgian Law", *International Financial Law Review*, December 1983;
- Karen P. Williams, "On Demand and Conditional Performance Bonds", *LL.M. Journal of Business Law*, January 1981;
- David Duckworth and Ian Blackshaw, *Troubleshooting: International Business Problems* (Oyez Stationary Ltd. 1980);
- Societe Generale de Banque, *Monthly Review*, December 1980;
- ICC No. 400, *Uniform Customs and Practice for Documentary Credits*;
- ICC No. 325, *Uniform Rules for Contract Guarantees*;
- ICC No. 406, *Model Forms for Issuing Contract Guarantees*;
- *Guide on Bank Guarantees*, a guide by the Working Group on Legal Affairs of ORGALIME, Brussels, July 1987 (editeur responsable T. Gay, Sécrétaire génèrale de l'ORGALIME);
- Report of the Working Group on Bonding Requirements, London April 1984—British Overseas Trade Board, Overseas Projects Board;
- Rechtsanwalt Dr Herbert Stumpf in collaboration with Rechtswalt Claus Ullrich, *Bank Guarantee (Contract Guarantee)* (VDMA, 5th revised ed. 1987), published by Machinenbau-Verlag GmbH;
- "Article Chronique de droit bancaire privé", *Revue de la Banque*, No. 9, November 1989; Lucien Simont and André Bruyneel, *Les Operations de banque: garanties independantes* (1979–1988);
- "*La Garantie a Premier Demande—Analyse Descriptive*", Dossier 2, Association Belge des Banques, Brussels, September 1985;
- M. Vasseur, "Rapport de synthese: le droit des garanties bancaires dans les contrats internationaux en France et dans les pays de l'Europe de l'Ouest", Colloque de Tours;
- *The Treasurer*, April 1988 (official publication of the Association of Corporate Treasurers, London).

(See *Joint Ventures in Europe* (Ellison and Klings, eds:)—a practical guide to the selection and use of differing joint venture structures in France, Germany, Italy, the Netherlands, Spain, Switzerland. Based on experiences of leading commercial law firms in their home jurisdiction. Published by Butterworths, £75.00.)

Appendix B

USEFUL ADDRESSES

General

Association of British Insurers (ABI)
Aldermanbury House
Queen Street
London EC4N 1TU
Tel: 071–248–4477

ORGALIME
Organisme de Liaison des Industries Métallique Européenes
Rue de Stassart 99
B–1050 Bruxelles

(The Organisme de Liaison des Industries Métalliques Européennes (ORGALIME) groups the central engineering and metalworking trade associations in 15 European countries and provides liaison between these bodies in economic, legal, technical and other matters of concern to the industries they represent.)

Insurers of Bond Risks

Export Credits Guarantee Department
PO Box 2200
2 Exchange Tower
Harbour Exchange Square
London E14 9GS
Contact: Bonds Branch

PanFinancial Insurance Co. Ltd.
International House
World Trade Centre

1 St Katherine's Dock
London E1 9UN

Lloyds of London
Lloyds Building
Lime Street
London EC3
Contact: via a Lloyds Broker

Federal Insurance Co
50 Fenchurch Street
London EC3M 3JY

American International Underwriters (UK) Ltd.
120 Fenchurch Street
London EC3

NCM Credit Insurance Ltd.
Crown Building
Cathays Park
Cardiff
CF1 3PX
South Wales
(NCM purchased the short-term branch of ECGD on December 1, 1991.)

(This is not a comprehensive list of insurers.)

List of Surety Companies That Issue Bonds

General Surety and Guarantee Co. Ltd.
Hawthorn Hall
Hall Road
Wilmslow
Cheshire SK9 5BZ

Seaboard Surety Company
Warnford Court
Throgmorton Street
London EC2N 2JQ

Sun Alliance Insurance Group
50 Fenchurch Street
London EC3M 3JY

(This is not a comprehensive list of surety companies.)

Brokers of Bond Risk Insurance

Bain Dawes Credit Ltd.
Bain Dawes House
15 Minories
London EC3N 1NJ

Berry Palmer Lyle Ltd.
24/26 Minories
London EC3N 1BY
(Lloyds Brokers.)

Chandler Hargreaves Ltd.
Chandler House
3/7 Marshalsea Road
London SE1 1EF
(Lloyds Brokers.)

Hogg Robinson (Credit & Political) Ltd.
13 Grosvenor Place
London SW1X 7HH

Furness-Houlder (Commercial Services) Ltd.
Bankside House
107/112 Leadenhall Street
London EC3A 4AA

Jardine Credit Insurance Ltd.
Thames House
1–4 Queen Street Place
London EC4R 1JA

Sedgwick UK (National) Ltd.
Sedgwick Credit
Sedgwick House
The Sedgwick Centre
London E1 8DX

Steven Backhouse and Co. Ltd.
Chronicle House
72/78 Fleet Street
London EC4Y 1HY

(This is not a comprehensive list of brokers.)

Bond Risk Consultants

Export Risk Control Ltd.
Park View Road
Woldingham
Surrey
CR3 7DN
Tel: 0883 652047

Bond Support Advisers Ltd.
48 Southwark Street
London SE1 1UN
Tel: 071–403–6166
(Arranges support for bonds under its own bank guarantee indemnity scheme.)

Bond Risk Management Systems
Adaps Consultants
Quadrant House
7/9 Heath Road
Weybridge
Surrey KT13 8SX

INDEX

Abusive calls *see* Unfair demands
Accessory obligations, 18
Advance payment guarantees,
 coming into force clause, 77
 development loans, 75
 German law, 91–92
 import licensing schemes, 72
 percentage of contract value, 7
 reduction clauses, 71, 178
 specimen texts,
  documentary demand, 87
  simple demand, 87
 text examples of, 47–48, 56–59,
  72–78
 unreduced value of, 10, 73
Agents,
 benefits of local, 184
AIG and PanFinancial, 207
Assignment, 159
 German law, 159
Attachments (German law) *see*
 Unfair demands

Back-to-back bonding *see* Sub-
 contractors
Bank charges on demand
 guarantees *see* Demand
 guarantees
Bank demand guarantees *see*
 Demand guarantees
Bank guarantee indemnity scheme
 (1982), 156
Banks,
 advice to exporters, 159
 company analysis of banking
  business, 265
 competitive charging policy, 25
 foreign banks, 140–141

costs of guarantees *see* Demand
 guarantees
demand guarantees *see* Demand
 guarantees
drafting requirements, 45–46,
 110
follow-on guarantees *see* Tender
 guarantees
as guarantors, 8–9, 14–15
 commencement of liability,
  179
 to sub-contractors, 120–121
as instructing bank, 9
as issuing/correspondent bank,
 9
 contractual relationship to
  instructing bank, 235–236
 overseas, 26–27, 141, 142–144,
  162, 174
joint venture banks, 143
knowledge of local laws, 183
overseas branches, 144
overseas subsidiaries, 143–144
recognition and control of risks,
 220–221
relationship to issuing bank,
 141–144
risk asset ratios, 24–25, 140
selection by exporter, 174
Basle Agreement, 220
Beneficiaries *see* Buyers
BGI *see* Bank guarantee indemnity
 scheme
Bid bonds *see* Tender guarantees
Bond issue support schemes,
 153–156
 eligibility for, 153–154
 indemnity agreement, 155

recourse-worthiness, 154
Bond risk cover *see* Unfair
    demands
Bonds,
    bid bonds *see* Tender guarantees
    completion bonds *see*
        Performance guarantees
    customs bonds *see* Customs
        bonds
    definition of types, 5–8
    freight bonds *see* Freight bonds
    payment bonds *see* Retention
        bonds
    performance bonds *see*
        Performance guarantees
    retention bonds *see* Retention
        bonds
    surety bonds *see* Surety bonds
    tender bonds *see* Tender
        guarantees
    warranty bonds *see* Warranty
        guarantees
    see also Demand guarantees
Burgschaft (German law), 90
Buyers,
    beneficiary of guarantees, 8
    conflict of interests with
        exporters, 9–10
    drafting objectives, 39–40
    fair demands *see* Fair demands
    terms for, 5
    unfair demands *see* Unfair
        demands

Comfort, letter of *see* Letter of
    comfort
Committee of London and Scottish
    Clearing Banks (CLSCB), 12
    draft code on demand
        guarantees, 225, 228
Completion bonds *see* Performance
    guarantees
Compliant demands, 21
Conclusive evidence clause *see*
    Counter-indemnities
Confederation of British Industry

(CBI),
    checklist for bond provision,
        275–276
Consortia, 132–133
    risk control, 175
Contingent liability, 3–4
    analysis of risk, 262
    aggregation of guarantees, 10–11
Contract guarantees, uniform rules
    for *see* Uniform Rules for
        Contract Guarantees
Corporate guarantees, 213–218
    commercial considerations, 216
    continuing liability of, 214–215
    internal guidelines for, 215–216
    letters of comfort, use of,
        216–218
    provision for liabilities, 218
    return or cancellation, 214
Correspondent bank *see* Banks
Costs of demand guarantees *see*
    Demand guarantees
Counter-guarantees,
    French law, 35–37
    Counter-indemnities, 29–31
    conclusive evidence clause,
        28–29
    inter-bank, 11, 31–32, 236
    joint ventures, 131
Cross-indemnities,
    joint ventures, 131
Currency fluctuations *see* Exchange
    rate fluctuations
Customs bonds,
    purpose of, 8

Declaration of renunciation *see*
    Demand guarantees
Default guarantees,
    dependent on contract, 18–20
    English law, 82
    European law, 18–19
    independent of contract, 20
Demand guarantees,
    abuse of, 160, 224
    see also Unfair demands

advantages to buyer, 17
aggregation of, 10–11
assignment of see Assignment
bibliography on, 278–279
cancellation, 177–178
   on return, 138
capital assets of bank, 24
charges for, 25
code of practice, 12
coercive power of, 161–162
contingent liability, 163–164,
   167–168
contract statement on, 175, 177
costs of, 135–147
   bank charges, 141
      correspondent bank, 141
      exporter's bank, 139–140
      foreign banks, 140–141
   hidden, 145–147
   insurance cover, 144–145
   legal drafting, 136
   local taxation, 141
   variables affecting, 135–136
and creation of contingent
   liability, 3–4, 262
credit ceiling, 15
currency fluctuation risks, 126,
   146–147, 152
default see Default guarantees
development since 1970s, 2–4
direct, 26
dispute settlement procedure,
   194–195, 235
drafting requirements, 40–43,
   45–51
   approval by insurers, 204
   costs of, 136
   dispute settlement clause,
      50–51
   protection in text, 49, 137,
      175–177
   risks of, 51, 158
effect of unreduced values in, 10
expiry/validity date of, 11,
   137–138, 180–184
   extension, 137–139, 144–145,

160–161
458 Rules provisions see
   Uniform Rules for Demand
   Guarantees
late claims against, 180–181
local laws, 138, 182–183
   see also Extend or pay claims
first demand see First demand
   guarantees
follow-on guarantees see Tender
   guarantees
French law, 35–37, 88–90
German law, 90–100
hidden risks to exporters, 10–11
high-risk texts, 48–50
indirect, 26
issue procedure, 17, 27–32
   CBI checklist, 275–276
   specimen text for company
      policy, 267–274
local guarantee required , 212
local legislation, effect of, 11
low-risk texts, 41–47
maximum liability
   consideration, 177–178
misuse of, 160
non-return of, 145–146, 234, 259
operative period of risk, 179
origins of, 4
project see Project guarantees
reduction clauses, 177–178
   self-liquidation provision,
      183–184
renunciation of, 146
risk exposure control see Risk
   exposure control
specimen texts, 83–85
   company policy for issue and
      control, 267–274
   German, 89–91, 106–107
   international models, 99–106
sub-contractors, 120–121
   see also under Sub-contractors
terminology, 4–5
text of, 11, 17
   guidelines, 273–274

examples, 42–77
top-up clauses *see* Performance
    guarantees
types of, 17–21
unfair demands *see* Unfair
    demands
use by exporters, 4
validity date *see* expiry date
value of the guarantee, 136
    built into contract price,
        184–185
    risk control, 260–261
    text relating to, 137
Dependent-contact guarantees *see*
Default guarantees
Direct guarantees *see* Demand
guarantees
Documentary credits *see* Uniform
Customs and Practice for
Documentary Credits

ECGD *see* Export Credit Guarantee
Department
Exchange rate fluctuations, 126,
    146–147, 152
    risk analysis, 265–266
Export Credit Guarantee
    Department (UK),
    bond issue support scheme, 151,
        153–156
    unfair calling cover, 203–206
Exporters,
    assistance from insurance
        brokers, 195–196
    coercive pressure on, 9–10, 23,
        158, 161–162, 167, 173
    commercial risks to, 158–162
    conflict of interests with buyers,
        9–10
    contingent liability, 163–164, 168
    counter-indemnities required, 11
    drafting,
        negotiations over, 46–47
        objectives in, 40
    financial risks to, 163–164
    local laws, difficulty of, 162,

182–184
    political risks to, 164–165
    principal to guarantees, 8
    recourse-worthiness *see*
        Recourse-worthiness
    risk management *see* Unfair
        demands
    technical risks to, 162–163
    unfair demands *see* Unfair
        demands
Extend or pay claims, 11, 138–139,
    144, 160–161
    458 Rules provisions, 234
    French law, 180–181
    German law, 145
    as hidden cost, 145
    private insurers, 210–211

Fair demands,
    circumstances of, 171–172
    insurance cover, 205
First demand guarantees, 20–21
    categorisation in 458 Rules,
        232–233
    independent documentary, 22
    independent of contract, 23–24
    simple demand, 22–23, 46, 52
        autonomy from supply
            contract, 224
        English case law on, 82–84
        458 Rules provisions *see*
            Uniform Rules for Demand
            Guarantees
        fraudulent claims, 84, 197–202
        risks of call on, 171
    types of, 21–23
    uniform rules and practice *see*
        Uniform Rules for Demand
        Guarantees
Foreign currency risks, 126,
    146–147
458 Rules *see* Uniform Rules for
    Demand Guarantees
Fraudulent claims *see* Unfair
    demands
Freight bonds,

purpose of, 8
French law,
    abusive or fraudulent claims,
        197–202
    demand guarantees *see* Demand
        guarantees
    guarantor's rights, 19, 86–88
    inter-bank guarantees, 35–37

Garantie (German law), 90–100
German law,
    demand guarantees *see* Demand
        guarantees
    injunctions and attachments *see*
        Unfair demands
    standard texts, 91–93
    types of guarantee, 91
Grading of risk *see* Risk exposure
    control
Guarantees,
    advance payment guarantees *see*
        Repayment guarantees
    bank demand guarantees *see*
        Demand guarantees
    corporate *see* Corporate
        guarantees
    default *see* Default guarantees
    demand guarantees *see* Demand
        guarantees
    dependent *see* Default
        guarantees
    first demand *see* First demand
        guarantees
    independent *see* Default
        guarantees
    interim payment guarantees *see*
        Repayment guarantees
    issuing bodies, 8
    maintenance guarantees *see*
        Maintenance guarantees
    parties to, 8–9
    performance guarantees *see*
        Performance guarantees
    retention guarantees *see*
        Retention bonds
    tender guarantees *see* Tender

guarantees
    types and uses of, 5–8
    warranty guarantees *see*
        Warranty guarantees
    see also Bonds
Guarantors,
    rights in European law, 19
    terms for, 5

High-risk texts *see* Demand
    guarantees

Independent guarantees *see*
    Default guarantees
Indirect guarantees *see* Demand
    guarantees
Indulgences,
    advance consent by guarantor,
        19
    granted by buyer, 19
Injunctions (German law) *see*
    Unfair demands
Insurance brokers,
    address list of, 281–282, 283
    assistance to exporters, 195–196
Insurance companies,
    as surety companies, 13
Insurance cover *see* Unfair
    demands
Inter-bank counter-guarantees *see*
    Counter-guarantees
Inter-bank counter-indemnities *see*
    Counter-indemnities
Interim payment guarantees *see*
    Repayment guarantees
Interlocutory injunctions (German
    law) *see* Unfair demands
International Chamber of
    Commerce (ICC), 12
    specimen guarantee texts,
        104–108
    325 Rules *see* Uniform Rules for
        Contract Guarantees
    458 Rules *see* Uniform Rules for
        Demand Guarantees
    uniform rules for contract bonds,

237
  uniform rules for surety bonds,
    17
Instructing bank *see* Banks
Iraq,
  outstanding guarantees
    problem, 221, 236
Issuing bank *see* Banks

Joint ventures, 130–132
  risk control, 175

Letters of comfort, 10, 216–218
Letters of credit,
  expiry date, 138
  stand-by, 32–34, 229
    specimen texts (USA), 111–112
Lloyd's of London, 207
  restrictions and exclusions,
    209–210

Maintenance guarantees,
  as coercive factor, 162
  definition and purpose of, 7
  risks of, 170
  Manifest fraud *see* Unfair
    demands

NCM Credit Insurance Ltd, 207

Organisme de Liaison des
  Industries Metalliques
  Europeenes (ORGALIME),
  model texts produced by,
  101–104

Payment bonds *see* Retention
  bonds
Penalty bonds *see* Performance
  guarantees
Performance guarantees,
  definition and purpose of, 6
  German law, 92–93
  ICC specimen text, 107–108
  international model texts,
    102–103, 104

as letter of credit, 84
  reduction and cancellation, 178
  risks of, 169
  specimen texts for, 86–87
    German, 109
  sub-contractors, 120–121
  text examples of, 43–44, 54–55,
    65–71
  top-up clauses, 162, 177
  unfair call on, 179
Pre-emption *see* Unfair demands
Progress payments,
  percentage of contract value, 7
Project guarantees,
  consortia, 132–133, 175
  financial exposure limitation,
    117–118, 175
  joint ventures, 130–132, 175
  structure of project, 118–119
  sub-contractors *see* Sub-
    contractors

Recourse-worthiness,
  bond issue support *see* Bond
    issue support schemes
  considerations affecting, 149
  currency fluctuation, 152
  exporter's balance sheet, 150–151
  inflation effect, 152
  related balance sheet, 150–151
  third party security, 150–151
Reduction clauses *see* Demand
  guarantees
Renunciation, Declaration of *see*
  Demand guarantees
Repayment guarantees,
  arbitration on, 169
  definition and purpose of, 6–7
  ICC specimen text, 106
  international model texts, 102,
    103–104
  risks of, 168–169
  specimen text (German), 109
Retention bonds,
  definition and purpose, 7
  unreduced value of, 10

Risk exposure control, 259–276
  analysis of bank business, 265
  computer software packages for,
    266
  contingent liability analysis, 262
  expiry and cancellation analysis,
    264
  grading analysis procedure,
    261–264
  high–risk territory analysis, 263
  quantative control of value,
    260–261
  recording and control systems,
    259–260
  specimen document for
    company policy (text),
    267–274

Secondary obligations, 18
Sellers,
  terms for, 5
Simple demand guarantees *see*
  First demand guarantees
Stand-by letters of credit *see* Letters
  of credit
Sub-contractors,
  back-to-back bonding, 123–124
  bank as guarantor, 120–121
  bond issue support, 156
  claims by main contractor, 129
  cover against unfair demands,
    123–124
  drafting of bond text, 126
  expiry and validity dates,
    129–130
  nominated by buyer, 124–125
  overseas position, 128
  relationship to main contractor,
    119–120, 122–123, 127
  risk analysis by main contractor,
    266
  surety bonds, 121–122
  value of guarantees, 125
    currency risks on, 126
Surety bonds, 9–10
  acceptance by buyers, 14

arbitration delays on, 16
benefits of, 15–17
drafting of, 42–44
ICC uniform rules for, 17
proof of default, 16
text examples of, 42–43
underwriting considerations, 14
Surety companies,
  address list of, 282
  definition of, 13
  experience advantage of, 16
  as guarantors, 8–9
    to sub-contractors, 121–122
  underwriting considerations, 14
  United States, 110–112

Tender guarantees,
  cancellation, 178
  definition and purpose of, 5–6
  drafting, 42
    specimen texts, 85
  extension of, 166
  follow-on guarantees, 167–168
  German law, 91
  ICC specimen text, 105–106
  independent evidence for claims,
    77
  international model texts,
    103–104, 105
  replacement by performance
    guarantees, 6
  risks of, 165–168
  security for, 165
  specimen texts (German),
    108–109
  text examples of, 42–43, 52–54,
    59–64, 77–78
325 Rules *see* Uniform Rules for
  Contract Guarantees
Top-up clauses *see* Performance
  guarantees

UCP *see* Uniform Customs and
  Practices for Documentary
  Credits
Unfair calls *see* Unfair demands

Unfair demands,
  abusive or fraudulent claims,
    197–202, 224
  attachments (German law),
    94–95, 98–99
  bibliography, 277–278
  coercion factor, 161–162
  commercial risks, 158–162
  contingency fund against, 184
  cover for sub-contractors,
    123–124
  dispute settlement procedure,
    194–195, 235
  documents required, 179
  English cases, 114–115
  European cases (schedule),
    113–114
  extend or pay claims *see* Extend
    or pay claims
  financial risks, 163–164
  injunctions (German law), 94–98,
    100, 189–190
  bibliography, 277–278
  insurance cover, 144–145,
    145–146, 185, 203–211
    address list of brokers, 283
    brokers' role, 195–196
    ECGD cover for UK exporters,
      203–206
    private insurers, 207–211
      eligibility and risks, 207–208
      period of cover, 210
      premium costs, 211
  international model texts,
    101–110
  legal remedies, 187–194, 224–225
    Belgium, 191
    France, 190–191, 193–194
    Germany, 94–100, 189–190
    Italy, 192
    Luxembourg, 191
    Netherlands, 192
    Switzerland, 190
    United Kingdom, 188–189
  nature of, 170

  political risks, 164–165
  pre-emption in contract, 177
    exporter's procedures for,
      186–187
  protection against, 10, 12,
    81–115, 177–194, 224–225
  risk control of, 173–174
    see also Risk exposure control
  technical risks, 162–163
    see also Fair demands
Uniform Customs and Practices for
  Documentary Credits 1983
  (ICC), 33, 112, 138, 223, 229
Uniform Rules for Contract
  Guarantees 1978 (ICC : 325
  Rules)
    disadvantage to banks, 222–223
    legislative history of, 12, 20,
      221–223
    text of, 238–249
Uniform Rules for Demand
  Guarantees 1992 (ICC : 458
  Rules)
    acceptance of, 230
    application of, 229–234
    categorisation of first demand,
      232–233
    choice of guarantee, 230–231
    draft objectives of, 226–227
    expiry provisions, 233–234
    legislative history of, 12, 226–229
    objectives of, 235
    settlement of disputes, 235
    text of, 250–258
    voluntary nature of, 236
United Nations Committee on
  International Trade Law
  (UNICTRAL), 12, 219, 221, 229
United States law, 110–112

Warranty guarantees,
  as coercive factor, 162
  definition and purpose of, 6–7
  risks of, 170